BABY STAR SIGNS

Your Guide to Better Parenting is in the Stars!

First published by O Books, 2008
O Books is an imprint of John Hunt Publishing Ltd., The Bothy, Deershot Lodge, Park Lane, Ropley,
Hants, SO24 0BE, UK
office1@o-books.net
www.o-books.net

Distribution in:

UK and Europe
Orca Book Services
orders@orcabookservices.co.uk
Tel: 01202 665432 Fax: 01202 666219
Int. code (44)

USA and Canada
NBN
custserv@nbnbooks.com
Tel: 1 800 462 6420 Fax: 1 800 338 4550

Australia and New Zealand
Brumby Books
sales@brumbybooks.com.au
Tel: 61 3 9761 5535 Fax: 61 3 9761 7095

Far East (offices in Singapore, Thailand,
Hong Kong, Taiwan)
Pansing Distribution Pte Ltd
kemal@pansing.com
Tel: 65 6319 9939 Fax: 65 6462 5761

South Africa
Alternative Books
altbook@peterhyde.co.za
Tel: 021 555 4027 Fax: 021 447 1430

Text copyright Chrissie Blaze 2008

Design: Stuart Davies

ISBN: 978 1 84694 124 5

A CIP catalogue record for this book is available
from the British Library.

Printed in the US by Maple Vail

O Books operates a distinctive and ethical publishing philosophy in
all areas of its business, from its global network of authors to
production and worldwide distribution.
No trees were cut down to print this particular book. The paper is
100% recycled, with 50% of that being post-consumer. It's processed
chlorine-free, and has no fibre from ancient or endangered forests.
This production method on this print run saved approximately
thirteen trees, 4,000 gallons of water, 600 pounds of solid waste,
990 pounds of greenhouse gases and 8 million BTU of energy. On its
publication a donation for planting a tree was sent to The
Woodland Trust.

BABY STAR SIGNS

Your Guide to Better
Parenting is in the Stars!

Chrissie Blaze

BOOKS

Winchester, UK
Washington, USA

CONTENTS

Books by Chrissie Blaze are *Workout for the Soul: Eight Steps to Inner Fitness*, AsLan Publishing, Inc., November, 2001; *The Baby's Astrologer: Your Guide to Better Parenting Is In the Stars*, Warner Books, 2003; *Das Baby-Horoskop. Die besten Erziehungstipps stehen in den Sternen* (Broschiert) Ullstein Tb; Auflage: 1 (Dez. 2004) *Power Prayer: A Program for Unlocking Your Spiritual Strength*, Adams Media, 2003 (co-author, Gary Blaze; Foreword by Marianne Williamson); *How to Read Your Horoscope in 5 Easy Steps*, O Books, 2008, *Mercury Retrograde: Surviving Astrology's Most Precarious Times of the Year*, O Books, 2008; *Superstar Signs: Sun Signs of Heroes, Celebrities and You*, O Books, 2008.

I dedicate this book to my enlightened Spiritual Master,
Dr. George King, who taught the mysteries of the deeper aspects
of Life and Love, and whose incredible global Mission helped
secure the future for our children's children.

FOREWORD

As a national radio broadcaster, I have had the privilege for the past twenty years of interviewing pioneers in their own field. So it was an honor, after interviewing Chrissie Blaze on several occasions regarding her work in human development and the great international efforts of The Aetherius Society, to be asked to write an introduction to her wonderful book, *Baby Star Signs*.

Sharing a professional interest in astrology, I was delighted to learn that her book on using astrology for babies and toddlers was a book everyone could use. Its simplicity is the result of Chrissie Blaze's own astrological acumen and decades of practice in this interpretive art.

If this were a radio broadcast I would probably open the show with these sentences: '*Find out from astrologer Chrissie Blaze whether your baby will be an early walker or later talker, whether they will be picky or adventurous eaters, whether you should sleep for six months before they are born because they won't like sleeping too many hours in a row after they arrive!*'

Baby Star Signs is like having a nanny in the house who can offer parents or caregivers lots of insights into the bundle of joy they now love so dearly, but who on occasion they may have trouble understanding.

Baby Star Signs is a wonderful contribution to the field of astrology in general and to parents who want to have a deeper understanding of their baby. As Chrissie makes clear, from the moment of our birth we visibly and invisibly are impacted by the cosmos. Her appreciation for the fact that the arrangement of planets at the time of our birth, or our children's births, is not a fixed static pattern but can show tendencies, natural likes and dislikes, attributes and challenges.

Chrissie explains, in this beautifully-designed book, that our birth charts do show us tendencies, strengths, and weaknesses. As a parent or guardian of any young children or person, knowing their sun sign and the placement of the moon can help us understand the basic way each person expresses themselves to the world through their behavior, and how they react to the world in terms of their feelings. Using astrology as a backdrop to our understanding enables a spiritual as well as practical appreciation for our baby's soul and personality.

Baby Star Signs makes it possible for anyone to identify how our deeper soul (some might equate with the moon sign) influences our personality, or sun signs, our likes and dislikes. Chrissie also gives a reader the opportunity to look at their family members, not as undeveloped children, but as precious individuals, born with a full palette of qualities. These may not be at first visible but, like the current in a river, they influence the children's movement, direction, and power. Astrology is like all interpretive arts, exactly that. Chrissie Blaze offers a profoundly simple but insightful and broad spectrum of ways we can utilize the stars in discovering the mystery already imprinted into the life of our loved ones.

As a practical book, *Baby Star Signs* gives clear instruction for determining the sun sign of each child and their moon signs based on their day of birth. Each chapter addressing each of the twelve Zodiacal sun signs details certain characteristics exhibited by each sun sign (Aries, Taurus, Gemini, etc.) and examines how this energy shows up in behavior.

This cute book is always there to offer creative tips to soothe or arouse curiosity in our toddler or infant, pointing out why one child only likes one food at a time and another likes to combine them. *Baby Star Signs* shows how your baby's dispositions show up in their style and way of sleeping. Do they wake a lot or sleep soundly through the night early on? Do they tend to explore with ease, using their body comfortably or might they take a bit longer to feel confident clambering up and down the steps or walking safely to and fro? Taking time to discuss the baby's language skills and the way each baby likes and benefits by learning is a wonderful asset. And of course how our babies interact with each other and the world is clearly discussed for each sun sign.

This will be a fun tool to use as your child comes into contact with their siblings and with other children. When my own children were younger, I found it remarkably helpful to know what was going on astrologically. It helped me see why a sensitive Pisces did not want to be a leader like their sister Aries. *Baby Star Signs* answers questions about our baby's development, not as a question of right and wrong but, instead, what occurs based on the influence of both solar and lunar qualities. While some may consider astrology a game more than a science, I regard it as a sacred art that enables fuller and deeper appreciation for our shared divinity and that of our children.

Chrissie Blaze makes it a fun exploration for everyone who is curious about each other and their children. It is an honor to introduce her book to you, and it is my sincerest hope that, just as those many young families I once counseled about the potential talents and difficulties for newborns, talking of them as though they were fully present beings, this book will remind you, the reader, that all life is precious and our babies reflect the universe in their persons. We, if we are quiet enough, can see a reflection of their soul's desire and their natures, even years before they are grown to full maturity. Chrissie Blaze teaches us how to do that, what to look for, and how to interpret what we see. Astrology is not a permanent pattern but a valuable guide for being conscious in their journey we make with our children, in love and awareness.

Zohara M. Hieronimus
Host of *Future Talk*, Nationally Syndicated Radio Program
www.futuretalkradio.com

ACKNOWLEDGMENTS

To my wise and honorable husband, Gary Blaze, who inspires and supports me.

To my adored parents, Phyllis and Tom Shafe, who have taught me so much about the joys and sacrifices of love. Even though my mother has passed away since writing this book, she will always live within my heart.

To the delightful children and babies who have inspired me in writing this book, particularly MorningStar Angeline Wilson-Chippewa and Georgia Alice Holder.

To Zohara Hieronimus, friend, originator, and host of the important and futuristic radio show, *Future Talk*, for writing the Foreword, and to Anita Chu, for her friendship, support, and enthusiasm.

To John Hunt and everyone at O Books.

To all parents throughout the world: may God bless and guide you on your journey of parenthood.

PART I

YOUR UNIQUE BABY

INTRODUCTION

I was in the supermarket by the jars of honey when this book was born. There was a harried young mother standing next to me pushing a stroller with one hand, with a tiny toddler hanging from her other arm, as she was trying to reach a honeycomb on the top shelf. I grabbed the honeycomb and put it in her basket. Her thanks were drowned by a sudden loud wail from the tiny toddler. Ten minutes later we met again as we both reached for a bag of frozen peas. She said, nodding in the direction of her infants, "I wish they came with guidebooks. I feel like such a novice at all this." We both laughed, but I could see a distraught look underneath the smile. I assured her she was doing a great job and seemed to be a wonderful mother, and we parted.

Her words haunted me for a few days. I am sure you have had the experience when somebody says something and the words resonate and seem to go deep inside you for no apparent reason. Well, that happened to me.

Two days later I was tossing and turning in bed and suddenly "Eureka!" – a flash of inspiration. I sat up and said to the night, and to my sleeping husband "They DO come with guidebooks!" I felt like an idiot for not having thought of it before, having studied astrology for most of my life.

Astrologers know that the birth chart, drawn up from the moment and place of your birth, is indeed a guidebook for life. Your astrological traits do not suddenly become real the moment you decide to have your birth cart drawn up. They are real from the moment you draw your first breath. In most cases, however, we do not become aware of the value of astrology until we are older and wiser.

I knew it was important to offer to parents of new babies some understanding of the vast and intricate study of astrology. Even some simple astrological tools could help them during those vitally important first three years, when so much of their infant's personality is formed.

I was fortunate that my own mother was enlightened in the ways of astrology. When the nurse told her she had a daughter, my mother's reply was: *"Yes, yes, that's fine – but what time is it?"* The nurse casually told her it was about 2:00 P.M. and went on to explain that I was a lovely, healthy baby girl. My mother, now irritated, said, *"Yes, that's wonderful, I know it's a girl, but I need the EXACT TIME!"*[1]

Well, this book was written for all those parents and grand-parents and all those who love and care for babies everywhere who (even though they may not know the exact time!) are open-minded enough to give astrology a chance when it comes to understanding and nurturing the newborn infant in their care.

In this book I describe, through the wisdom of astrology, the unique personality, habits, patterns, past, present, and future of these tiny, unfurled souls.

Discovering the Unique Person Who Is Your Baby

Pre-parenthood, you may think of infants as just small humans who cry, gurgle, squeal, sleep, and generally make a mess. However, parents and caregivers soon realize that, from early on, distinct personalities emerge. Maternity nurses are able to see this within the first few hours of birth. They can spot the willful ones, the placid ones, or the timid ones. When we emerge into this world, we already have a personality; it just takes a decade of four to discover fully what this is.

I recently gave an astrological consultation to an elderly lady of eighty-seven. She is an amazing soul, an eternal student, who told me afterward that she could now understand herself as she never had before. My consultation, she said, had given her an "honest look at herself and her potential." She was now raring to go out and use it! Well, better late than never. I wrote this book for enlightened parents, teachers, and guardians to ensure that their child does not have to wait eighty-seven years!

I am sure all parents wonder what kind of person their child will become. They know he will be handsome, brilliant, charming, and talented, but they don't know what problems and challenges he may be faced with, or in what area his talents may lie. They will give him the best of care and love him more than they thought possible – but may ask themselves, "Who is he really?"

It is widely known that astrology gives a practical understanding of the types of personalities, psychological dilemmas, and life experiences we all face, but it is not generally regarded as a useful tool in the developmental years.

This book is to introduce you to the unique person who is your baby. Besides helping you to understand who your child is, this books is written to help you understand the wisdom and enlightenment that astrology can bring to parenthood.

Why Is One Child Different from Another?

Your children are not your children.
They are the sons and daughters of Life's longing for itself.
They come through you but not from you.
And though they are with you yet they belong not to you.

You may give them your love but not your thoughts.
For they have their own thoughts.
You may house their bodies but not their souls.
For their souls dwell in the house of tomorrow,
Which you cannot visit, not even in your dreams.
You may strive to be like them, but seek not to make them like you.
For life goes not backward nor tarries with yesterday.

-Kahlil Gibran, The Prophet

It is a commonly held belief that a combination of genetics and environment mold our personalities. However, most parents will admit that a newborn baby is pretty much herself from Day One. Many astrologers, including myself, regard reincarnation as a fact and the birth chart as an outline of the talents and strengths we bring with us from our journeys in previous lives; the challenges and obstacles present lessons we still need to learn on our paths to enlightenment. The birth chart also shows the direction of our soul's growth and much more. Astrology does not predetermine our fate so much as incline us toward certain behavior and directions. It describes rather than prescribes.

Although parents give their children the gift of life, they do not create the underlying intelligence, or human spirit, that is their child. This aspect already exists. Almost one hundred years ago, a team of research embryologists in Vienna made the following astounding discovery. They found that the first fertilized cell in a human being does not grow into an embryo, as happens with animals. Instead a baby first develops into different layers. Only at about the seventeenth day does the growth of the embryo take place. Following this it takes another twenty-three days before the formation of the organs begins. Finally, there is a period of forty days before the foundations of the body are laid. The scientists realized that a baby is not, therefore, born in the same way as an animal, as had been previously thought. They realized that, while an animal is *born* from an embryo, a baby *incarnates* in different stages.

In other words, the human being has a different origin and a different destiny from that of animals.[2] The incarnating human must depart from his spiritual home to return to the world of form. It is interesting that many believe this forty-day period is a period of adjustment between the spiritual and physical states. In legends and myths, and according to the Bible, the period of forty days is associated with a change of consciousness.

How This Book Can Help You As a Parent to Help Your Children

The first three years of life are formative ones because it is a time when a person's innate tendencies can either be nurtured so that they flourish in later life or can be ignored. Your baby is rather like a seedling. The seed packet gives directions on the best way to water, fertilize, or prune the plant and how much or little sunlight it needs in order for the seed to flourish into a beautiful plant. Without the instructions, the seed may never see its fully glory.

The birth chart is like the directions on a seed packet, and it shows the beautiful person that your baby can become and how best to nurture and care for him. It enables you to be objective about your baby's strengths and weaknesses and can, therefore, free you from some of the anxiety you may have in raising your children.

According to all astrologers and also to expert in the science of ethno pediatrics, which brings together medical, developmental, and social science, "babies are not just unformed adults, but beings in their own right."[3] Parents, of course, have always known this!

Baby Star Signs is based on this principle that a newborn baby is not just a cuddly bundle, but also a soul that has come into this life with strengths and potential to be developed, weaknesses to be overcome, and a unique destiny. We all have a soul, which transcends the limitations of the intellect. The warmth of our divine soul qualities allows the intellect and other parts of our nature to blossom.

Parents can help develop soul qualities within their babies by expressing love in practical, intuitive ways from fantasy play to bonding meditations. The role of astrology is to bring under-standing, the harbinger of love. Some knowledge of astrology can be of great assistance, especially to parents of preverbal children. As parents you can use this book to help you understand your baby's unique character and destiny. You can use it to help point him in the right direction for the flowering of his genius and talents in later life. The influence of the planets affects the way we think, communicate, love, relate, and even eat our first solid food! Unfortunately, popular Sun-sign astrology is rather generalized, and this often puzzles parents who consult astrology books. Other astrology books are far too complex. This book will bridge the gap between the two.

Baby Star Signs takes into account not just your baby's Sun sign, but also her Moon and Rising signs as well as several other interesting factors. From this, you can understand your baby's personality, emotional needs, and relationship to the environment, as well as past and future talents and potentials.

Also, please note that I have used, throughout the book, each gender alternatively for each sign, starting with "he" for Aries, "she" for Taurus, etc.

For example, even before he is born, the Aries baby makes himself felt with restless kicking and poking, as if impatient to come into the world. After birth, he makes his needs and desires felt very quickly. The little Pisces baby, however, is a gentler soul who may benefit from a soothing water birth. While she may delight in sucking and proceeding slowly and cautiously, the Aries baby will thrash his legs and arms when angry, seemingly frustrated at his slow rate of development.

Baby Star Signs also looks at the child from a spiritual viewpoint as an emerging soul, with intelligence and intuition as well as a past and a future destiny, as an individual and as part of a generation. This destiny can be ascertained from the day the baby takes his first breath.

Why Astrology?
Surprisingly, there are few astrology books for babies. Probably because we assume it is more important to feed, clothe, and generally nurture our baby than to try to understand him at a

deeper level. Modern child psychology is useful, but no general rules on parenting can sufficiently honor the unique personality that each little soul possesses. It is here that astrology can make a profound and creative contribution.

Astrology is now accepted as a valuable psychological tool. Jung asserted that astrology had a great deal to contribute to psychology and admitted to having employed it with some frequency in his analytic work with clients. In cases of difficult psychological diagnosis, Jung would draw up a horoscope in order to adopt a point of view from an entirely different angle. "I must say," he once told an Indian astrologer, "that I very often found that the astrological data elucidated certain points which I otherwise would have been unable to understand."

This new psychological approach to astrology, pioneered in the last few decades, is increasingly capturing the attention of the layperson. Astrology is gaining popularity by the minute as people learn it is an invaluable tool that can increase understanding, is a practical guide for life, and offers a deep spiritual perspective.

One thing astrology teaches is that children are not blank slates upon which their environment writes; they are not a bundle of responses to stimuli, nor just the product of their genetic coding; they are souls incarnating into this world with personalities, likes, dislikes, talents, weaknesses, and strengths. Each soul has the free will to choose his own path in life. Astrology inclines, it does not compel.

All babies have within them seeds of genius that may blossom or may wilt and die. At best we can assist the souls in our care to manifest their unique genius and grow into wonderful human beings. At worst we can, through ignorance, push them toward insecurity, fear, and discontent. Bringing babies into the world is a huge challenge. Astrology is a nonjudgmental framework that parents can use to assist them in making wise choices for their babies and infants.

It is hard to imagine that every newborn baby brings into this life her own inherent blueprint for life. As she gazes at you with her clear eyes, she seems so innocent and pure. However, just as we are influenced by the great cosmic energies that course through space from the Moon, the Sun, and all the planets, so, too, are our newborn infants. Despite the fact that children may have the same parents, the same social and economic background, and the same education, they each express different personalities and different emotional responses. The reason we are all influenced in different ways is complex and profound. However, it can be summed up in one word, *karma*.

Karma is one of the Laws of Creation that states that action and reaction are opposite and equal. In other words, through all of our actions and thoughts, we mold our future. This law applies to everything in Creation, including even our newborn baby! This may seem difficult to comprehend, but we should remember there is an underlying Intelligence that organizes the infinity of things happening in the Universe. The philosopher Manly Hall put it succinctly: *"Astrology is the study of the anatomy and psychology of God."*

Your Baby Chooses You

The intricate karmic web your soul has created through many pervious lifetimes is like a cloak of many threads. Some of the threads are strong and resilient, some broken and fraying, others spun out of sheer gold. When we are ready to reincarnate, our higher self chooses to don this cloak in physical form. It does so at a certain time in order to have the benefit of the influence of the planets aligned in a particular way. This moment in time is significant; for it helps the soul to gain those experiences it needs in its journey through life.

As well as choosing the best time, the incarnating soul also chooses her parents. We may think we choose to have a child at a certain time, but in fact our child chooses us in order to gain the experiences she needs.

I know a child who was born into a humble working-class family in England. From an early age she acted as if she was a member of the Royal Family. She would expect her mother to wait on her with a platter of food for breakfast. She would stand patiently and wait while her mother selected her clothes and would help her dress and braid her hair. As she grew older she realized this was her past, not her present. She was convinced she had been a member of a royal family in a past life and that her mother had been her beloved lady-in-waiting!

How This Book Can Help

The birth chart of a baby is a map or blueprint of past patterns and future potential. This potential is easily stifled by conflicting family demands or ignored through lack of recognition. Encouragement of an infant's potential can help her develop so that she won't be so easily "conditioned" later in life by school or society at large.

This book is designed to help parents and guardians assist and understand the babies in their care. The children will then be better prepared for life with a greater sense of purpose. They will not have to waste years of their lives "finding themselves."

Like adults, babies possess inner conflicts and insecurities. It is natural for them sometimes to feel afraid. Astrology can assist parents in pinpointing these fears and anxieties from the moment of birth. Similarly, each child possesses emotional needs that may be different from those of her parents and mentors. A Taurus baby needs lots of hugs and kisses, while a Gemini infant responds well to verbal communication and reassurance.

Rather than trying to be perfect parents in order to create perfect children, this book enables you to honor and support your baby's right to be himself. Astrology does not provide a map of your baby's fate, but gives an outline of the best route he can take through life.

Baby Star Signs is particularly essential now, as people are now more sophisticated in their needs. Before, parents struggled to feed and clothe. Now, in the Western world, we spend millions of dollars on self-improvement. People seek new and better ways to bring awareness and spirituality into their lives and the lives of their families. This book can help you do this by examining astrological trends operating in your baby's life. It also provides simple tables by which you can understand what these trends are and what they mean. *Baby Star Signs* is like a psychological and spiritual self-help manual for parents and their babies.

As mentioned, when I was born my own mother was more concerned with my sign than my sex. Despite the nurse's raised eyebrows and disapproval, she *insisted* on the *exact* time so that she could have an accurate birth chart drawn up for her darling daughter. Astrology is in my genes. I am hoping that it will also become a helpful guide for you, as it is for me.

There is a lot of complexity *Baby Star Signs* could go into but doesn't. If you want that, you will find books on astrology that analyze everything from aspects to quadruplicities. This book is designed to be simple and illuminating – not complex and overwhelming. It gives enough detail to be a fascinating guide to a baby's personality and enough simplicity to be enjoyable.

CHAPTER ONE

Sun Sign, Moon Sign and Rising Sign

"We are born as tiny infants, innocent and pure,
Yet imbued with the energies of the Cosmos coursing through
our veins,
Urging us to become the person the Creator intends us to be –
As majestic, noble and brilliant as the Sun, the Moon and Stars."

-Chrissie Blaze

The question "What's your sign?" is no longer considered odd. People now realize it's a more accurate way of sizing somebody up than by their occupation. At one time a doctor was a certain type of person and the local grocer another. Now the grocer may also be a writer and the doctor may spend his time volunteering in a third world country. Every other person is "in computers" and in Hollywood, where I'm writing this book, everyone and his dog is an actor.

While having an accurate birth chart is important to reveal all the deeper, intricate nuances of personality and possibilities that await your tiny infant, you can learn a lot about your baby through his Sun sign. Even so, Sun-sign astrology is pretty limited. Suddenly your baby and about 500 million other people are exactly the same. You know that's ridiculous.

Sun-sign astrology is a useful, though broad, guide for adults; for babies, however, knowing just their Sun sign is not enough. Moon signs and Rising signs (also known as the Ascendant) are just as important in determining traits, character, and potential. *Baby Star Signs* explains what, for example, the Sun in Aries, Moon in Gemini, and Leo Rising really means for you and your infant. Tables are provided so you can quickly and easily ascertain your baby's "astrological makeup."[4]

The Sun Sign

When people ask you what your baby's sign is, they are referring to his Sun sign, or the sign of the Zodiac the Sun was in when he was born, as seen from Earth. Without the Sun, there would be no life. The Sun's rays sustain and nourish and give us all we need to gain experience. They provide us with live, creativity, drive, and an inner sense of purpose. Your baby's Sun sign describes his core self. It represents his character and creative drive.

If your baby son is a Leo, he is confident, dynamic, active, boisterous, desiring to be in the limelight. If he is a Taurus, he is loyal, steadfast and cautious, preferring cuddles to noisy expression.

Don't worry if you disagree. You're right – it's not quite that simple. I know two Cancer babies who were born on the same day. One of them, Georgia, is "typical": reserved, shy, cautious, and sensitive. The other, Vanessa, is colorful, extroverted, and already a budding actress. They were born only two hours apart but Georgia is a Cancer Sun with Cancer as her Rising sign, whereas Vanessa had the more flamboyant sign of Leo Rising when she was born.[5]

Although the surface behavior of these two children is very different, when you look deeper, you will find they have a lot in common. Georgia and Vanessa both cling to their toys and snuggle up to their dolls in the nurturing, sensitive ways of the Cancer Sun sign.[6]

Babies gradually grow into the qualities of their Sun signs. We are here to learn certain lessons and, as we mature, our character and creativity develop. It is then that we can draw upon the "steel" of our Sun sign.

Because of this, don't be surprised to find your baby alternating between expressing his Sun-sign qualities and his Moon-sign qualities. The Moon sign represents his basic personality and how he responds to life through his feelings, habits, and emotions. That is why, if your baby has an Aries Sun and Taurus Moon, you should study both the Aries and Taurus sections of this book to give you a better understanding. Then add the Rising-sign section to give you a "richer mix."

In order to check your baby's Sun sign, please refer to Table I below.

The Moon Sign

Your baby's Moon sign is the sign of the Zodiac the Moon was passing through at the time of birth. The Moon moves very quickly, much faster than the Sun, and whizzes through each of the twelve signs in a couple of days. To find your baby's Moon sign, please refer to Appendix 1 on page 191.

The Moon sign highlights your baby's emotional needs. While the Sun represents who he really is, the Moon represents his feelings and reactions; how he likes to establish routines and his physical and emotional sensitivity. Does he like the feel of wool against his skin; does it make him cry or smile? Does he like to be fed regularly like clockwork – or only when he's hungry? When your baby is born he is a bundle of responses and emotions. Life is simple. When he is hungry, he cries; when he is happy, he cries. When he is wet, he yells! And then he smiles – and all the cries are instantly forgotten! Since the Moon represents this response to life, a baby's Moon sign is very important. Your baby will express his emotional nature more freely than you. As adults, we are conditioned to keep our emotions in check and our reactions "politically correct."

One should never underestimate the power of the Moon, which can affect our own watery makeup[7] just as easily as it affects the ocean's tides. As the Moon has such a strong effect on us, the Moon sign can significantly temper the tone of your baby's Sun sign, especially in the first few years of life. As your baby matures and becomes self-conscious, you will see more of her Sun sign as it sets over the horizon of her dawning consciousness.

How will you be able to distinguish between the Sun and Moon signs? Once you get a feel for the qualities of the different signs, you will notice your child exhibiting traits of his Moon sign, Sun sign, Rising sign, and then some.

Ariadne is two-years-old; she has the Sun in Aries and the Moon in Taurus. She has a classic Taurean need for the comfort and security of the tried and true, combined with a classic Arien desire for new horizons. Unlike many babies who drop their toys when confronted with new ones, Ariadne is fiercely loyal to her old, chewed-up toys, but still reaches eagerly for and embraces new ones. The result is that her crib is stuffed full of soft toys that grow in number by the week! As she matures, she will probably still hold on to her stuffed animals but will also translate her tendencies into other areas of life.

An adult I know with the same combination has been married three times but remains close friends with her former husbands; she lives six thousand miles from where she was born, but is in constant daily contact with her family abroad. Taurus needs roots, whereas Aries needs new pastures and challenges. It is fascinating to see how opposing desires can and are contained within us without conflict. You will find the same with your baby.

The Rising Sign

As the Earth spins around, your baby's Rising sign is the one of the twelve signs of the Zodiac that was coming up over the eastern horizon at her place and time of birth. Because the Earth rotates, Rising signs are changing all the time. Because there are twelve signs of the Zodiac and twenty-four hours in the day, as a general rule, the Rising sign changes about every two hours. It starts at sunrise, so if you were born between 6:00 A.M. and 8:00 A.M., your Rising sign would be the same as your Sun sign, since the Sun comes up over the horizon at approximately 6:00 A.M.

Therefore, if you are a Leo born at 6:00 A.M., you would also have Leo on the Ascendant, or Leo Rising. If you were born at 8:00 A.M., you will probably have the next sign of the Zodiac rising, i.e., Virgo. If it was between 10:00 A.M. and 12 noon, it would be the sign after that, e.g., Libra, and so on throughout the day.

This is why your friend's child can be born on the same day and in the same hospital as your own child, but they have completely different temperaments. You may say, *"It's in the genes!"* That's part of the story, but it's also because she probably has a different Rising sign, as well as other differences in her birth chart. Likewise, a baby born on the same day and the same time, but in a different place, would also have a different Rising sign. So what does this mean?

Your baby's Rising sign describes the very first impression she makes on other people and her physical appearance. Is she tough and feisty, sweet and saucy, shy, romantic, strong-willed, dramatic? I know all babies are cute, but watch closely, and yours will soon make her distinct mark. Her Rising sign indicates her very specific and personal "signature" on life and how others see her.

If your baby has sunny Leo rising, she is likely to come across as happy and bright, with a desire to be the center of attention. She will project her basic character, as determined by her Sun and Moon signs, in a dramatic Leo-like manner. If, on the other hand, she has a more gentle introspective Rising sign, such as Pisces, she will seem more sensitive, vulnerable and quieter, even though her Sun and Moon signs may be the same.

To see what your baby's Rising sign is, turn to Appendix 2 on page 297.

The Sun-Moon-Rising Sign Combination
When you know the Sun sign, Moon sign, and Rising sign of your baby, you have a good foundation from which you can begin to understand your baby at a deeper level. If, for example, your

baby has a Cancer Sun, Aquarius Moon, and Capricorn Rising, you should begin by reading the section on his Sun sign – Cancer. Next, read the section on Aquarius – his Moon sign, and finally the one on Capricorn – his Rising sign. Remember, he is not just influenced by his Sun sign, but also by his Moon sign and Rising sign – and a whole lot more as well. You may find that some of the things in the Cancer section just don't "ring a bell," but the Aquarian section more aptly describes your baby's reactions and emotions. You may also notice that his Rising sign characteristics come into play more when he is interacting with other people. Do not be surprised to find that, as he grows, he will develop more and more of the characteristics listed in all three sections. You may well find that he seems much more like his Moon sign than his Rising sign or more like his Sun sign than his Moon sign, etc. However, as he grows, you will eventually see characteristics of al three prominent aspects of your baby's chart, and can guide him toward their positive expression.

CHAPTER TWO

BABY SIGNS – ARIES TO PISCES

This chapter is in twelve sections, one for each of the signs of the Zodiac from Aries through Pisces. If your baby has his Sun in Aries, with his Moon in the sign of Scorpio and his rising sign is Sagittarius, you should read each of these three sections – Aries, Scorpio and Sagittarius – for a better idea of his potential, personality, and approach to life.[8]

In each of the twelve sections, there is a general introduction to each sign, followed by specific stages of your baby's growth from 0-1, 1-2 and 2-3 years, in the areas of sleeping, eating, learning, motor skills, socialization, and language. I call these your "Survival Guide." From this guide, you will see that a two-year-old Gemini baby will, for example, have different eating and sleeping habits from her Capricorn counterpart. The Survival Guide outlines the different tendencies of your baby at different stages of development, according to her sign. Remember, this is only a general guide. For a better picture, you should read the Survival Guide for your baby's Moon sign and Rising sign, as well as for her Sun sign.

Also, as mentioned earlier, please note that I have used each gender alternatively for each sign, starting with "he" for Aries, "she" for Taurus, etc.

At the end of each section is a journal for you to keep notes on how your baby's development correlates with the astrological profile.

Baby Aries

March 21 – April 20

You probably didn't notice it when your newborn baby was first thrust into your arms. You were filled with the euphoria of birth and saw only a tiny, cuddly, harmless bundle. It might not even dawn upon you during those first few days. However, you will soon see the glint in his eyes and feel the iron will of this feisty little scrap. So small, so cute, yet ever so definitely the boss.

Your Aries baby is born to follow no star but his own. He is Number One and will strive to remain that way. You can tell him what to do, cajole him, manipulate him, raise your voice to him, or ever so pleasantly ask him, but whether he is one-week-old or sixty-years-old, your Aries baby will do exactly what he wants, when he wants to.

No, I am not confining you to a life of misery. You know how cute your baby is. He is quite possibly the cutest baby in the hospital. I am just telling you not to expect a humdrum life. With his strong, active body and bright, alert mind, your Aries baby seeks excitement. If it's not provided, he will provide his own.

He will be willing to try anything and usually does so with gusto that borders on hyperactivity. While his playmates may be content to gurgle and smile, your Aries baby will already be seeking active ways to entertain himself. There is a tinge of the loner about him no matter how sociable he appears to be. He has a good head on his tiny shoulders and, even as a toddler, he will take initiative while others wait to be told.

Be glad your Aries baby is destined to be a leader, not a follower. Be glad he knows his own mind before he can even speak. Be glad he is mark, sassy, and fascinating. Just don't expect him to follow orders.

One thing you can expect from your Aries baby is impulsiveness. He will not seek a measured balanced approach to life but a colorful one of extremes. The combination of incredible energy and a passion for life makes for a little fireball of activity and a tendency for scrapes, bruises, and especially accidents to the head. Do not fear, the Aries rush and crash is inevitably concluded with a bounce: Their ability to bounce back after accidents, injury, sickness, or heartbreak is phenomenal. They just don't have time for self-pity; life is too exciting and there is too much to do and discover.

The result of the innate Aries desire for speed, combined with an honesty and candor that are refreshing as well as irritating, is the famous full-frontal attack. Be prepared for this. Your baby may not be cooing sweetly in his crib, but very soon he will be talking. Soon after that the frontal attacks will be launched.

Sara, a charming little Aries baby with steel blue eyes and black curls, was the prettiest two-year-old you could imagine. People would sidle up to her in her stroller, beam, and say: "Oh, she's adorable, she looks just like a doll!" Recognizing an insult, the little dear would stick out her tongue, and scream: "I hate you!"

Love and hate are near neighbors to the Aries child. You will forgive him anything when he throws himself at you and passionately tells you how much he loves you. The Aries child's style of self-expression is simple and refreshingly honest and continues throughout his life to charm and upset all those in his path!

You may think this scenario is typical of all children. The difference is that, while the rest of us mature into "socially acceptable adults," your Aries baby is more likely to retain his magical childlike innocence, directness, and enthusiastic self-centeredness into adulthood.

All this energy, combined with the Aries' impatience, makes for a pretty demanding child. There will be frustrating periods when your child is beginning to walk and talk but is not quite there yet. At that point, his willpower and desires will be stronger than his abilities, and he will cry and scream and make his frustrations known. Be patient; he will master things quickly and confidently and will not linger or whine like other children his age.

Aries is the sign of beginnings. It is the first sign of the Zodiac, and your Aries baby will be the first one to develop, the first one to try new things, but also the first one to become impatient and move on to new pastures. As your baby grows into a child, he may leave behind unfinished homework, and you should encourage him from an early age to finish projects. He understands more than you think. When I was only two, my grandmother would explain to me (an Aries child) how every thought and action was a living thing that, if left unfinished, would hang around me waiting to be completed. She explained that, as soon as I finished something, it grew wings and life and could fly off and perform its magic. This appealed to the sense of wonder and magic that is often innate to the Aries child.

You can help your Aries baby grow into a fine adult by taking a fair but firm approach. Eva-Maria was such a vociferous and forceful baby that her gentle parents constantly gave in to her demands. Unfortunately, she is now a spoiled child with frazzled parents. The Aries child needs intelligent discipline. He needs to learn right from wrong and that he is not the center of the Universe. One way to instill in him a sense of discipline is to appeal to his warm and fair heart.

He is nothing if not contrary. If you tell him he can't do something, he will instantly try to do it. There is no point saying "no" to your Aries child without a reason. Although on the surface he may be brash and confident, underneath, your Aries child is a softie. A friend of mine has a two-year-old Aries baby, Mandy. Recently, Mandy was screaming in a store because she wanted something that she was not allowed to have. When my friend told her she couldn't have it, she screamed more. Finally, my friend said, "Darling, I am very tired; I have a bad headache, and your screaming is making it worse. You are also giving everyone in the store a headache." Mandy instantly stopped screaming, threw her arms around her mother, and said, "I'm sorry, Mommy, I'm sorry, Mommy."

Like Leo and Sagittarius, Aries is a fire sign. All those born under the fire signs have a need to express themselves, and because Aries is what is known as cardinal fire (cardinal being the most outgoing and expressive), this trait can emerge as self-assertiveness or aggression. Later on, it may develop into competitiveness. One of the best ways to control this "edge" is to find channels for the Aries, such as competitive sports and games. If the energy is suppressed, it can emerge in negative ways, such as temper tantrums or fighting with friends. You can help light the creative spark in your Aries fireball and allow it positive expression through positive reinforcement and intelligent praise.

Another way you can help your Aries child is through developing his awareness of the world around him. Astrologers teach that we are born under a certain Sun sign to develop certain qualities. Because of this innate striving to develop self, your Aries child can be self-centered, and there is a need for him to practice awareness of others and their surroundings. Take the emphasis away from your Aries child's innate self-centeredness by appealing to his warm heart, and you will help him to grow into a kind compassionate human being who is passionate and strong and willing to fight for the underdog. He will then transmute his selfish traits into selfless ones. You can also help through observation games you can play together. These can take the form of looking and describing other people and their surroundings.

Harry Houdini was an Aries. As a child, his father would take him past store windows, then ask him to name and describe all the objects in the window. He quickly developed a photographic memory and could describe every item in the window with only a glance!

Your Aries child may not become a Houdini, but in his own

special and unique way, he will overflow with potential and talent. There is a sense with the sign of Aries that it is all potential – more than most. Your job is to help the potential to manifest and flourish: The danger with Aries is that it can lie dormant without the correct guidance and channels for expression. Two Aries children I know have regular school reports that say: "This child has great potential." Whether your Aries baby develops his full potential is, in part, up to you. It requires just a little help in the right way – through firmness, intelligence, and understanding. Appeal to his sense of fairness and warm-hearted nature, and give him expression for his energy and positive reinforcement. He can then become the creative, enthusiastic, charismatic, sincere, intuitive, intelligent, and brave adult that he has the potential to become.

YOUR ARIES BABY SURVIVAL GUIDE

Birth to One Year

Eating – Your Aries baby has a healthy appetite and won't like to be kept waiting for his food – or anything else, for that matter. Don't worry; he'll let you know loudly when he's hungry. This is the baby who will usually end up with food smeared all over his face. His impatience, combined with his bobbing head, makes it difficult to accurately reach his mouth!

Sleeping – It may be difficult to get this bouncing rattle-banging baby to sleep, but he will delight you with his tremendous enthusiasm for life and all experiences. He is like a rubber ball, bouncing back from his constant scrapes and falls with courage and zest. It is important to allow this high-energy baby to exercise so that he can sleep better. These babies will not enjoy being constricted in playpens.

Motor skills – He is a restless soul, always moving, kicking, and vigorous even before he is born. Aries is the first sign of the Zodiac, and this little bundle loves to be first at everything. He may surprise you by pulling himself up and grabbing onto things in an early attempt to walk before others babies his age. Don't be surprised if he is walking by nine months. He will revel in his newfound independence, and once he is moving around, you will begin to see your baby's individualism emerge.

Language – This baby will say his first words before all the other kids on the block. He loves to tease, and you will quickly see this mischievous quality developing in your fun-loving baby. It is not unusual for these babies to play teasing games with Mommy and Daddy as early as nine months old.

Learning – His fine intelligence shines through his clear focused gaze. His speed of learning is impressive, but don't be surprised when his face turns red in anger and he pounds his little fists. His desire to succeed outweighs his ability to do so, and he is easily frustrated with himself.

Socialization – This infant is not shy, unless he has a more sensitive Moon or Rising sign. He is bold and brave with people and has no trouble expressing his many needs! He delights in life and in people. He loves to be the center of attention and makes his presence felt from the moment he is born.

One to Two Years

Eating – He is strong-willed and demanding about his food. He wants what he wants when he wants it. This can create a battle of wills. He is learning to do things like scoop and pour, so dinnertime can be messy! Teach him the value of compromise and negotiation.

Sleeping – He has natural vitality and lots of energy, so he doesn't seem to need much sleep. He finds it hard to relax, unlike some of the more passive signs. He is either rushing around or completely tired, and he finds it difficult to know when he *is* tired. Teach him about rest, recuperation and, above all, balance.

Motor Skills – This little fireball is likely to ignore your cries of restraint as he climbs the furniture, leaps from the coffee table, and rattles doorknobs. Remember, he is an adventurer. If something is forbidden, he will enjoy it all the more. You can take the doorknobs off, but he will often manage to outwit you with his dexterity and will to succeed. Just be sure the outside doors are locked so that he doesn't escape onto the street when your back is turned.

Language – He will have a growing command of language, which will assist him in asserting his strong will. One thing you can teach this little dynamo is that you are the boss, not him. If he doesn't learn this early on, you'll be in trouble! As it is, he will make many of his own decisions, such as when to stop wearing diapers. Learn to control him with humor, not a heavy hand. This is a toddler who loves to laugh and chuckle.

Socialization – He can be demanding and disobedient and loves to do his own thing. He is also exuberant, enthusiastic, and charming. His playmates will be impressed with his bossy zest for life, while adults of faint heart may fret. Keep him on the straight and narrow by gaining his respect. Praise him for his daring feats, but watch him closely.

Two to Three Years

Eating – At this age, he is learning massive amounts of information, and ordinary activities provide him with opportunities to learn. At lunchtime, introduce him to new skills, such as comparing things: "Daddy has this big spoon for his ice cream, Mommy isn't having dessert and so has no spoon, and you have this little spoon." It is a good opportunity to teach him that eating is a social occasion where other people have needs apart from his.

Sleeping – The ability for make-believe is developing now. Entice him to bed with storytelling; allow this bright toddler to make up stories for you. Three-year-old Aries Sadie loves bedtime because she equates it with telling noisy, laughter-filled, make-believe stories until she's so exhausted that she just conks out, leaving the rest of the household in peace!

Motor Skills – He is now learning the limits of his own strength – both physical and mental. He will be a challenge and a handful, especially if you spoil him. When you are short of time and need to get him to the bathroom, don't force him. Tell him there's no time for him to wash today, and he'll be there in a shot, scrubbing his shiny little face and cleaning his teeth. Once you understand his perverse ways, you can help control him.

Language – He is witty, clever, and quick off the mark. He loves to tease and be teased and is a bundle of fun. He has realized by now that he can boss other people around, and they will often obey him to keep the peace.

Learning – He is quickly learning about the themes of power, will, and might. Noisy things, like tractors and helicopters, impress him, and he is likely to imitate them loudly in his play. He is learning about his own power, and he will enjoy competitive play. Supervise his games to ensure that he doesn't become overly aggressive.

Socialization – There's no denying this kid's a handful, but he will gain admiration wherever he goes. He is ahead of the pack, independent, aggressive, and funny. His natural exuberance can now be channeled into his play with other children. He will strive to be the leader of his pack and number one in every game and adventure; he knows it's his natural place!

Aries Lessons Growing Up: Constantly teach your Aries child about thoughtfulness to other people. Remember, he is easily bored but also easily inspired. He is innately a warrior but can grow into the most chivalrous knight. He will only respect those people who win his respect. He does not respect or care about position for the sake of it. However, you can teach him to appreciate the beauty that lies within all folks, despite their weaknesses. He will need this lesson, for he does not suffer fools gladly. Also, his speed and impatience must be focused into constructive channels. Show him the value of follow-through and completion. This child needs lots of love and discipline. He generally has an overdose of confidence, so it helps him to know that he isn't the most important person in the world. Then his mischievous tendencies can be replaced by thoughtfulness for others. As an impulsive firebrand, it is particularly helpful for him to learn from a very early age that all his words and actions have consequences.

YOUR ARIES BABY JOURNAL

Baby Taurus

April 21 – May 21

Taurus is like the calm that comes after the Aries storm. It is the element of Earth and is calm, steady, solid, and enduring. You may be amazed at the serenity of your newborn – until she erupts – and then you will be equally amazed at the sheer power of this tiny scrap of life. Like volcanoes or earthquakes, the eruptions may not occur frequently, but when they do, they will be memorable.

She may learn and think more slowly than her faster counterparts. However, what she lacks in speed she makes up for in her steadfast attachment. Watch that she doesn't become attached to her favorite food to the exclusion of all else. Taurus baby's loyalty to things she likes is legendary, funny, and – sometimes – irritating. Alice, a Taurus two-year-old, would eat nothing but her favorite foods until she was sick. Her mother tried to interest in her healthy snacks, but as much as she would try and force her, Alice would resist, preferring ice cream, caramel corn, and hot dogs. Give your Taurus baby delicious healthy alternatives using nourishing foods, such as yogurt, honey, and dried fruits. It is far easier to tempt her into submission than to persuade her.

Once tiny Taurus makes up her mind, it is difficult to force her to change. Like Aries, she is strong-willed. Aries, however, will quickly bore and move on to new pastures, whereas Taurus can dig her heels in. Prepare yourself to learn patience with your warm, loving, stubborn Taurus child: You'll need it.

She may easily build the strong stocky build the Taurus is famous for. As well as tasty food and snacks, also provide her with plenty of activities and affection. If you do this, overeating should not be a problem.

A more difficult task is to persuade your growing infant to get sufficient fresh air and exercise. Taurus baby can be so pleasure-loving and relaxed that she doesn't feel the need to move around. She is not really lazy, just charmingly at home with her own comforts!

Born under an earth sign, she is attuned to the material world and to nature. She may enjoy riding on a tricycle, watching the world go by, and get her exercise at the same time. This is the type of activity Taurus likes, rather than competitive games and sports.

Taurus babies enjoy nature and feel happy and peaceful in the countryside. If you live in the city, do take her on leisurely walks with her favorite dog. Taureans are affectionate and love to touch and are good with pets; she can express her sensuous nature by stroking and hugging her loving companion.

Taurus is the builder of the Zodiac, and with her artistic flair, she could later make a talented interior designer or architect. Provide her with building blocks, as she loves to see the fruits of her labors take shape. A friend's son, Edward, would spend an entire day at the seaside sitting in a hole in the sand with his bucket and spade, endlessly making sand castles, while his Aries sister, Felicity, would zoom around the beach, knocking them down. With endless patience, Edward would quietly pick up his little spade and start digging all over again!

You may be amazed at how your little Taurus can continue doing the same thing until her steam runs out. She has masses of determination and reserve energy, so this can take hours – or even days. Be assured that her dogged persistence will pay dividends later in life. What does not come easily to her, however, is new ideas. The world of ideas seems rather abstract to this "material girl," who is so attuned to the solid world of form. Explain the purpose of things to her in practical down-to-earth terms.

She is so loyal and persistent, it is important that you express the same consistency with her. She will feel insecure with a lifestyle that involves changes of residence, emotional change, or inconsistencies in general. If you are a Gemini with a Sagittarian husband and you love to argue and go on adventures, do remember to curb your impulses around your infant. To her, sameness and routine represent security. When this is threatened, she may become extremely possessive, hanging on to her toys as a crutch.

However, we all go through changes at times, and some of these may be unpleasant. As long as you are aware of the effects on your infant and can help ease her way through them, you will be impressed with her tremendous strength of character, which seems way beyond her years. She can be extraordinarily mature, supporting you with affection and devotion during your own trials. It will be then that you see the truly wonderful qualities of your Taurus child. All she will ask in return is that you hug her, love her, and value her.

Taureans are exceptionally magnetic and, because of this, make very good healers of people, plants, and animals. They seem to carry with them a storehouse of quiet vitality that they can channel, using their good concentrative abilities, to help and heal others. Even as a baby, you can feel her quiet strength and magnetic energy.

You can see by now that your baby Taurus is the sweetest, most loyal and thoughtful child. However, if she feels she is not valued – by you, her teacher, or her playmate – the world had better watch out! Once you see an emotional storm brewing beneath her calm exterior, prepare for the fact that your world will never seem the same again.

This does not mean you should live in fear of upsetting her, but always be there for her on some level. Respect her and allow her to express her emotions so that she can let them go and move on. The worst thing is to push her into doing something she doesn't want to do or feel ready to do. Just support her, and eventually she will change.

Victoria was a Taurus three-year-old who loved to dance, as is often the case with this artistic sign ruled by the planet Venus. Her mother was thrilled by Victoria's potential and believed she had the talent to become a ballerina. Victoria enjoyed her mother's encouragement and asked to join a children's dance class. When the big day finally arrived, she looked adorable, kitted out in her pretty tutu and ballet slippers. Her mother proudly took her into a room full of children, when suddenly Victoria dug her heels in and screamed, "I want to go home! Take me home! I want to go home!" at the top of her lungs. The more her mother pushed Victoria into the room, the more she dug her heels into the floor. She just wasn't ready to dance in a crowded room full of strangers. Her fear of new situations overwhelmed her, and she displayed tremendous resistance.

A better strategy for Victoria would have been for her mother to have taken her to watch the dance classes a few times, then to introduce her to the other children. In this way, the dance class would have become a part of her own routine. Because she felt forced into doing it, she ended up refusing to do it. Over fifteen years later, Victoria has never set foot in a dance class again!

Every sign has a strength and beauty within it. On the positive side, Taureans are loving, loyal, strong, and contented. As she matures, she will lend her strength and support to others, bringing balance and healing. She has the ability to bring things to completion, which is so essential to success in life. She will bring magic into your life with her innate ability to cherish even the most mundane things. She sees beauty in a little daisy or a blade of grass. Encourage her patiently in her love of life and appreciation of nature, and she will blossom into the strongest, finest, most ethical person you could ever hope to meet.

YOUR TAURUS BABY SURVIVAL GUIDE

Birth to One Year

Eating – Your Taurus baby will eat her food with gusto. She is the master chef and gourmet in the making. You may be amazed that such a tiny scrap can consume such vast amounts of food without a pause. Just make sure you don't run out of her favorite flavor, and keep her meals on schedule. From an early age, this placid yet strong-willed infant will know exactly what she likes and exactly what she doesn't in the food department.

Sleeping – Baby Taurus also loves to sleep. Being an earth sign, she is attuned to the pleasures of daily life from a very early age. Make sure you establish a good regular sleeping routine for this loving child. She is a creature of habit who craves routine. If you keep her up too late or put her to bed at the wrong time, she will definitely let you know. Give her what she wants and needs, and in return, she will give you peace!

Motor Skills – She is placid, easygoing, loving, and slow to learn. She is more of a tortoise than a hare, and, like the tortoise, she will always get there in the end. Be patient with her and give her lots of hugs and kisses. She is affectionate and loves to be touched; it helps her to grow strong and true. While other children are crawling, she may still be sitting and smiling. In fact, you may find she never crawls as much as other children and may go straight from sitting to walking.

Language – Your Taurus baby may be inclined to whimper rather than cry or scream. However, if she is ignored or feeling wet and uncomfortable , the whimper may quickly increase to a resounding bellow. Although stubborn, she is easily comforted with soothing words and strokes.

Learning – As Taurus is grounded in the material world, she learns through her five senses. If she can see, hear, touch, or smell something, she will be more inclined to learn. When you give her a toy, she will hold it to her nose and smell it, squish it with her hands, and plainly enjoy the feeling of it.

Socialization – This contented, loving, self-contained child is always popular. She is the baby other adults secretly wish was theirs. She smiles for everyone, gurgles and chuckles and is pleasant and sociable right from birth. She likes people and is born a charmer.

One to Two Years

Eating – You have gathered by now that your Taurus baby likes nice things. Give her a Winnie the Pooh bowl and pretty cup; she will appreciate her own things, and the prettier they are, the more inclined she will be to enjoy her food and not spatter it all over you.

Sleeping – Be aware that this physically-attuned baby is highly sensitive and can be irritated by man-made fibers. Give her nice all-cotton nightclothes and woolen blankets. This will help her to sleep deeply and soundly.

Motor Skills – Although she may not be the fastest kid on the block right now, she can outshine her playmates as time goes on through her sheer determination and willpower. She is not inclined to physical movement or dashing about. When she does finally begin to walk, she is likely to carry with her a favorite teddy bear, not wishing to be parted.

Language – You may notice that she gazes at you with tremendous focus. This is not necessarily just because she adores you, but that is how she learns to talk and communicate. She has surprising powers of concentration and observation. Although she may not be chatting as quickly as some other children (unless she has a Gemini Moon or similar), she may gain a wide and interesting vocabulary. She is an artistic soul who enjoys the power of words.

Learning – Give her toys of varying textures and also practical toys from which she can learn. Taurus is the builder of the Zodiac, and she likes to feel that her efforts will last. She may be possessive with her belongings, as they represent security to her. Encourage her to join in games with others, and you will help her learn the important lessons of cooperation and sharing.

Socialization – She is obedient and well-mannered. Although she does things her way, she also adores harmony and can fit into a team of playmates. She is popular but not pushy. But at this age, she may prefer to spend time playing on her own.

Two to Three Years

Eating – By now, she knows that when she is good, she gets candy or cookies. Conversely, when she wants to get 'round you, you will feel a sticky sweet pressed into your palm. Touch and food are very important to her, and a barometer of show well she is doing. Watch her diet, replacing candy with fresh fruit.

Sleeping – She is able to rest and sleep easily and readily, as long as there is comfort and routine in her life. She does not like her sleep or her mealtimes disturbed. Two-year-old Taurus Kevin always tugs on his mother's sleeve when they are way from home at a relative's house, saying, "Isn't it time I was in bed?"

Motor Skills – She loves nature and the great outdoors but is physically rather lazy. Because of this, she is not inclined to run around but prefers to go for a ride. To ensure she gets the exercise she needs, take her to music or dance classes. She will enjoy this much more than rough-and-tumble play. She responds happily to music and rhythm.

Language – Your Taurus child has a naturally sweet voice and should be encouraged to sing. This is a great way for her to develop her language skills and increase her socialization. She has a good ear for music and may be one of the rare kids who actually enjoys her piano lessons. If she likes the teacher and enjoys herself, she may continue to play for years to come.

Learning – She enjoys saving money once she understands how it works. Buy her a piggy bank and encourage her to save, as well as spend wisely. Set up a savings account and use it to teach her the price and value of things. Also teach her about love and the importance of values such as honesty, integrity, and courage.

Socialization – She is now more inclined to want to play in a group than before. She prefers a harmonious little group of two or three friends to a large, noisy, highly-strung group. Her high level of concentration, combined with a healthy dose of imagination, enables her to play with her friends for hours with tea sets and finger paints.

Taurus Lessons Growing Up: Teach your Taurus baby about the value of sharing with others. She is inclined to be possessive and holds onto her toys as security. If you give her plenty of security in the form of love, hugs, and endearments, she will not need her toys in the same way. She is kindhearted, so if you encourage her to share her toys with those less fortunate, she will respond. Teach her about the purpose of money, its pitfalls and limitations. She understands money from a young age but can become overly concerned about it. Give her a plant to water or a little bit of your garden to tend; she relates to the Earth and gardening is soothing for her young soul. Teach her that love is more important than money, and give her a good and solid code of ethics by which to live her life.

YOUR TAURUS BABY JOURNAL

Baby Gemini

May 21 – June 21

For your Gemini baby, variety is the spice of life. If you are trying to get him into a more regular schedule for your benefit, it might be difficult. Try distracting him by rocking him on your shoulder or carrying him. When he is twisting, squirming, and rolling all over while you are trying to change his diaper (common for all babies that age), try talking to him enthusiastically about what's going on in your life. You may be surprised that his delighted responses, although incomprehensible, resemble real conversation so much that you are sure he understands everything you are saying. And indeed he might. One Gemini child told me that one of the most frustrating things he remembers as a baby was that adults talked to him in garbled baby talk. He said he could never understand why they didn't talk to him normally!

Another way to calm your Gemini baby is to give him a stack of toys or objects to play with. Make sure there are several because once he has probed and banged around the first one a bit, he will be ready for more. Also, Geminis love movement and motion, so just put him on your shoulder and walk around, bouncing him up and down, or put him in a bouncy chair.

Be prepared to put your skates on once baby Gemini arrives. Unlike the slow patient Taurus, your Gemini child will be fast and everywhere at once. Your main challenge will be learning how to keep up with him. Gemini is the sign of the twins, and you will feel as if you have at least two children, not just one. This baby can out-talk, out-walk, out-think, and out-smart almost everyone else. Despite the arsenal of games you may have for him, he will rapidly zip through them all and be eater for more. He loves to play, and he loves to communicate.

Unless your Gemini baby has a Capricorn Moon, or some other more grounded aspects in his chart, he will love to chatter and talk as he rushes from thing to thing and person to person, evading even your most ingenious attempts at discipline. Keep him occupied with plenty of challenging activities so that his energy fizzles out before yours does!

Wait until he is crawling and talking; then you will really feel the high-pitch energy of the Gemini. You will be amazed at his ability to do several things at once, occupying his hands, his brain, and his mouth. Don't be surprised to see him playing a game, listening to music, talking aloud, and paying attention all at the same time! He may miss half of what you say, but he will get the gist of it. He is not a plodder; he will not hang on to your every word, but he catches on quickly and doesn't want or need long exhaustive explanations.

There is no doubt that your baby Gemini is bright, alert, and intelligent. You realized that as soon as he first gurgled in delight at something you said. If you happen to be a slower, more thorough type of person, don't expect your infant to be the same. He may rarely finish a game he has started, but he will make up for it by dazzling adults and playmates alike with his wit and cheeky remarks.

As soon as he is able to chuckle and say, "Mama, dada," there begins his lifelong love affair with language. Even before age two, you may find him animatedly "reading" to himself from memory the stories you have read him. He is wired fast, so watch that he doesn't overextend himself in his restless attempts to do too many things at once an take on too much. Get him to slow down for regular rests and refueling. Unlike Taurus, rest does not come naturally to Gemini and food is definitely not his main priority.

Life offers so many exciting distractions for your Gemini baby. His sparkling eyes gaze at the world with more aliveness than those of other babies. This baby is ever alert to opportunity. This can be a source of joy or a source of irritation, as you find yourself following his path of discarded toys. Teach him to pick up his toys, but try not to be upset by his scattered approach to life. Your

Gemini baby's way of understanding what the world is all about is to examine as many details as possible, then to gradually organize them into a coherent pattern. He may not be orderly in the way that the Virgo infant is, but do not fear his future school grades. He is bright enough to pass his exams – and then some.

Taming your curious Gemini infant is rather like trying to catch the wind. Your best bet is to reason with him. Even as a toddler, he is quite mature in this area and will be happy to discuss things with you. One mistake, however, is to present him with choices. Making decisions is not his strong suit. He enjoys the diversity and richness of every new experience, so choosing just one is an impossible task.

When life becomes exasperating, talk to him like the two-year-old adult he is and tell him how you're feeling. You will be surprised at his understanding. By the way, although your infant may at times seem more mature than you are, the Gemini adult remains a child forever. If you can work this out, you are well on the way to understanding the diversity of Gemini.

Your Gemini baby has a way of keeping you youthful and up-to-date. Prepare yourself for constant questioning about the relationships between things. "What's that?" "That's a tree." "Why is it green?" "Why does it look so old?" "What is the tree's name?" As soon as your baby can talk, he will open your eyes to life and a whole new way of looking at the world. He is precocious, intelligent, and always eager for information or in pursuit of some object of his curiosity, in the way that other children are eager for candy or toys.

Your Gemini baby's nervous system is wired fast, and *wiry* may be a good way to describe his characteristically slight alert physique. Although you may be a harried parent with several other demanding children, do respect your infant's constant needs to express himself. If you just do not have the time for constant communication, then set aside a special time each day to converse with him. Even when he is is as young as two-and-a-half to three-years-old, you can collaborate with him in composing limericks or playing question-and-answer games. Even better, ask him to tell you a story. All this is excellent discipline for the tremendous mental energy your Gemini infant possesses. Apart from that, he will entertain you and give you a well-deserved laugh at the end of a long day!

Humor is his middle name. He can see the funny side of even the most serious situations. This will get him into trouble but also make him a champion with his playmates. He will be a popular child because he is always bright and witty and never one for long, boring, tedious explanations. He can be a brilliant mimic, and when you are telling him off, just make sure he is standing where you can see him!

My hairdresser's precocious three-year-old Gemini son, Jason, was a great mimic. When my hairdresser was mad, he would stand behind her with his hand on his hip as she did, imitating her wagging finger and facial expressions. With Jason around, she could never stay mad for long!

If you lose your temper in his presence, beware. It will become one of the ever-growing repertoire of amusing incidents that he will use to entertain his family and playmates alike. He will not spare your feelings, but he will always cheer you up.

On the subject of feelings, don't expect him to be particularly sensitive. While is intellectual side is well-developed, his feeling side is not. He is more rational than emotional, and if he upsets you, do not bother to sulk. The effect will be lost on him, as he will not understand what you are doing. It is far more effective to let him know how he has upset you. He will appreciate this and will be eager to learn about the diversity of people and their feelings and reactions. Although he seems bright and mature, he will generally have much to learn in the area of human emotions.

Although not overly emotional, he can be moody. He is a chameleon, ever changing, as if there were a whole bunch of children rolled into one. Remember that variety is his constant, and you will understand him better. If he becomes angry or irritable, distract him and lead him in the direction you want. He is malleable and can change as quickly and easily as the breeze.

As soon as he can crawl, your toddler will be in and out of every room, cupboard, nook, and cranny in the house. He loves to travel. As he gets older, he will be happy to go on walks, visits, and excursions. He is not the child to drag his feet when visiting Aunt Freda. He will enjoy the visit and be able to hold a grown-up conversation with any of the adults. Just make sure the journey is not too long and you have plenty of books and games in the car, for as soon as you have turned the corner from your house, he will ask, "Are we there yet?" Bring a good supply of books, toys, and games. If he goes quiet, it is probably because he has discovered your Aunt Freda's kitchen cupboard and is busy opening up all the interesting pots and jars.

As he gets older, you'll just have to learn to be tolerant of experiments on the floor and obstacle courses around the house. He does not need expensive state-of-the-art toys (though he'll ask for them as soon as he goes to school and learns about them from his classmates). As a baby, he is equally at home with a spool of thread, a jar, and a few household objects as the latest and greatest toy. Todd, an ingenious three-year-old Gemini, recently constructed a working model night-light from odds and ends his father had given him.

YOUR GEMINI BABY SURVIVAL GUIDE

Birth to One Year

Eating – Food is not your Gemini infant's main concern. The world around him is just too distracting for him to waste time eating. Do not expect mealtimes to be regular routines. Establishing any kind of routine for this fascinating and fasci-nated infant is quite a challenge!

Sleeping – This is another interesting challenge. He is not the baby who is happy when you turn off the light. There is too much still to investigate. Gemini's love words, so try rocking him to sleep while reading or singing softly to him. Then, as soon as he dozes off, make a quick exit before he changes his mind!

Motor Skills – Your Gemini baby will be eager to move around and play with his newfound toes, waving his legs and arms around excitedly. He can't wait to start crawling and getting into all those forbidden places.

Language – This little mercurial infant adores language. By the time he is one, he may well be learning new words every day. It is important you spend time talking to him because communication is his *raison d'être*. Don't restrict yourself to baby language; he will take in every word and mimic it; far better to expand his vocabulary as soon as you can.

Learning – He has tremendous mental curiosity. He is a natural explorer, always seeking new and varied experiences. As soon as something captures his attention, he will seek to understand it – and then move on to the next experience.

Socialization – Because he loves to chatter and smile in his friendly mischievous manner, he will enjoy the company of others. He is naturally sociable and will grow to become the life and soul of the party.

One to Two Years

Eating – Food does not provide emotional comfort for this little one but is a distraction. Life itself is food for him. Offer small bites of new foods and let him decide if he wants more. Expose him to new foods as you both explore what he likes to eat. You can offer foods he has previously refused; he quickly changes his mind about his likes and dislikes.

Sleeping – He tends to get overtired and doesn't enjoy switching off to go to sleep. There is too much to see and discover. At this age, he loves repetition. Repeat his favorite songs and nursery rhymes as a way to get him to bed.

Motor Skills – I knew a Gemini baby of almost eighteen months who would insist on climbing up onto the kitchen table. There was something about that rickety table that appealed to his sense of adventure and curiosity, despite his mother's insistence to the contrary. You have to stay alert to catch up to this little quicksilver.

Language – While a sharp "Don't do that!" won't cut it with this intelligent child, a short explanation on reasons why not will stand more chance of being heard.

Learning – While he devours facts and information about the outside world, he is not so good at learning about himself. Because of this, you may find regular routines, such as toilet training, a challenge. Encourage him to let you know when he feels the urge, or he may get out of the habit.

Socialization – With his sharp mind and observation skills, combined with a natural curiosity about people, this little one makes friends easily. He loves fun and games and will soon learn that his funny antics and faces can make you laugh.

Two to Three Years

Eating – He prefers to talk rather than eat, and as soon as he can toddle around, it may be difficult to get him to sit still. Explain to him the benefits of relaxed eating; otherwise, it will set up a pattern in his life in which he will always be eating on the run, causing him to run out of steam. Get him interested in mealtimes by letting him help set the table or pour out water for people.

Sleeping – Warning signs that he is overtired are that he will chatter incessantly and also run around doing many different things at once. You can start now to teach him about his body and about why he needs sleep. The more he understands the benefits, the more likely he is to fall asleep.

Motor Skills – It is important to give your Gemini baby stimulation and variety. When you are showing him some new skill, you won't need to belabor the point. He is a very quick learner. He will enjoy crafts that allow him to cut and paste, color, string things, and build.

Language – His language skills are growing rapidly, so spend time talking to him every day; use everyday opportunities, such as folding the laundry or peeling the vegetables, to converse with him and ask questions. An occasional television program can be good discipline. Join him and engage him in conversation about what's happening on the show. If he gets frustrated and upset about something, help him to identify it by expressing the cause in words.

Learning – Do not offer him too many choices. Instead, let him know the plans for the day. If he objects, have a second choice ready up your sleeve. Gemini's at any age are not good with choices; unfortunately, at this age, choices are impossible.

Socialization – Provide him with plenty of opportunities to play and social time. As he can see both sides of an issue, he may take on the role of referee with his friends.

Gemini Lessons Growing Up: Bright, intelligent, and dexterous, this little fun-filled person can lack focus and concentration. It is important that he enjoy variety while being shown how to focus his mind and the importance of follow-through. He is witty and clever but needs to learn the lessons of tact and diplomacy and to get more in touch with his feelings. One of the best things you can teach him is the value and beauty of listening to others, especially those who are ore slow-witted than he is (most of us!). He loves to talk, but listening does not come easily. Explain that communication is a two-way process and we have two ears and only one mouth for a reason!.

YOUR GEMINI BABY JOURNAL

Baby Cancer

June 22 – July 23

While Gemini is friendly and bright as a button, baby Cancer is sweet, sensitive, cautious, and retiring. Do not expect your baby to take instantly to strangers. While baby Gemini operates in the world of intellect, your Cancer baby operates in the just as real world of emotions and feelings. If she does not feel like being friendly or sociable, she won't be. As a child, it is that simple. Do not be embarrassed if your baby clings to you and hides in your skirts when a kindhearted stranger stops to say how pretty she is. Cancerians do not take kindly to new things and people. They need time to adjust. They can be just as sociable, amusing, and witty as anyone once they have matured, but never rush them into things. As a baby, she needs lots of nurturing, encouragement, and security.

You will be pleased to hear that, as your baby's keynote is feeling, she will have a type of "psychic antenna" toward any difficult people or potentially dangerous situations. This intuitive sensitivity needs to be developed, not ignored, so that she can evolve in the world of her feelings and stay safe and secure. Do take heed of her feelings, and don't ignore them for appearing illogical.

This serious infant has a softness about her, and she needs the coziness of a secure home, close by her mother's side. The sign of Cancer is symbolized by the crab; like the crab, she may display a hard outer shell to protect her inner softness and vulnerability.

This outer shell is her home, and she has a way of making a home wherever she is. As soon as she can crawl around and play with toys, you'll see her gravitating toward doll's houses and even building little houses for herself out of chairs and plastic bricks. It's as if she knows her home represents the protection she needs from the harsh world outside.

She may be crotchety and moody at times. Perhaps you have been late with her food (definitely cause for concern for the Cancer baby who thrives on routine, especially with regard to meals!). Perhaps she is upset about something. Give her lots of cuddles and kisses and surround her in a cocoon of love and nurturing. Cancer baby will blossom in the presence of home and family, and her childhood years will be among the happiest of her life.

Later on, you will be surprised at how many details she will vividly remember and recount from her early childhood, long after you have forgotten them. She is a wonderful storyteller because of this and can always get an audience for her amusing true-to-life stories. Through this ability to retain and recount events and memories from the past, Cancerians draw people around them from a young age.

Your Cancer baby loves to collect and hold on to things. Don't be surprised if she refuses to let go of her first teddy bear, which is now well-chewed and dirty. Your best bet is to wait until she is asleep and prise it away from her to wash it and return. Just make sure you don't wake her in the process, or you may have a struggle on your hands.

All objects hold sentimental value to your Cancer child. Make sure there is plenty of room in your house for the seashells she gathered, her dress-up clothes, and all the dolls and soft toys. With her wonderfully vivid imagination, she will give names to everything and invest life and love into them all. A brand-new walkie-talkie doll does not necessarily get pride of place over the dusty old tattered one. Your little Cancer infant is not impressed by surface appearances.

Although she likes to hold tight to what is hers, she will also solemnly declare that she is giving everyone gifts from time to time. These gifts may not be impressive to you, but accept them in the spirit they are given. Giving away her old toys is a big deal for her, and it represents a sense of connection to those she loves.

Another way you can help your Cancer baby to develop healthily is by helping her overcome her insecurity and timidity in new situations and with new people. You cannot keep her in a cocoon, as much as she may want that. She will grow by facing the new, and if she is insulated too much as a child, she will have a hard time when she eventually ventures into the world. Her fear can manifest as crabby moods and silences that even she does not really understand.

If you respect and understand her, the Cancer baby will grow into a thoughtful, helpful, and affectionate person. You cannot pull the wool over her eyes; she responds to you emotionally, will feel what is really in your heart, and will resist being manipulated. If her emotions are thwarted and she is upset about something, you may find her with a spate of tummy upsets. Cancers are particularly vulnerable in this area of the body, which is rather like the soft underside of the crab!

You can help her toward a deeper understanding of her fluctuating emotions by helping her gain perspective at a very young age. In other words, encourage her to channel her deep feelings. Teach her the value of kindness and the importance of helping and caring for others. She may have a tendency to be wrapped up in her own private feelings, but as she is naturally kindhearted, you can easily touch her heart and encourage her to think of others. This will help her balance her emotions, instead of bottling them up with tears and moods.

Encourage her to be responsible with her dolls, siblings, and friends. Even at a very young age, she has a protective instinct and sense of responsibility. I recently met parents of a Cancerian toddler. Emily was only two-and-a-half, but they told me how she would watch them carefully while they changed her little brother's diapers, then she would ask them to do the same.

Another way you can help your Cancer baby is literally to place her in her element – water. Give her a bath or take her to the ocean. Little Thomas would sit in his paddling pool for hours, just gurgling happily to himself. Water is his natural medium, and it is here that he feels peaceful and secure. Cancer enjoys melodious soothing music and natural sounds such as the rain, the ocean waves, and the rustling branches in the wind.

All infants love fairy tales, but she will be especially drawn to this magical world. She likes to make everyday life into a romantic expression of her inner dreams. Encourage her to do so, while also teaching her about the practical necessities of life. Never squash her imagination but give it full rein. Allow her to spin dreams and she may one day become an inspired artist or writer, bringing dreams alive in the minds and hearts of others.

While you might have to scold the headstrong Aries, the stubborn Taurus, or the quicksilver Gemini child, you may never need to scold your Cancer child to get your disapproval noticed. She will be perfectly aware of your anger and will be the first to give you a big hug if you let her. She does not like to see you upset. She will probably feel bad enough about her behavior as it is.

While her sensitivity can cause her discomfort and her irritable displays and moods may be frequent, she can light up your life with her generous affection, love, and caring. Even as a tiny baby, she will cheer you up when you are down, and when you are happy, she will bask in the reflection of your joy. Encourage her in her rich world of feeling and imagination, introduce new adventures into her life, help her to overcome her shyness and extreme caution, and she will grow into a caring, compassionate soul who will bring light into your life and into the world.

YOUR CANCER BABY SURVIVAL GUIDE

Birth to One Year

Eating – Your adorable Cancer baby may be a mystery to you. Just remember she lives in the world of her feelings and so is as changeable as the wind. Her moods are erratic, and she will be crying one minute and gurgling the next. Her feeding may be equally erratic. Don't worry about it; just accept that it's her, not you. Don't try and rush her into solid foods – or anything else, for that matter. She is in no hurry and will get there in her own good time.

Sleeping – This child loves to be nurtured and may even fall asleep in the bath; she is in her element and enjoys the gentle soothing feeling of the water. She will love to be rocked asleep or cuddled, as her tactile senses are very strong. You may try a crib-hanging toy, such as an aquarium.

Motor Skills – This is the age when tremendous changes take place extremely rapidly, and you may see sudden spurts in development. However, don't be impatient that she is not moving around as much as other babies her age. She loves to lie silently, soaking up impressions of her new world, and needs plenty of time to rest and absorb.

Language – Take extra care to speak in soothing tones, and don't keep her in an environment with lots of loud music, anger, or noisy chatter. This is not the baby (and I really don't think there are any) to take with you to the latest war movie.

Learning – She may wail particularly loudly when you leave the room, rarely giving you a minute's break. During these first few months, she is learning about who cares about her and who is a stranger as her attachments and feelings deepen. Above all, your Cancer baby seeks a reliable and constant source of love to give her the environment she needs in which to learn. Play hide-and-seek, go-and-fetch, and peek-a-boo games. These help her learn that people and objects disappear and return.

Socialization – Give her the chance to be with other children as often as you can. This is healthy for this loving but rather clingy child. She will also enjoy a friendly pet, especially if it is gentle and cuddly.

One to Two Years

Eating – When she is happy, she will eat well. If the emotional peace of her environment or of herself is disturbed, her eating habits will be also. She is very sensitive to atmospheres, and if you have a large noisy family, you may notice her go off into her own world and start playing with her food. Provide a calm loving atmosphere to avoid eating disorders later in life.

Sleeping – She enjoys being held and cuddled. This provides her with physical as well as emotional comfort. She likes to be tucked up in bed and sung to or held close and rocked. She loves to feel secure and cozy.

Motor Skills – She will delight in her newfound ability to walk and find special corners for herself. Like her symbol, the crab, she will carry her home around with her. This may take the form of pillows and assorted chairs – anything to create her own private place. You had better have an invitation before you visit!

Language – Sometimes she will chatter incessantly, and sometimes she will seem shy and withdrawn. Her communication is based on how she feels. How she feels is usually based on nothing you can fathom. She may be jealous of the new cat or anxious that you spent too much time away from her. Don't try to talk her out of her moods. They are not born out of stubbornness but emerge from somewhere deep inside her. Even she doesn't usually understand them.

Learning – She is learning that the world is very big and dangerous. People come and go and sometimes never return.

Teach her about security. Allow her to bring something with her from home, such as her favorite toy or blanket, to let her know that home is still part of her day.

Socialization – She is shy with strangers but affectionate with those close to her, including her toys. She may have one toy to whom she chatters and who goes everywhere with her, including bed. She is quite possessive of her belongings and concerned that they are safe. Darwin, a Cancer two-year-old, would place his teddy bear in the bread bin every night. This was teddy's nest; he would cover teddy with a pink-spotted tea towel and leave the bin open just a crack so that teddy could breathe.

Two to Three Years

Eating – More and more, she will want to be a "big girl." As a Cancer, she is attuned to the home and the joys of mealtimes and delicious food. Encourage her to help you with food preparation. She will enjoy putting the raisins in the cookie mix and putting her sticky fingers in her mouth!

Sleeping – Make sure she is calm before she goes to sleep, and she will sleep well. Take her out onto the porch and get her to smell the flowers and listen to the sounds of early evening before retiring.

Motor Skills – She may have been rather jealous of her siblings. By now, those feelings have probably been resolved and replaced by tremendous loyalty. She is kind and concerned about those she loves. Never pressure your Cancer child to relate to a stranger. She will accept others in good time, relying heavily on her impressions.

Language – You may find her chattering away to an invisible friend. Often natural psychics, Cancer children may indeed be talking to the fairy in the garden. Just accept this as part of life, and she may happily share with you her latest adventure. This is a good way for her to develop language skills, as well as her wonderful imagination and psychic abilities.

Learning – She is now starting to learn what works for her and what doesn't. She is more secure and probably no longer wails every time you make some change in the home or invite a new friend round for tea. She no longer cries at the drop of a hat; she is learning to work out why things upset her and to trust her acutely sensitive nature.

Socialization – She often prefers quiet play by herself to the more active social scene at nursery school. She is not especially outgoing but may develop strong links with her teacher and playmates as they become part of her extended family. The more confident she becomes, the more at home she will feel – and the bossier she may become! Cancers like to be in control and may fuss over others they are close to.

Cancer Lessons Growing Up: More than with any other sign, a happy home life and good, loving, and secure relationships with parents is important for the Cancer child and will guarantee a well-adjusted adult. These sensitive souls need to learn to care for and share with their friends and siblings without feeling threatened. Even at a young age, they need a channel for their strong feelings and nurturing abilities. Encourage your kindhearted Cancerian to offer support and comfort to others. I know a three-year-old who collects all the used bottles and cans (they are great collectors) in the household and insists on their being recycled; he dutifully saves up the coins he receives to buy a Christmas gift for the elderly, housebound, next-door neighbor. A wonderful example to us all!

YOUR CANCER BABY JOURNAL

Baby Leo

July 24 – August 22

Probably even from before he is born, your Leo baby will make his presence felt. Your little Leo king is like the sun. He generously radiates warmth, joy, and zest for life to all, expecting to be the center of the solar system! He is extremely lovable, and nobody can fail to be warmed by his sunny disposition and easy laugh. You will feel proud of your adorable and adored infant, and others will gather 'round his stroller. Even as a baby, he can attract a crowd of adoring females, and this trend will continue throughout his life. He is graceful and strong and draws admiration with his handsome looks.

He will expect to be the leader, and leadership comes naturally to this regal sign. He will expect to be obeyed by his friends, members of his play group – and even you. However, it won't be a chore. His bossiness will have a playful air about it, and you will enjoy his gregarious personality and exuberant charm.

You may have realized by now that your Leo baby is meant for stardom. He needs to shine and fly high; he needs expression for his zest for life and generosity. So far he sounds perfect, but, as with all the signs, there are weaknesses as well as strong points. The weaknesses may be quite well hidden by the confident air of authority he exudes from the moment he can first make his presence felt. However, weaknesses they are, and when you scratch the surface, they'll come tumbling out. Better that you are aware of them before he completely bowls you over with his charm into thinking he's perfect. You can help him fly even higher if you know his weak points as well as his strengths.

Your Leo baby can become so used to adoration and unquestioning loyalty and support that he grows up thinking the world is his oyster. That everyone is here to do his bidding. He can become full of himself and his own importance. It is your job to ensure that your Leo baby becomes the talented, creative, gregarious, warmhearted, generous leader that he really is.

His tendency toward arrogance is more than compensated for by his generous displays of fun, love, and magnanimity all rolled into one. People are entranced by your Leo infant and happy to let him take charge. He will lavish so much warmth and affection on his playmates that they are happy just to stay and bask in the Leo sunshine. Love him and adore him, but always be aware of this trait. Baby Leo will seek the limelight, which is his birthright. However, if he starts creating dramatic scenes to gain center stage, beware. While it is not a good idea to quench Leo's natural enthusiasm, it is good to introduce discipline and respect at a very early age. More than most, he will seek power. You can teach him that power comes through being a good person, rather than through bullying others. But, if you see him fighting his playmates, do not embarrass him by shouting or sending him to his room.

Baxter was three when his parents would often invite all his playmates 'round for tea and games. One favorite game was hospitals. Baxter was the doctor in change, and his job was to make all the patients feel comfortable and ensure that all the nurses and other doctors worked well together. It was amazing to see him in action, organizing and informing his playmates of their roles and acting as their magnanimous leader. He showed them all a good time, and giggles could always be heard. By acting out this role, Baxter was learning the value of taking responsibility for others and showing fairness to all.

Another thing Leos love to do is dress up. As a natural actor, life is all about making impressions. Don't throw away your old feather boa, fireman's helmet, evening tiara, or costume jewelry. Leos will dress up in just about anything that sets them apart from the norm.

If his innate need for show and drama is not met – beware! The father of two-year-old Amanda had to lock himself in the bathroom to get a moment's peace from her constant demands for attention!

One thing you should never do with your bright Leo infant is embarrass him – especially in front of others. Self-respect and respect for others are tied up together in your Leo baby. He needs to be able to respect you, just as you should respect him.

In his first few years, he will look to you as his role model and turn to you for guidance. He will expect wisdom and maturity from you and will watch you closely in your dealings with others. If you treat others with consideration and generosity, he will strive to follow your example.

Leo can be as regal as they come, but he also has an innate love for all life and all people. His generosity embraces the world and everything in it. He is not petty or small-minded about anything and may give away his most precious toy or possession – just because he lives to give. Don't discourage him in his generosity, but applaud it.

Because of his sensitive ego, he hates to be ignored or dismissed. However, your sunny Leo infant won't usually sulk; he just needs a big hug, and all is well again. If he trusts and respects someone, he can always forgive them, no matter how mean they may have been. Leo wants to love people; it is his natural state. He can forgive and rise above pettiness or nastiness. If you teach him that everyone should be respected, no matter what their position, status, age, color, creed, or nationality, then these values will form the basis of his life and will constantly stoke the fires of love that are so much a part of his nature.

Like all those born under the fire signs, he is naturally expressive. He may be a chatterbox, always wanting to share with you his latest discovery or adventure. Life will be fun with your Leo infant, and he will share his hugs, affections, and feelings for you just as readily has his candy or details of his new friend.

Encourage him to paint and draw and color, to sing and play an instrument, to dance and tell stories. He loves to do everything on a grand scale, so get plenty of art paper – and as large as possible! You will be impressed by his artistic talent and may wonder where his creativity came from. Creativity is his essence. Just as Cancer is attuned to the world of feelings, so Leo is attuned to the world of creation. If he is not artistic or musical, you can rest assured that he will be creative in some other way. Justin had no apparent artistic talents as an infant, yet he grew into an amazing inventor. At the age of eight, he invented a board game that won a national competition and was bought by an international company.

Your Leo baby will shine like the sun and light up your whole family. You will see him basking in the love he receives from those around him and throughout his life. Positive vibrations are like food for the Leo soul. But if a Leo baby is given the love and affection he craves, his deep attachment to the family will be great, and he may find it hard to leave and venture into the world. You can help him overcome this hurdle when the time comes for him to go to playschool by showing him that his love can continue to be given as a gift to all he meets. If you do this, then your Leo baby will grow full of love and have a zest for life, with the ability to inspire and impress everyone he meets.

YOUR LEO BABY SURVIVAL GUIDE

Birth to One Year

Eating – The first thing to remember with your Leo baby is that your world and the world in general should center around his every move, chuckle, dribble, and mouthful. This little dramatist in-the-making loves an audience. You may feed him in the early hours, sleepy and half-awake, but he will still desire lively company!

Sleeping – The planet that rules Leo is the Sun, and your tiny Leo baby will relish a stroll in the park in his stroller or backpack on a fine summer's day. He will gurgle and chuckle in delight and soon nod off to sleep as the warm life-giving rays (in moderation, of course!) soothe his soul.

Motor Skills – What motivates your Leo baby is a desire for interaction with others. At first, this will take the form of chuckles, flashing delightful smiles, and waving arms and legs. Later, he will want to crawl to the nearest adoring person.

Language – This same desire to be noticed encourages him to be heard as well as seen. If he is not the center of the household, he will soon scream and later shout – if you let him – with frustration and authority. As soon as he starts to talk, he will enter into every conversation.

Learning – Your Leo baby will learn best in front of an admiring audience. Watch him and praise him when he first grabs his feet, pulls himself up, or utters his first word, and he will be only too pleased to give you an encore.

Socialization – Leos are born convivial. They like people and bask in the attention of adoring adults. They seem impressed by baby talk and answer with giggles and lusty chortles. Everyone adores this little one because he adores everyone. What could be more irresistible?

One to Two Years

Eating – He is beginning to serve himself snacks and drinks. Provide him with the utensils to do so and give him plenty of praise for his efforts. He will respond well to your approval, will usually be happy to try new foods, and enjoys the fun of it all. Mealtimes are usually a jolly affair, though not necessarily neat and tidy!

Sleeping – With his vitality and high spirits, he can suddenly crash in the middle of the day. You might want to create a soft indoor play area with pillows, mats and mattresses he can use to nap during the daytime.

Motor Skills – His sojourn in to the world of the high chair can mean much noisy flapping of arms. He will enjoy lording it over the dining room and all those around him. Be prepared as he flicks his food with enjoyment and abandonment from his seat of power. Cover your carpet with plenty of newspapers; this could be a messy affair.

Language – Almost as soon as he learns to talk, he also learns how to take charge with his regal air. Remember that he is the boss, and you will fare better. Instead of trying to order him around, get into the habit of giving him choices. It will be better for all concerned.

Learning – He will learn if his attention is captured. Like all the fire signs, he is easily bored and, just as he is a dramatist, so, too, does he like drama. Make sure his bedtime stories are full of dragons and magic castles, color and adventure, and he will lap them up.

Socialization – As your Leo toddler is a great entertainer, he needs to have an audience. He is pretty good at imitation and loves to make you and anyone else in the vicinity laugh with his antics. He is the life and soul of the party.

Two to Three Years

Eating – These infants love to have fun. Make mealtimes happy gregarious affairs, and he will enjoy himself immensely. He does everything with gusto and enthusiasm and enjoys his food. Notice what he eats and make a point of telling him how well he has done.

Sleeping – He has lots of energy and vitality and rushes around before you can catch him to go to bed. This is not his favorite activity, and it will behoove you to play make believe that his bedroom is a castle. He will invite you to assist him in getting ready for bed and will particularly enjoy it if the family pays him a visit to say good-night and give him a kiss before he goes to sleep.

Motor Skills – He may not always have the patience to tie his shoelaces. He is not one for details. However, he is athletic and will love to run around and show you how fast he is and how good he looks.

Language – Your Leo child is a great communicator. Unless he has the Moon in a more conservative sign, he will tell you every detail of his day, as well as his plans for tomorrow. His language is rich and colorful, full of punctuation marks and drama.

Learning – Learning has to be a fun thing for your Leo toddler. He is determined to enjoy himself to the fullest extent, and if he is bored at this play group, he won't learn much. You may want to get him a pet. Having to look after another living thing will be good for this child and assist him in learning the lessons of caring and sharing so essential to his healthy growth.

Socialization – At this age, he will need lots of reassurance that you love him as much as his siblings and like him better than all his playmates. He may constantly ask you if you love him and may sometimes tell you, "I don't love you today," just to get your feedback. He needs to know he is loved constantly. Insecurity can sometimes plague the Leo's life and is one reason why he seeks to be good at what he does, so he will be admired by all.

Leo Lessons Growing Up: Your Leo child needs to learn that he is not the center of the Universe and that other people should be allowed to blossom and grow and express their power also. You may see him at the center of a group of playmates, lording it over them. He should be taught how to wield power responsibly from a young age. Teach him about the value of others and point out to him their talents. Encourage him to share his limelight with them, and you can help him to grow into the generous loving philanthropist and leader that is his birthright.

YOUR LEO BABY JOURNAL

Baby Virgo

August 23 – September 24

Whatever you may have heard in the past about Virgo children being fussy, reserved, and picky is true. However, you should never underestimate them. Your Virgo baby may be more crotchety than most about her soiled diaper or sticky fingers, but underneath, there's a heart of gold. Right from the word *go*, your precious Virgo baby needs every bit of encouragement and praise she can get. Unlike Ms. Leo, there is little chance her head will swell. She is born with innate modesty and humility. In this world, where glitter and fame are mistaken for greatness, hers are precious virtues that can too easily be overlooked.

You may have a challenging task as parent or guardian of a Virgo baby. However, your efforts can produce a genius who can excel in any field to which she puts her considerable intellect and superior practical ability.

She is naturally reserved and shy and getting close to her can be difficult. Once she warms to a person, however, she will be the most helpful, kind, and thoughtful child you could hope to meet. While she does not have the open friendliness of many other children, she can be the most loyal companion. She may not rush in and yell, "I'm hungry!" and tell you what she had for lunch, what her friend said and what the teacher did, but she will lap up her schoolwork and engage in intelligent conversation with you just as soon as she can talk at all.

Sometimes, when you're sitting quietly at home with your Virgo infant, you may get the distinct impression you're being examined and scrutinized inside and out. I know a Virgo child, Emma Jane, who would give out marks for everything that she and her mother did. If her mother cooked a delicious meal, she would dutifully get out her notebook and give it a score. Then, if the next meal was a disaster, Emma Jane would scan her notebook with furrowed brow and announce to her mother that, although she could only give her two out of ten for today's dinner, last Tuesday, she gave her nine. In her persnickety, yet kindly Virgo way, she was trying to make her feel better!

Life can be overwhelming for your Virgo child, for she feels the need to analyze and make sense of all the everyday details. Her endless lists and scores provide her with a solid structure from which to base each day. As soon as she can scratch words across a page, make sure you provide her with notebooks and plenty of colored pencils, pencil sharpeners, rules, and pens. These are her tools for life. By doing this, you will help this highly-strung infant to unwind a little, and you will assist her in becoming the most efficient sign of the Zodiac in later life. If she does not have the tools she needs or is discouraged from keeping all her lists and tallies, then her love of detail may get out of hand and overwhelm this sensitive child.

The mother of a Virgo toddler I know always asks her child to help her with the weekly shopping lists. It amazes me to see Carolyn calmly sitting with her little notebook, drawing pictures of cherry ice cream or opening the cupboards to check that there is plenty of soda pop. She loves to help with tasks like this. Virgoans are not lazy and will put a tremendous amount of energy into selflessly helping other people. In later life, this will develop into a truly spiritual quality if correctly nurtured as a child.

Constantly praise your Virgo child for helping you and for her excellent efforts. Never take her for granted. Notice how carefully drawn her pictures are and express your praise. Just as she will notice everything about you, pay special attention to her. She will regard this as a high compliment that will boost her morale and raise her spirits, and she will flourish with your thoughtful praise.

Unfortunately, the Virgo baby may perceive herself as not being liked or highly regarded. Unlike the Leo child, she does not expect to be the center of attention or the most popular child at playschool. She is imbued with an intense and sincere modesty and because of this may believe she is nothing special. If you do not pay special care, then her confidence may be lower than it should be as she grows. She could, without fuss, take subordinate positions in life and do all the boring tasks that others reject. Work on her self-worth and channel her obvious intelligence into creative channels.

Your Virgo baby can grow into a talented writer, for example. She notices every detail, has an innate understanding and command of language, and can put together an orderly well-written essay. This natural ability should be encouraged, along with any other talents she displays.

While your Virgo child can be the most talented and brilliant at all manner of tasks, her strong self-criticism may make her give up all too easily. Sometimes she may give up on a task even before she attempts it, just in case she fails. Encourage her to figure out how something works before she tries it – whether it is tying her shoelaces or doing up her belt buckle. It is very important to her that she succeeds at everything she undertakes. Once she has succeeded, praise her for her dexterity (and explain to her what the word means; she loves difficult words).

When you first take your Virgo baby to playschool, she will not rush up to the teacher and boldly assert her identity (unless she has the Moon in Aries!). Often slim and slight, she may try and disappear in the crowd or answer the teacher with a shy mumble. Once she gets to know the teacher, however, she can "talk the hind leg off a donkey" if the mood takes her, since she is ruled by the planet Mercury. However, despite her reserved demeanor, the teacher should never underestimate this astute child. She may prove to be the brightest and best in the class, one who pays attention instead of fiddling and giggling in the corner.

Although you will need to help your Virgo infant loosen up and have fun, you should not belittle her constant striving for perfection. It is an essential part of her nature, even at a young age. She will have lots of energy, but not the same type of energy as the flamboyant Leo or the headstrong Aries. This will be energy to help with practical things. All children hate doing chores – except Virgo children. Getting her to assist you with little chores around the house will actually benefit her. Show her how to lay the table and change her little brother's diapers. You will be surprised at the results. Her affinity for work and attention to detail make her a valuable assistant. Above all, she will feel useful, and this is a very big deal for this child.

Virgos make wonderful nurses. Even your little baby has a healing touch. If you have a headache, ask your Virgo infant to put her hand on your brow. You will instantly feel better because not only will she really care about your headache, she also has a soothing touch that can help the world seem lighter. She has a real desire to see tangible results for what she does. If she sees you suffering, she will do all in her power to make you better. For Virgo, it's as simple as that.

You may begin to feel that your Virgo child is mature beyond her years. She wants you to talk to her like an adult, giving her all the details. She wants to assist you and do everything to the best of her ability. However, do not forget that she is a child. Just as any other child, she needs her share of sunshine and play, perhaps more than most. This child is tightly wired and needs plenty of relaxation worked into her busy day. Along with ballet lessons, piano lessons, and gym class, she also needs regular trips to the countryside. Nature is good for children of this earth sign. The green grass and trees feed her soul and nurture her. It helps her active mind to turn off and her highly-strung nature to relax. Also, make sure you give her good wholesome food from an early age. Sodas and junk food are no good for her; her health can be delicate unless treated with proper care at an early age.

Although she loves to be organized and help around the house, young Virgo never quite seems to get where she is going and is often lost in an endless myriad of detail. Jackson drives his parents crazy with his mounds of toys. They call it organized chaos. At least Jackson knows where everything is. His parents dare not enter his bedroom and move anything, or they'll be in trouble. The piles of scraps of paper with rainbows and houses and stick men all mean something and are highly significant to Jackson.

Just give your Virgo baby lots of love and praise; encourage her when she's down; teach her to help and care for others, and your tiny child will grow into one of the kindest, most thoughtful, and talented people you could ever hope to meet.

YOUR VIRGO BABY SURVIVAL GUIDE

Birth to One Year

Eating – Although your Virgo baby can be as good as gold, the first three months may be quite a strain just because she can be colicky or prone to allergies. This is one sensitive infant.

Sleeping – Your Virgo baby may be a poor sleeper: it may take a long stint of cradle rocking before she nods off to sleep. Also be aware that the slightest noise can wake her up, such as a creaky door or the barking of a dog several blocks away.

Motor Skills – She has a delicate touch. Watch her when you give her a teething biscuit. Instead of crumbling it in her fingers, she will lick it delicately, as if trying to find out what it tastes like before making any commitment on her part. She approaches life in the same way. She also enjoys things that she can fiddle with, such as crib pullers, knockers, bells, and beads.

Language – Don't hold back on your conversations. Like baby Gemini, she is ruled by the planet of communication, Mercury, and has a love of language. By talking to her gently, you can help her overcome some of her resistance to the foods you're trying to get her to eat that her discriminating palate doesn't like.

Learning – Your Virgo baby seems to observe everything carefully – suspiciously, you might think – and may resist your efforts to play with her hands and feet. It's as though she wants to figure out the world completely before she gets involved in it. A Virgo needs and craves as much stimulation as any other baby; just giver her some time to warm up.

Socialization – She is finicky about everything, including people. If you let a stranger peer at her too closely, it can distress her for some time afterward.

One to Two Years

Eating – She is prone to anxiety, so do create a "safe" or "secure" base from which she can explore new foods and tastes. Offer her carrots or apples for dessert. She will delight in this opportunity to make decisions, but give her plenty of support and feedback, as she lacks confidence.

Sleeping – If you are away on vacation or she is sleeping in a strange cot, she may have a difficult time getting to sleep, as she craves routine. It gives her a feeling of security. At least ensure that your own routines involving her bedtime are on schedule, and this will help.

Motor Skills – Here is a combination of intelligence and the ability to learn quickly, with a certain reticence and insecurity. It may appear that she is slower than other children in her overall development. Just give her plenty of reassurance, and she will do fine. She is a bit of a fidget, who may squirm and squiggle when you try to hold her.

Language – Your Virgo toddler is probably just beginning her lifelong interest in language and learning the names of things. She will enjoy your reading to her and love to help you turn the pages. She particularly likes books with lots of pretty pictures.

Learning – She learns by exploring. Children of this Mercury-ruled sign have inquiring minds and will not only explore mentally, but are also prone to exploring all your private cupboards and hideaways.

Socialization – She may be a little shy and unsure of herself with others. Humility is part of the Virgoan nature, and she may be hard on herself, even at this young age. The secret is not to apply pressure to her over such things as toilet training, but give her plenty of warm encouragement for her efforts.

Two to Three Years

Eating – She is naturally modest; if you give her a big meal, she may feel daunted by the sheer size and feel guilty if she can't finish it. This little one prefers tasty morsels to big meals. Encourage her to chew her food well and concentrate on what she is eating in a relaxed fashion. She enjoys wholesome food and is sensitive to anything that may not be quite fresh.

Sleeping – She may be the untidiest child on Earth, but she appreciates a neat tidy room in which to sleep. Encourage her to keep her room clean and neat and instill in her the importance of an orderly environment.

Motor Skills – Your Virgo toddler is learning tremendous dexterity. She can be quite brilliant in working out puzzles and intricate games and furnishings for her dollhouse. She loves to put order into things, such as sorting out drawers to keep all her dolls' clothes in, etc. Challenge her with this ability by giving her plenty of stimulating games and also an interesting environment, such as a bedroom with lots of drawers and cupboards.

Language – Don't be surprised to find your baby sitting in the corner, talking to herself. Her conversations can be pretty long and complex, as if she is trying to sort things out in her mind. Learning to tell time may be beyond many at this age, but she is interested, and you can start her off by mentioning the hour.

Learning – Even at this young age, she likes order and routine, and she learns best in this environment. Try and provide this for her or, if there is a change in her routine coming up, give her plenty of advance warning. If she is subject to constant change, she can become tense and nervous and, to a certain degree, "shut down" her learning abilities. With order in her life, she will really shine.

Socialization – She likes to keep up a good image in the company of others, and it is rare that you will find this pretty little girl with a chocolate mustache or dirt on her blouse. She does not make friends easily at playschool, but she is loyal to those special friends she has. Although she may not always be willing to participate in group activities, she will probably be the teacher's darling. She is a doll: always kind and sweet and thoughtful.

Virgo Lessons Growing Up: You will need to help your Virgo child to be easier on herself. She is a taskmaster, especially with herself. She also can be critical of others – just because she notices every little detail. You definitely need to put more emphasis on her successes, rather than her failures. She is quite well aware of her failures and doesn't need to be reminded – especially in public. She also needs to know that learning through trying is more important than getting perfect results. You can tell her stories about this so she knows you are serious and not just saying so. She will know if you are just saying things for effect or to make her feel better. It will not be easy to pull the wool over her eyes. She is intelligent, smart, and discriminating and will keep you on your toes! She loves to help others, and this is a wonderful virtue that should be encouraged. Also encourage her to love herself in a healthy way.

YOUR VIRGO BABY JOURNAL

Baby Libra

September 24 – October 23

Your Libran baby loves to be loved. Although he may never have a problem with this, with his good looks, fine manners and charm, popularity is for him a lifelong concern. Some of the first words you may hear him say are, "Do you like me?" Libra is the sign of relationship. Librans are forever seeking balance with another person and work best in partnerships and teams. Libra is the opposite sign from Aries and, while Aries loves to compete and win, Librans seek the cooperation and approval of the team. While Aries is irritated when Mom straightens his clothes, believing that only he should do it, your Libran infant will smile back at you as you do so.

From an early age, you will see that your little Libran is sensitive and attuned to what the family and his playmates want. He is cheerful and friendly and has a way of bringing out the best in others. While Aries may be the one who places a tack on the teacher's chair, your Libran child is the teacher's pet. Strong discipline is rarely needed for this good-tempered sweet-natured infant; other parents will look enviously at your baby's spotless clothes and polite manner.

If at all possible, avoid any discord at home. Your sensitive Libran baby will feel this very deeply and, just as soon as he can, he will act as the mediator for the entire family. He seeks harmony above all else and will strive to obtain this at all costs. If you happen to be a feisty person born under a fire sign who likes a little banter and battle now and again, try to abstain from argument within earshot of baby Libra. Ill feelings unsettle him, and he may feel he is the cause of it. He will urge you to be nice to each other and will have a pained look on his face as you argue over the washing-up or some other minor thing.

Your Libran child is a social being and will feel most at home with a playmate or in groups. He will enjoy going to school and will relish organizing games and social settings. Other children can sit playing with their toys for hours on their own, but your Libran baby is not happy doing this. His true gift is as an arbitrator of mediator. He needs people in order to do this, although early on his toys will do nicely. You will chuckle to yourself as he seats his toy soldiers, teddy bears, and anyone else he can find 'round the kitchen table for a tea party. He will be the charming host, conversing with them all and passing them tea and cake. If you care to join in, he will be delighted and will politely ask the other guests to make room for you at the table.

By now, you may be thinking that your Libran baby is just about perfect. Along with all the other signs, however, there are just a few things you can help him with. He loves harmony so much that he will shrink from conflict. While not weak, he just cannot stand people arguing with each other. He is not the person who will make a stand for what he believes is right no matter what public opinion. He may even be prepared to compromise himself, rather than stand up to you in open combat. This can become his greatest problem. "If only he would not say yes every time I ask him to do something," complained one mother, "I'd be better able to deal with his actual resistance. At least I would know right then and there that I had to do it myself, instead of finding out an hour later, when it's still not done."

Librans just want to please, and he will accommodate himself with seeming pliability, rather than stand up to you. He can be just too reasonable. He can bend like bamboo to please you, instead of openly admitting what he really wants and needs.

The surface sense of compromise often conceals a strong determination to have his own way. He would, however, much rather achieve this with diplomacy than through openly admitting his desires.

Mimi is a Libran and Sadie an Aries. Sadie would see the candy on the table, stand square in front of it, and scream until you gave her a piece, if only to shut her up. Mimi would sit in her high chair and gurgle and coo and smile so sweetly that you just couldn't resist popping a candy into her mouth. Librans work by using the attraction principle. They may not always let on what they want, but they sure know how to get it.

His soft sugar-candy coating impresses all but the most discerning. Only a few see the firm determination and strength that lie beneath. He may not be the best at school and has a lazy streak, but despite that, he will have glowing school reports.

While your Virgo child may enjoy the household chores, do not expect little Libran to be the same. He would far rather hold a tea party for his toys, while others do the washing-up. Sweating and toiling are not for him.

He is born with an interest in human nature and very quickly will learn the best way to twist you round his little finger. When you say no for the very last time, he will not stamp his feet and scream. He will dimple and smile up at you with his big eyes wide and appealing as he says, "Please could you play with me just one more time, please Mommy, I would really like that." How can you resist his charming appeals? He knows hot to melt your resolve and will use this approach throughout his life, earning him the description of "the iron fist in the velvet glove."

Yet for all his strength, intelligence, and charm, your Libran infant's greatest difficulty will be learning to make up his mind. Like his fellow air sign, Gemini, he is only too aware of the myriad of opportunities and challenges that life presents. He embraces them all and swings hot and cold between them, unable to choose.

This is one of his biggest challenges and one you can help him with from an early age. Because he finds it so difficult to decide, he prefers not to choose, and because he does not choose, he cannot act. That is why you will sometimes find the talented charming Libran remaining on the sidelines of life, while his more focused fellow signs are out in the front, making the most of what life brings to them.

This blowing hot-and-cold and swinging between one thing and another may infuriate you at times. However, start by giving him simple choices, such as what color sweatshirt to wear, and be patient while he dillies and dallies between his choices. It may be a good idea to walk away while he decides, and once he emerges (it could be quite a while later!) in his green sweatshirt, compliment him on his choice. If time is short, then your best bet is to make the choices for him but don't make a habit of this. It may be easier for you, but he does need to learn decision-making and the younger he starts, the better! Also, encourage him to follow through on things, instead of giving up halfway through because he can't decide what to do next.

My friend found her two-and-a-half-year-old Libran, Annie, sitting in her bedroom surrounded by toys, with tears streaming down her cheeks. When asked what was the matter, she replied that she did not know whether she should move Pinkie (her favorite elephant) into the playpen with the other animals, or whether she should sleep with her dolls as she normally did. This was only because her uncle had jokingly remarked that he thought Pinkie would prefer to be with the other animals. She was completely floored by this and just could not decide the right course of action. Fortunately, being a natural communicator, she shared her problems with her mother, and together they found a reasonable solution.

Your Libran infant will always be reasonable, and by discussing problems with him, you can usually find solutions. The solution, in this case, was to move Pinkie in with the animals by night but to let her play with the dolls during the daytime! A typical Libran solution is to find the best of both worlds.

He will love to be fair, and even when he is at this most demanding, you can usually get him to stop by appealing to his innate sense of justice. Try and get him to understand the consequences of his actions. If he keeps his friend's toys, explain why this is not fair to his friend, and he will readily give them back.

He hates to be thought of as unfair or unjust, even as a toddler.

Just as your Libran baby is born with a desire for harmony in his friendships, so, too, is he born with a desire for harmony in his physical surroundings. This sense of harmony is an aesthetic sense also. Emotional clutter disturbs his finely tuned sensitivity, and so does physical clutter. Although he loves to have nice toys and clothes, he dislikes it when they start to clutter his bedroom. While he is not neat and fussy in the way Virgo is, he has a strong aesthetic sense and an innate feeling for what looks good.

A little Libran friend, Nova, has dozens of dolls with hundreds of different outfits of all colors and styles. She is in her element dressing up her dolls for hours on end and experimenting with the different looks and colors. Whether or not the colors and outfits match each other is of serious importance to her. She enjoys it if she can hook a consenting adult to approve of her fashion antics and tell her how clever she is! Nova enjoys the soothing harmony of music and dance, just as she loves the harmony of color.

YOUR LIBRAN BABY SURVIVAL GUIDE

Birth to One Year

Eating – Your Libran baby will probably not be thrilled at his first taste of solid foods, but just make a fuss of him and you are likely to win a smile. He loves being made a fuss of, no matter what he is doing. However much chocolate he sprays over you, he will always charm you into thinking he's perfect. Your Libra toddler at age one may prefer you to keep feeding him rather than feed himself. He just likes the give-and-take, and it will be easier for you to just keep feeding him. Later on, he will be happy to hold his spoon, but then you may have the challenge of getting him to eat!

Sleeping – He will happily coo and gurgle and splash around in the bathtub, but sleeping may not be quite so exciting, as he doesn't yet like to be left alone. Just smile at him and rock him gently and pay him lots of attention, and he will happily nod off. However, when he awakes in the night and finds you not there, it may be another story.

Motor Skills – Your Libran baby is a people person. He may first start crawling at about nine or ten months, when he sees you disappearing from view, as if to say, "Hey, I'm here, wait for me!"

Language – His nonverbal language can be very powerful. He may coo or scream to get your attention, but get your attention he will. He may start communicating early because he seems to understand instinctively his role as ambassador, diplomat, and general charmer.

Learning – Your Libran baby learns to "read" your words, gestures, and facial expressions quite quickly. He will increasingly look your way and pause to consider your reactions before doing anything. Approval is second nature to him.

Socialization – One way to keep him quiet is to give him a mirror. A client, Astrid, worried that her two-year-old Libran daughter, Diana, was going to grow up completely vain because, as a baby, she loved to look at her reflection in the mirror. I told her it was just that people thing; with a mirror, nobody is ever really alone!

One to Two Years

Eating – He loves approval and thrives on harmony. Even as a baby, he wants mealtimes to be social harmonious affairs. Encourage him and tell him how good he is when he eats up his dinner.

Sleeping – He will be quite good at going to bed on time, as he doesn't like to be disobedient. He likes to please you and keep you happy.

Motor Skills – By about eighteen months, you may find your Libran baby dancing happily by himself to music. He also enjoys playing games with older children and adults. Peek-a-boo can be a favorite for this one.

Language – Learning to talk is a great breakthrough for your little socialite. He hates to be alone, and you will soon learn that his calling for a kiss or glass of water just means he is missing you. He may become particularly talkative at bedtimes for this reason.

Learning – He is just beginning to learn from what he sees other people do. You may demonstrate the use of a particular toy, such as blowing a whistle or placing a peg in a hole. While your toddler may not repeat the action immediately, he may display it in some form at a later time in the day or week.

Socialization – Play is also a social activity for your Libran toddler, and he will enjoy your participation. Provide him with plenty of paper and crayons. He has a feeling for color, and even though he may not yet be a budding artist, he will enjoy the process. Just admire his work and make sure he is not eating his tools! Even at this age, Librans enjoy people. Sabrina loved to look at pictures of family members from years back and point out who they were.

Two to Three Years

Eating – He will appreciate it if you lay the table nicely with a clean linen tablecloth and nice china and may enjoy helping you put things in their correct place. He will probably like to eat what you're eating, so don't make the mistake of saying it is overcooked! He will suddenly lose interest in the food.

Sleeping – Although good at going to bed, if he is engrossed in a game, you may find it difficult to tear him away. Try negotiation. Librans have an instinctive understanding of the power of negotiating to bring compromise. Try "If you finish your game and come to bed now, I will read you your favorite story."

Motor Skills – The third year of your Libran's life is an active one, both physically and verbally. His movement skills increase dramatically, and he will particularly enjoy make-believe or imaginary play. Evita would sit for hours at the bottom of the garden, playing with the fairies. As an avid believer in the realms of the fairies myself, I did not dismiss her games as "purely imaginative" but encouraged her in her play, as indeed her mother did. Later in life, Evita developed into a gifted psychic and never lost her natural ability to see beyond the physical.

Language – Home life with your Libra toddler is not always stress-free. Like baby Gemini, he may chatter endlessly about the daily decisions and which course of action he should take. You might be surprised at his verbal dexterity, as he weighs whether he should eat the fish sticks or the quiche. However, you may need to nudge him toward making a decision. He is practicing for the time when he can adroitly weigh both sides of an issue, but his decision-making skills may definitely need development!

Learning – Music, color, light, and form all interest this little artist in the making. While you may be unable to disengage his siblings from the television set, you can take this one outside and show him things in nature, which he will enjoy. Even quite subtle things, like the play of sunlight on the dewdrops in the morning, will fascinate this sensitive child.

Socialization – Your Libran toddler may enjoy a playgroup and quickly learns etiquette, responding politely to the teacher's greetings and imitating her charmingly. Although he may not be so charming with his playmates, you may one day find him starting to share his toys. Even at this young age, he will happily play the role of mediator in his group when arguments occur.

Libra Lessons Growing Up: If you could sum up the desires of your Libran baby with one word, you could use the word balance. Gracefulness, charm, harmony, and a desire to please are wonderful attributes. You can truly help him by teaching him that courage is just as important as harmony and that truth is as essential as fairness. Encourage him to remain true to his sense of justice, to be thoughtful to others when things do not go his way, and to express his desires openly, and he will blossom into the marvelous person he truly is.

YOUR LIBRA BABY JOURNAL

Baby Scorpio

October 24 – November 22

There's something ever so mysterious about this tiny scrap: your Scorpio baby. Although she is small and still, and possibly even quiet, you sense that there are hidden depths beneath her innocent surface. If you have witnessed the volcano of feelings beneath her placid demeanor, you will understand why *emotional intensity* describes the Scorpio child. An air of subtle mystery surrounds her throughout life, and you may never fathom the depths of this complex, talented, intense child. If you are a delicate soul, toughen up.

Your Scorpio child is strong-willed and powerful from an early age. She needs to respect you and will have an instinctive knowledge of all your weaknesses and how to press your buttons. Not out of malice, but just because she wants to know how things work and why they are as they are. Your Scorpio infant will never let you get away with things, so be prepared. A friend's three-year-old, Katie, followed her quietly round the pharmacy, good as gold. Then, suddenly, as her mother discreetly picked up her prescription for diet pills, Katie yelled at the top of her lungs, "Mommy, why do you take those diet pills? My friends think you're fat, but I like you all pudgy."

Your Scorpio infant may make you cringe with embarrassment – not because she is unkind, but if she senses you are hiding something from her, she will be sure to find out what it is and why. Mysterious herself, she cannot tolerate mystery in others. She is a born investigator, and it is almost impossible to pull the wool over her eyes.

When she makes a point, it is with force; emotional intensity is her fuel. Make sure you stoke up her fires with plenty of love and affection. Relate to her; this baby does not mind if you don't chat to her all day – unlike the Gemini baby. She does, however, want a close emotional relationship with you. She may not show her feelings openly. They are all stored away, along with her passion for life, until life demands it. Encourage her to share her feelings with you at an early age because her emotional intensity can be bottled up and cause her problems later on.

Your Scorpio baby will exude a magnetism that is beyond her years. From her first breath, she will naturally draw people to her, and this powerful force of attraction will remain with her throughout her life.

One mother told me of when her son, Luke, was telling her about his friend at playschool, who had a deformity. He was describing Thomas to her in the typically unkind manner of a child, when suddenly he burst into tears. He sobbed for a few minutes with empathy for his poor playmate, then stopped, wiped his eyes, and carried on describing him as if nothing had happened! She said Luke would not hesitate to criticize or embarrass her in public, but was also the kindest sweetest soul you could meet. Scorpio's feelings run deep.

Unlike the free-spirited Sagittarian, your Scorpio infant does not need a happy carefree childhood in the same way. Her happiness stems from expressing the intensity she feels. She thrives on this, and meaningful superficial pursuits do not interest her. This does not mean she doesn't like to play. She loves to play, and her games have plenty of drama and imagination. Her play-acting will be serious stuff, and you may wonder if your child is a Richard Burton, Julia Roberts, or Leonardo di Caprio in the making (all of them are Scorpios).

Another type of play she enjoys is one in which she wields the power! Your Scorpio child will not want to be the nurse or patient in the childhood game of doctors and nurses. She will be the doctor or surgeon, administering orders to the nurse or drugs to the patient. While other children play for fun and amusement, this little kid knows about power plays from the moment she first beguiles you with her calm, steady, and hypnotic gaze.

These complex children have an innate and intuitive understanding of psychology and are students of human nature. You may sometimes feel she knows just what you are thinking, especially if you are trying to keep something from her. As you sit absorbed in a problem she will look at you with her clear intelligent eyes and ask, "What is it, Mommy?" You may think you could never explain your problems to your two-year-old, but do try because you may be amazed to find that, on some level, she understands. Even at a very young age, she can be a wonderful counselor with her intuitive perception and understanding of people.

Because of the intensity of their feelings, these children are more capable of love than most. It will not be the warm, earthy, huggy love that you'll receive from your Taurus infant, but you will feel it as a force that seems to know you inside out. She may chide you, criticize, and even bully you, but there is nothing superficial about her love. Make sure you appreciate that from Day One, so that you can make the most of probably the deepest relationship you may ever have. Be sure you nurture and appreciate her love. She needs to trust you, and if ever you destroy this trust, the Scorpio intensity can turn to ice. She may forget, but it is hard for this child to truly forgive. This is where you can help her by explaining the importance of forgiveness of herself, as well as others. You may have guessed by now that to truly help this child, you must brush up on your own enlightenment. She will test your mettle, and superficial answers will not satisfy.

What a complex, richly intense, and fascinating child this is. As with all the signs, she may harbor negative emotions, especially if a playmate has crossed her in some way. If you see her plotting a cruel revenge on a friend or teacher, find out what happened. She will readily share her nefarious schemes with you. As one three-year-old put it: "I hate Ella (his two-year-old sister). I hate her, I hate her, she stole my panda. I am going to pull the ears off her Heffelump and throw them away. Then I will cut the hair off all her ugly stupid dolls. Then I will cut her silly red hair off."

Be particularly aware if another baby arrives in the family soon after your little Scorpio. This can be an emotionally charged situation, and you can take the sting out of it by preparing your sensitive possessive Scorpio child. You can encourage her to share in everything, including the excitement, so that she feels the new baby is a part of her, just as much as you. It is when she no longer feels she belongs in the same way that problems can start. This is a child who is not afraid of responsibility, so you may want to map out an area of responsibility for her with her new sibling.

When a Scorpio friend, Remy, was a young child, his parents ran a children's home. They also had several more children themselves. Instead of being the apple of their eye, he was one of dozens of other children. The children all ate together, opened their gifts together, and life became one long communal event. Had this child been an Aquarian, he would have taken it in stride and enjoyed it, but this tiny Scorpio felt abandoned. This feeling of abandonment remained with him into his adult life. Your Scorpio child's natural home is in the world of emotions. Make sure this offers her the loving security and stability that she craves for her healthy emotional growth.

The deeper our feelings, the more easily we are hurt. Scorpio children prove the rule. She hides her sensitivity under a cool façade but is extremely vulnerable to slights from her more fickle friends. A chance unkind remark can leave lasting damage. She may not always be the friendliest child (unless she has a more gregarious Moon sign) and is slow to warm to people. However, once she has warmed, her loyalty is immense.

She chooses her friends carefully, even at an early age. Don't worry that she'll be taken in by the pesky bigheaded boy next door. She won't. She has tremendous discernment when it comes to people. She goes for the inner stuff. It's as if her laser-like vision (her symbol isn't the eagle for nothing) can penetrate right through to a person's soul. Once she accepts and likes you, she will love you intensely forever – unless you betray her, and then it's as if all her powerful feelings turn to ice, which nothing can melt. Nothing she does is half measure. Her love is immense and her vengeance lasting. It is particularly important that you teach these children a spiritual and moral code just as soon as you can. She has a natural inclination for the spiritual; it satisfies her desire to unravel the mysteries of life.

I know a young father, Dennis, who is deeply religious. He has a Scorpio two-year-old, Birgitta, who would always want to sit with him while he said his prayers. Birgitta would bring in her favorite doll and seat it next to her dad and, after the prayer session, she would lay her hands on the doll and say, "You're healed. Now get up and walk!" Birgitta explained that, when she prayed, her hands got "all hot and tingly, and she could make people better." Dennis didn't know where she had heard such things because he had never mentioned them himself.

Do not laugh or take such things lightly. Scorpios are so magnetic that they are natural healers; encourage them to channel this power. Encourage her when she brings in a bird with a broken wing. She will gently nurse the bird back to health, lavishing love and attention on the wounded creature. This channeling of emotions is vital to her confidence and self-worth.

You don't have to worry too much about this tough little cookie. Sensitive she may be, but weak she is not. While she may shed a tear over another's pain, she will rarely shed tears over her own. You will be amazed at her strength. She has a strong body and forceful energy, and this combination endears her to rough play with monsters, witches, soldiers, or dragons – or perhaps all of them at once!

Little Rafael would line his soft toys up and make-believe they were chained in a dungeon, set upon by a wicked witch, until a fire-breathing dragon came along and melted their chains so they could escape. "Strange scenarios for such a tiny innocent soul," I thought. Until I discovered he was a Scorpio. *Innocent* is not a word to describe a Scorpio, however blue-eyed and deliciously dimpled he may be. I later discovered from Rafael's father that he read him fairy tales every night and that Rafael's make-believe stories were a more gruesome version of the stories he had been told!

YOUR SCORPIO BABY SURVIVAL GUIDE

Birth to One Year

Eating – You will learn that your Scorpio baby is passionate about life the moment she enters the world and lets out her first blood-curdling howl. When she wants milk, you had better not take her off the breast before she is ready. She doesn't like to be short-changed.

Sleeping – Similarly, rousing her from a peaceful slumber is not a good idea. This sensitive child knows how to make her disapproval felt. Though she may be the sweetest infant you have ever seen, she has a combination of strong will and emotional intensity, which together spell *beware*.

Motor Skills – Everything this child does is vigorous. When you give her a bath, she will kick and scream at first, then gradually calm down as she feels the water soothing her. Then she will love it. She is not one to expend unnecessary energy but instead will stare unblinkingly with her clear magical gaze.

Language – Your baby will be in no rush to talk. She will happily gurgle, chuckle, and scream; then, one day, when you least expect it, she will utter her first word. But don't try and rush her or cajole her. She will decide in her own good time when she is ready. When the world is ready for her word – it will come! In the meantime, she will enjoy pat-a-cake and giggle and squeal as soon as you start.

Learning – One thing your baby will soon learn are ways to siphon off the power and intensity that are a part of every Scorpio toddler. As soon as she can toddle around, you should move breakable objects and put safety plugs in the electric sockets. She learns by poking her fingers into things or rattling everything within reach.

Socialization – Your Scorpio infant is wary of strangers but will gaze at them for long stretches of time with her big unblinking eyes, as if searching the depths of the person's mind, heart, and soul.

One to Two Years

Eating – She will either love what you are serving her for lunch – or really hate it. There is no middle ground for this passionate soul. She may also love things one week and hate them the next. A lot depends upon her mood at the time.

Sleeping – Her sleep patterns are usually like her moods – up and down. She may go through long periods when her sleep is sound and unbroken, and then equally long periods when it is the opposite. She is highly sensitive and may like a night-light in her bedroom.

Motor Skills – At this age, she can become very attached to routines, and once she has learned a new skill, such as climbing up the stairs to bed, she will demonstrate an enormous tolerance for repetition – far beyond yours! Be patient, or her demand for repetition may drive you nearly insane.

Language – She may start uttering her first words around eighteen months, and she will also be developing receptive listening skills. Scorpios are innately good listeners, as they like to understand things and people. She will enjoy repetition in the form of her favorite bedtime story being read to her several times a night until eventually she tires of it.

Learning – If a pregnant friend comes to visit, you may be surprised at your baby's fascination with the birth process. She learns more from life than from books. From an early age, she has an innate desire to learn what life is all about and a passionate interest in its mysteries.

Socialization – You may find your Scorpio infant still shy and wary of adults. It's best not to leave her with baby-sitters until she has generally sized them up and offered her approval. She may enjoy playing with an older child, but watch that she doesn't become overly attached. With her sensitive nature, she can be easily upset when ignored by someone she has bonded with.

Two to Three Years

Eating – If she eats everything in sight one day and the next day just moves her food around on her plate, you can rest assured something is bothering her. Try to find out what it is before mealtimes, so that she can share her problem with you and regain her appetite.

Sleeping – These children are often highly attuned to the unseen psychic world and may have trouble sleeping at times. I knew a little Scorpio, Kristophe, who would see faces in the dark and would become very scared. His parents made the mistake of telling him there was nothing there, when, in fact, they lived in a house that they later discovered was haunted. Listen to this sensitive child; he needs understanding to sleep soundly at night.

Motor Skills – One of her favorite activities is dress-up. Don't worry if your little boy dresses up in your cast-off clothes. This is quite normal for a Scorpio of either gender. He will rush around as Batman or Superman just as soon as he can walk. Scorpio children delight in the world of imagination and like to play make-believe and imagine themselves in all sorts of different roles. Although the Scorpian girl enjoys play, like any other kid, she tends to get engrossed in just one or two toys, to the exclusion of all else.

Language – Not only will she playact various roles, but you may also find her talking to herself as a Power Puff girl. If you show any interest, she will enjoy drawing you in and wielding her magical powers over you. Scorpios love magic and the power that it brings them. Your little girl will enjoy saying "abracadabra" and turning you into a frog. Transformation is a keyword for Scorpio, and these little children enjoy transforming things and people.

Learning – Another fascination for Scorpios is the intricacies and intrigues of family relationships, and she loves to learn about these from an early age. You may often hear your child ask about her kittens' parents and siblings. She learns a lot from her own family and forms strong attachments. She can be good at learning new skills because she is tenacious and will keep doing a thing until she's got it. However, if she is tired or fed up, she may lose her cool and kick the thing that is causing her problems! She does have quite a temper!

Socialization – You will see her forming affectionate relationships with children her own age, provided she can be the dominant partner. She really likes to be the boss because she enjoys power and control, even at this young age. She also loves secrets and surprises, especially if they involve you or her friends.

Scorpio Lessons Growing Up: Imagination is our creative ability and a necessary tool for the mystical Scorpio. Always allow her plenty of scope for her imagination, and wean her on classic fairy tales, myths, and spiritual stories. These will enrich her all her life and allow her creativity to flourish. Another trait of your Scorpio child is a determination as fierce as that of her opposite sign, Taurus. You will not find her throwing away her puzzle in disgust because it is too complicated. With her capacity for discipline and ability to achieve, she will persist with it until she has accomplished her objective. As you might imagine, your Scorpio baby has all it takes to become a success at whatever she does in life. Her life may be a constant struggle with her own deep-felt emotions, but she has the will to overcome and the desire to succeed. All you need to do is love and respect her, give her security, trust, and wise counsel, and you will be providing the foundations for a spiritual giant to emerge.

YOUR SCORPIO BABY JOURNAL

Baby Sagittarius

November 23 – December 21

These children are as festive and outgoing as the time of year in which they are born. Like Aries and Leo, Sagittarius is a fire sign, and you won't doubt it for a minute. He is a little fireball – exuberant, enthusiastic, and always tripping up and scraping his knees. Your Sagittarian child is outgoing in every way. You will find his exuberance hilarious, annoying, and frustrating... but you will never be bored.

Unlike the cool Scorpio, your Sagittarian baby will express everything. He may irritate you with his endless questions: "What is that?" "Where are we going?" "Why are you wearing that?" or "What's that man?" but, unlike your Scorpio baby, you will always know where you stand.

The Sagittarius baby has a drive to understand and explore everything that life offers. As you can imagine, this often lands him in hot water – but with a smile or a few tears, he brushes himself off and starts over. He bounces back like a rubber ball, with an amazing capacity to take all life's challenges in his stride. He's not a sensitive cautious wallflower but a brave adventurer, with a warm open heart and enthusiasm for life.

The French described your Sagittarius baby when they coined the term *joie de vivre*. He has a zest for life that is unequaled. Surprisingly enough, he will never lose it. If he does, take it seriously, for it means he has also lost heart. Just as your Scorpio baby responds to the unseen world of feeling, so does the Sagittarian respond to life itself. The world is his teacher, and he constantly strives to learn its lessons. He's like a rubber ball, with an amazing capacity to fall down or make a mistake and yet recover almost instantly. Don't try to shield this little adventurer from the knocks of life. The more mistakes he makes, the more he will grow.

While the Cancer baby needs to feel close to home, do not restrict the freedom of your tiny Sagittarian. Try not to cover him up too much or strap him in unless absolutely necessary.

Sagittarius Callista is only six months and can just peek over the blankets on her stroller. She is still able to make it known to everyone around her when her blankets are restrictive or she is unable to wave her hands outside the covers. Freedom is her middle name, and restricting her freedom is like stopping her air supply.

Yes, I know there are times when you will have to do it in order to keep your baby safe. Especially with this child's boisterous nature and love of excitement combined with a lack of caution and very little thought of self-preservation, you will have to tell him when to stop. However, be mindful of how you keep him in check. When he is restricted, he can become destructive. When he is left to his own devices, he can also overdo it. So, wherever possible, let him roam free, keeping a watchful eye, rather than putting him in a playpen.

Although his antics and adventures may be a constant source of concern, try to remember his tremendous resilience. He does not need fussing over, just lots of love and freedom!

Another reason to let your Sagittarius baby roam free is because his abundant energy can wear you out! Keep him on the move and he will burn off some of his excess steam. Then, as soon as he can walk, engage him in games; he has a naturally athletic nature and is well-coordinated, with strong legs. Along with the other fire signs, Aries and Leo, he has a need to express himself physically, mentally, and emotionally.

Your Sagittarian child was born an optimist. However difficult life may be, he sincerely believes things will be better. He is one child who can smile and be happy during difficult times; this is because he is geared toward the future and the adventure of the unknown. The first day at school, a trip to the dentist, or a long journey is not a problem for him, as it is with more timid children.

He is a natural traveler and is always glad of an outing, wherever it leads. He just feels things are going to be good, even if they turn out not to be. This wonderful positive attitude brings him success and happiness in life. He attracts success to himself because he expects good things to happen. There is a simplicity about this child that comes from trust, openness, and hope. Life may knock him down, but he will always get up again with his inner strength intact.

As you can imagine, the problems that face your Sagittarian child are to do with overextending himself and over optimism. You will need to teach him certain basic things – such as the limits and routines of daily life. He would happily stay up at night, singing and dancing into the small hours, if you do not teach him the importance of going to bed by a certain time. Routine is not his strong point. He will happily clean his teeth, but getting him to do it at the same time, twice a day, may be a problem. Try and ingrain these routines into his daily life from an early age. Make them fun and enjoyable, and he will accept them more readily. Two-year-old Clarissa's parents get her to color in her tooth-brushing sessions on a jazzy chart in the bathroom. If she manages to get at least fourteen ticks in a week, she gets a prize!

You will also need to teach this one thoughtfulness to others. He can lift others with his high spirits but is not really concerned if they approve of him or his antics. This can get him into trouble. He may also think just a bit too highly of himself and his own capabilities. This is not a child whose confidence you will shatter easily if you tell him the truth.

There is another side to your growing Sagittarian, a natural inclination to study. Before you feel too delighted, this does not always take a conventional form. While his keen intelligence, combined with a desire to discover the truth about things, may lead him to bury his nose in books, he is also easily bored. Have plenty of books around (in later life, he may prefer to travel the world for his education, rather than learning about life from dusty tomes). However, despite his apparent lack of studying and apparent preference for fooling around, he will surprise you by obtaining good grades and passing exams with ease.

His natural tendency to adventure will express itself in daring physical sports later on, as well as a desire to soak up new knowledge. Uncharted territory has the most appeal for him, and, as a perpetual student, he may well aspire to higher education. You had better start saving money for his college education!

Although naturally intellectual, a Sagittarian is not good at details. He loves to face challenges, such as puzzles. However, if they are too complicated, he may become bored and move on to the next thing. Patience is not one of his virtues, but he can be incredibly inventive. Just give him a ball of string, some cardboard, and colored pencils, and he will produce all manner of strange-sounding machines and implements for you. And just as quickly as he thought of the idea and made the object, he will generously give it away and go on to the next challenge.

This is one area where you can be of great help. Because your Sagittarian child is so multi-talented and lacking in self-restraint, he can easily lose focus and concentration. When the magnificent bridge he constructed falls apart with the hour and he is about to discard it, encourage him to revisit the project and work out why it collapsed. Boost his confidence by telling him what a great idea it was, but also teach him the importance of details and of completing a task, as well as the joy of a job well done. *Fun* is a keyword for this child.

The father of a three-year-old Sagittarian, Aimée, aware of her tendency for speed and sketchiness, offered her a prize of a trip to the zoo if she completed her drawing of him in no less than an hour! This was quite a challenge to Aimée, and she and her dad had a lot of fun as she labored over the buttons on his coat and the freckles on his nose – details she would normally overlook. When she had finished, not only did she win the prize, but she produced an exceptional likeness of him, which he instantly framed and put in pride of place on the bookshelf. Aimée was supremely proud of her work, and this was quite a milestone for her. Whenever she tried to do things too quickly, her dad would point to her drawing to remind her of the excellence of which she was capable. Invariably, she would smile to herself, slow down, and prepare to meet the challenge.

This small success was more important than it might appear. At a very young age, her astute dad had helped her on a lifelong task of self-control. Your Sagittarian child is a visionary, with brilliant dreams and a touch of genius. However, her dreams will come to nothing unless you help her to make them a reality.

Sagittarius Damian would tell his mother frequently that he was going to become an "Art-y-tett!" His mother, Sara, a good friend of mine, would smile and say, "That's wonderful, Damian." I suggested she take him up on this. From then on, every time he mentioned the word, she gave him a block of paper and some pencils and asked him to design a new home for her. Eventually, he lost interest in the whole idea, but encouraging him to put his thoughts on paper helped him focus and concentrate. Once you help your child to establish these kinds of habits, he can grow to be a gifted and talented adult, capable of bringing his futuristic or visionary ideas to reality.

YOUR SAGITTARIUS BABY SURVIVAL GUIDE

Birth to One Year

Eating – Your Sagittarius infant will be cheerful and good-natured, smiling and laughing a lot. He dislikes being forced into eating things he doesn't like but is always happy to try new things and gets great pleasure from them. His first solid food is an adventure – for all concerned!

Sleeping – This baby loves the great outdoors and will sleep better if he has plenty of fresh air. Try and give him at least one outing every day, and he will delight in passing dogs, cats, strangers, and everything that moves – just as they will delight in this happy soul. When his restless energy has been spent, he is likely to have no trouble falling asleep.

Motor Skills – Unlike children of some other signs, this little baby will enter the world kicking and raring to go. He is impatient by nature and, early on, you will discover that tantrums result if you cuddle him too much or too long. He is not one for restrictions of any kind. One baby, Esme, would resent her elder brother pulling up the rain shield on her stroller so much that she remembered this long after she had grown up. It was very traumatic for this free spirit to be enclosed in any way. Changing diapers can be quite a struggle for you, as he will squirm around so much and try and escape. Quick to learn to walk and get going, he may be doing so by eight or nine months.

Language – He will probably learn his first words early on. Like Leo, he is an avid performer and loves to bask in applause and admiration. He will soon find out that the more he communicates, the more brilliantly he will shine – quite a motivator for this little star.

Learning – This little one learns quickly through his fearless approach to life. Between nine and twelve months, your baby will tell you in many different ways that he is growing up and learning about the world around him.

Socialization – He likes people and perks up when a stranger peers over his stroller and admires him. He will chuckle and smile for them as if they were part of the family.

One to Two Years

Eating – Like those born under the other fire signs, he has a zest for life and all it offers – including food! He may, however, devour a plateful of cookies and then feel queasy afterwards. His eyes are a lot bigger than his stomach. Teaching him moderation in his eating habits will not be an easy task but is a necessary one.

Sleeping – He does not wind down gradually but comes to a dead halt after hurting his knees or falling over. This often means he is overtired and ready for a rest. He puts out so much energy and is brave and accident-prone. This demands your attention, as he has no idea when he has overstretched himself.

Motor Skills – He likes to live life at a frenzied pace. He enjoys being noisy and reckless. Expect falls and tumbles and scraped knees; these will evoke a few noisy yells, then he'll be off – the injury forgotten – and on to the next.

Language – Sagittarians recognize that physical exploration alone is not sufficient to expand their knowledge, and at this age, they rapidly become fluent talkers. He will enjoy you reading simple storybooks to him, and even if he doesn't understand the story completely, the pictures will fire his imagination.

Learning – He is learning more about the world through his direct encounters. Unlike the more cautious or more introverted signs, he will seek out experiences and will learn quickly because of this. He is bright as a button.

Socialization – His fearless approach to strangers may rightly concern you at times. However, on the bright side, you won't have to worry about staying overnight at a strange house or hotel – he will adore the adventure and the new people, all there ready to admire him and his antics.

Two to Three Years

Eating – He has a healthy appetite but may well be attracted to all the things that are bad for him. Moderation does not come naturally, so give him plenty of wholesome healthy food and make sure he always has more than enough to eat. His zest for life burns up a lot of calories.

Sleeping – The more he learns to play, the more you might want to introduce afternoon naps into his daily routine. Don't expect that you will be able to get him to sleep early at night, though; you may have to wait until he runs out of steam.

Motor Skills – By this age, he may be difficult to control, as he is a high-energy high-boredom-level baby. Your best bet is to interest him in some competitive ball playing before dinner so that he gets rid of all that excess energy before spending the evening with you! If he refuses to leave his play and come in to eat, try racing him to the table. He loves a challenge and loves to win – it may pay you to let him!

Language – He does not "beat around the bush." He gets to the heart of the issue, and you may be surprised by his forthright communication style. This is a Sagittarian trait and a positive attribute. However, also encourage him to consider other more sensitive souls' feelings. A little Sagittarian I know, Corinne, would scream "I hate you!" to anyone she didn't love. This direct message was rather startling, and her parents told her how hurtful it could be. Very soon, she would smile at people instead, go up to them nicely, and whisper, "I hate you." She felt this was a great improvement. Remember, these children have lively senses of humor and will do anything to make you laugh.

Learning – Humor is a great way to teach your headstrong Sagittarian. Instead of telling him off, make a joke of his behavior, and he won't be able to resist a giggle. He certainly learns a lot better through understanding than he does through restraint. He will resist restraint at all costs but has an innate desire to understand the world and his place in it. From his early years, you can explain to him the meaning of life. He needs to learn that all actions have consequences and to understand why.

Socialization – Your gregarious three-year-old will be able to form friendships readily. He is high-spirited, with a tremendous capacity for enthusiasm, fun, and horseplay, all attributes that make him popular with his peers. His direct manner and lack of shyness also mean that he can get on in an adult world and seem quite grown up even at this young age.

Sagittarian Lessons Growing Up: His love of freedom does not attract him to forging close relationships with those who make excessive demands. He will have plenty of friends who enjoy his warmth, high spirits, and friendliness, but do not expect him to spend time exclusively with one person at this stage of his life. Instead, give him all the love and affection you can, along with plenty of enjoyment and fun, and help him channel his energy in constructive ways. Teach him about life, but don't force him, for he's a rebel at heart. He won't care if he has his sweater on back-to-front or inside-out. In fact, when you draw attention to it, he will probably just laugh and feel pleased with himself. Convention is not his guiding light. He is far more impressed with originality and being ahead of the crowd. Above all, he is a seeker of truth, and this will always be his guide.

YOUR SAGITTARIUS BABY JOURNAL

Baby Capricorn

December 22 - January 20

Your Capricorn baby may be a mystery to you. She will gaze at you with serious wise eyes and make you feel like the child. Unlike the scattered nature of those born under the previous sign of Sagittarius, Capricorn children have discipline as their middle name. Because of this innate understanding and need of discipline, it is important that you establish routines in your baby's life. Like those born under the other two earth signs of Taurus and Virgo, this little one also needs concrete structures by which to live her life.

Some say childhood is wasted on the Capricorn, as she is adult beyond her years. However, although she improves with maturity, she is still an adorable baby. She will not bother you with screams and fussing unless there is really something worth fussing about. You may notice a little frown and intent look in her clear intelligent eyes. Don't worry; your six-month-old baby is probably deep in thought, working out the next fifty years of her life! Capricorn is a planner, and underneath even the most jovial exterior, there always lurks keen ambition. From an early age, your Capricorn infant will strive for success in all she does.

I was recently at the ocean and noticed two children making sand castles. They were both about three-years-old. Their father was helping them by heaping up the sand. One of the children would pat it into his bucket and rush down to the ocean and pour, then kick the sand around for a bit, then toddle off again. The other one was very intent on the task at hand. He was building a large mound of sand and would neatly pat each section in place and shore up the sides of the walls neatly and expertly. After half-an-hour, he was still at it. He had not moved from his spot. I could not resist; I introduced myself as an astrologer and asked the father if this child, Antonio, was a

Capricorn. His dad told me he was born in June, making him a Gemini. I quickly got out my laptop computer and ran some calculations. Yes, indeed, this little child did indeed have the Sun in Gemini, but his Ascendant, Moon, and Mars were all in the sign of Capricorn, making him very much under the influence of this sign. The other boy, Juan, was a fellow Gemini. However, when I ran this chart on the computer, I saw that he had the Sagittarius Rising with the Moon in Aries, making him far more extroverted in nature.

The symbol for Capricorn is the mountain goat. You may notice this little surefooted creature in your baby as she grows. She can ascend the mountaintop of whichever task she is doing at the time, surely and patiently, always reaching her goal. You may guess that your baby will quickly ascend the developmental scale. You are correct. She may be among the first to walk and talk, draw and paint. She loves to see the fruits of her labors, and this will stay with her throughout her lifetime.

You may wonder what you can do to help your sturdy, clever, almost perfect little Capricorn. I said "almost perfect." Although she has masses of practical ability, discipline, and the focus to succeed, there is one area in which she often lacks. That is in the area of confidence. Although she can accomplish more than people of other signs, her self-image is usually lower than most. She is naturally modest and can be her own worst critic. She feels she should be perfect, and when she falls short, her confidence suffers.

Be generous with your praise and approval, and do not fear that your infant will turn into a big-headed child. Although she is self-contained and not needy as other children are, this child needs her confidence boosted far more than most. Make a point of praising her endeavors, even as a baby, so that confidence can grow within her from her early months and years. Tell her how wonderful she is, how clever and pretty. You cannot overdo it with a Capricorn. She is the type of girl who will look in the mirror and see a big nose, small eyes, and fluffy hair, while the boys are swooning over her brooding good looks and air of mystery! She is the type who will come top of her class at school but be disappointed that she only got 90 percent instead of 100 percent. She will rarely be satisfied with herself or her performance. The more you praise her, the more you will help build the inner confidence and self-love she lacks.

Another thing you can give your Capricorn infant, in addition to recognition, is responsibility. Rules, routines, and structure are what she craves. Freedom is for the birds in her book.

I have a friend, Maria, who runs a playschool. She told me about one little boy, Nash, who would sit in the corner with his thumb in his mouth and cry while all the other children skipped about, having fun and making a noise. I found out that Nash is a Capricorn. He just couldn't fit into this free, unstructured, happy environment. He couldn't find his place. I suggested to Maria that she give Nash some responsibility. She put him in charge of all the toys. This was a thankless task, but he undertook it with a will. Nash did his best to ensure that everyone had their fair share of toys, that they looked after them properly, and returned them to him when finished.

Nash blossomed with this new responsibility, and Maria made a point of praising his efforts. Soon, Nash became the leader of his group, and other children would go to him to sort out their disputes or to organize a game. Nash was in his element, and his parents were amazed at how their serious unhappy little boy had blossomed into a force to be reckoned with.

While she enjoys showing you how clever and trustworthy she is, do keep an eye on her to see that she is not overdoing it. She can become overburdened with worry about all the things she has to do and will not even mention it to you.

You may have become so used to your two-year-old with her twenty-two-year-old maturity, that you forget she is just a baby. If she starts to experience depression or dark moods, find out immediately what is wrong.

One young Capricorn, Tyrone, had taken it upon himself to look after his new baby sister, Michelle-Anne. She fussed and cried so much when Tyrone was with her that he felt it was his fault. He felt guilty that he couldn't make her happy when, in fact, she was trying to express that her diapers were wet! Tyrone's mother didn't know what was going on until she watched him closely and found out the source of his concern. She explained gently to him that Michelle-Anne's unhappiness had nothing to do with him. She showed him how he could tell when his sister was uncomfortable. Tyrone was delighted. He had learned something and had been let off-the-hook as far as his guilt was concerned. Your Capricorn infant was born feeling guilty. Do your best to alleviate her feelings of guilt and encourage her to play and enjoy herself.

You will have realized by now that your Capricorn child is not frivolous or flighty. However, you may have discovered that she does have a delightful sense of humor. As she grows, she may develop a dry wit that will keep you in stitches. She loves to make people laugh, and it is important for this little one to be surrounded by joy, laughter, and positive feedback. Surround your Capricorn baby with good humor and the feeling that everything is right with the world.

It is her nature to keep her feet firmly on the ground. She lives squarely in the here-and-now and is not one for fantasy or make-believe. Your efforts to introduce her to fairy tales may leave her cold. Find some stories that make sense and are reality-based, and she will enjoy listening and learning from them.

The same goes for her toys. She will enjoy practical useful things, such as building blocks or a hammer-and-nails set. Two-year-old Amber spends hours with her little tea set, making and pouring cups of tea for her dolls, and later clearing, washing, and tidying them. This encourages her sense of structure and order, while stimulating her imagination, which is extremely important for this reality-based child.

You should know that your relationship with your Capricorn child has a profound impact on her entire life. While this is the case with all children, it is even more so with baby Capricorn. She instinctively respects adults and strives to emulate their behavior and do all the right things. Watch your own behavior closely and make sure you are displaying all your positive attitudes, such as warmth, generosity, love, and optimism.

If you are in a particularly negative mood, beware. You may notice your child copying you. Try not to lose your temper; if you are particularly irritable, keep out of this child's way. She is more likely than most to adopt your attitudes and approach to life, so ask yourself whether you would be happy about that. If you have a low self-image, take steps to remedy this. Find out your own strengths and start living them, or there is a danger this will rub off on your infant.

Help your child to remain a child. Encourage her playful fun side. Give her masses of security and warmth, and don't hesitate to tell her how much you love and admire her. Be dependable and reliable and establish routines.

YOUR CAPRICORN BABY SURVIVAL GUIDE

Birth to One Year

Eating – Capricorn babies are quite businesslike about their feeding. They like to be on schedule, and in about ten or fifteen minutes, they are finished and ready to snooze. This baby will probably not go for long bonding sessions, unless she has a Cancer Moon or similar.

Sleeping – Her sleeping patterns will generally be quite good. She will sleep on schedule. However, if she is cutting teeth or needs burping, she will yell with the best of them. You can usually soothe her quickly, and she will be of to sleep again.

Motor Skills – She may focus her eyes in less than two weeks, but she may not be happy at what she sees! It will be a challenge for you to get this serious little infant to smile and chuckle, though when she first discovers her toes, she may think that's quite a hoot. With the expanded scope she gains from learning to walk, a Capricorn toddler seems determined to do the things you do as soon as possible.

Language – She won't rush into talking, as she likes to absorb things around her before attempting a new skill. You will see her watching and listening carefully, then one day she will speak. This will be just as exciting for her as it is for you! She is not a chatterbox by nature, unless she has a Gemini moon or similar.

Learning – Capricorn baby may be slow to learn, but she is persistent and keeps at a thing until she has mastered it. When she is first introduced to solid food or a new toy, she takes pleasure in it, as she likes to learn new skills.

Socialization – Although she is shy with strangers, she is more likely to watch attentively than to scream in terror.

One to Two Years

Eating – This baby loves the mealtime routine, as do those born under the other earth signs. She enjoys food, and feeding this one won't be too much of a problem, as she has a healthy appetite.

Sleeping – This is also a breeze. Just as long as her bedtime is not subject to your changing whims, she will be fine.

Motor Skills – As soon as she can toddle around, you should try giving her little responsibilities such as helping you with the washing. She loves to feel useful, and an adult's approval matters a lot to her. She enjoys useful toys, especially ones that look like your household implements. It makes her feel grown-up and important.

Language – Music can help her learn language; she enjoys this, so play your records for her, and you may hear her joining in the singing. She is not one to let her hair down in gay abandonment, but if she feels comfortable and secure, she will sing and chat with the best of them. Encourage her to do this, as it helps her to loosen up and lose her inhibitions in readiness for playschool.

Learning – She is smart and can master things quicker than most due to her innate ability to focus. She likes to achieve things and is proud of her efforts. Do remember to shower her with praise.

Socialization – You keep hearing that your Capricorn baby is shy and introverted, and you may disagree. Well, if she has an extravert Moon, perhaps she can chat up a storm. But underneath that, there is a reserved toddler who prefers people she knows and warms up to people slowly. However, once she likes a person, she will like him or her forever. This tiny one is no social butterfly; she is loyal and constant, and you will begin to see these wonderful qualities emerging even at this young age.

Two to Three Years

Eating – Don't be surprised if she gets hooked on certain foods and asks for her favorite fish cake and peas every single day. She likes what she likes, and feeding her won't be a problem. However, you should ensure she doesn't get hooked on junk food or diet sodas; encourage her to eat healthily from an early age. One thing about Capricorns: They just can't get away with eating the wrong foods or doing the wrong thing for long.

Sleeping – Three-year-old Peter would start to complain by 8:00 P.M. each night that it was past his bedtime. This disturbed him a lot, and he got particularly anxious when he was on vacation or staying overnight with friends. Take your Capricorn seriously; it is serious to her. You can gradually introduce later bedtimes on each birthday, as she understands the value of advancement, and by doing this, she will feel she is progressing.

Motor Skills – Like any other kids of two or three, this little one loves to play. She is not a great fan of frivolous toys. Provide her with challenging practical toys, and she will be delighted. With her good concentration, she can keep herself happy for hours playing "grown-up."

Language – One of the banes of the Capricorn's young life is a quest for perfection. This is a marvelous quality when older, but for a child, it can be daunting. Joshua was so worried about his vocabulary that, when his playschool teacher asked him a question, he remained silent. At first, the teacher thought he was an awkward child. It was many years later that he shared the real reason for this. Because of his innate desire for perfection, you may find that your child speaks slowly or hesitantly. Give her masses of encouragement, rather than criticism. She is her own worst critic.

Learning – Your Capricorn three-year-old will probably quite like school because of its inherent structure. She is good at role learning and may be the first child to learn the numbers one to ten. She will love to be first and enjoys admiration. She may have quite a fascination with numbers, and you can often get her to do things if you motivate her by counting. For example, when she refuses to come down to lunch, tell her she has ten seconds and do a countdown. She may rush down at the last second, giggling and triumphant.

Socialization – She may be shy and withdrawn during her first few days at playschool, as she feels awkward with new things and people. She doesn't know what is expected of her and may feel insecure. Don't worry, though. Once she gets into the routine and understands what it's all about, she will really shine. Watch that she doesn't worry too much. She may silently fret over whether or not she'll get to playschool on time!

Capricorn Lessons Growing Up: Always be there for her, as the loving caring parent that you are. Give her the praise she deserves and the responsibility she aspires to. Give her a practically based view of reality, but teach her the value of morals, ethics, and spirituality, so that she develops wisdom. If you do this, you will give your wonderful Capricorn child a tremendous gift. You will be a loving companion who helps her as she attempts the slopes and mountains of life. You will be a respected parent and wise guide. You will help your Capricorn baby to blossom into the thoughtful, conscientious, reliable, and honorable person that she truly is.

YOUR CAPRICORN BABY JOURNAL

Baby Aquarius

January 21 - February 19

However you prepare for your Aquarian baby, you will never be prepared. You may have found the best child-rearing techniques and the most efficient nanny; you may have established routines to keep everything running on schedule. You may erroneously think everything will go according to your plans and that you are in control. Think again! Baby Aquarius may only be a tiny six-pound scrap, but he sure does make his presence felt.

This is one child to whom upsetting apple carts and sacred cows is instinctive. Aquarius is the sign of the revolutionary, and it starts from Day One. Just as soon as he can blink, smile, gurgle, and charm you out of trees, he will make you realize you are not in charge at all. Unlike Capricorn, he has no respect for authority – unless you deserve it. Don't bother to tell him what to do because he'll decide what's best. And it may be a radical departure from what your family has done for generations; it may go against your more traditional vein, but just go with the flow.

This is one child who is completely original, with vision and intuition. You may worry that he will grow up to be a revolutionary. Don't worry about it; just accept that he will. However, what you do to help him now will decide whether his revolutionary ideas will change the world for the better – or get him into trouble. Just as soon as he starts to play with others and can communicate, you'll see that normal things don't impress him. While other children smile sweetly at the teacher and bring her apples, your Aquarian child will only be impressed if the teacher lives up to his standards on how a leader should act.

Your Aquarian infant is like a magnet for anything new and unusual. Don't think that hiding candy and cookies in out-of-the-way places will deter this child. While he is free-spirited, he also has a dogged persistence that allows him to achieve his objectives. As a baby, he will scream for the cookies until you give in. Then, just as soon as he can communicate, he will argue, with his clever logic, to convince you he has to have a candy bar. He may well succeed. Like those born under the other air signs, Gemini and Libra, he is a skilled communicator. He also has the strong will to push through and win an argument. Until he has mastered this, however, he may resort to temper tantrums to achieve his objectives.

I knew a lady who had a Cancer Sun with the Moon in Capricorn. Her name was Edna and her values were family tradition, authority, and self-discipline. She was conservative by nature and collected antiques. She was married to a Taurus male, Harold, who was active in politics and a great upholder of hierarchy and tradition. When they had their first children – twin Aquarian girls, Jane and Emily – their whole world was turned upside down. I almost felt sorry for them.

At first, they thought all babies must be noisy, demanding, fearless, and strong-willed. I remember going out with them one day. We were strolling in the countryside, and the girls were only one-and-a-half years old. Just ahead was a fairly wide stream. We were engaged in conversation when suddenly there was a splash, then another one. Jane and Emily had decided to cross the stream and landed in the middle. Unperturbed by the commotion and their dripping clothes, they rushed out and rolled in the mud like puppies, screaming all the time. They appeared to enjoy shocking their immaculately dressed parents. At only eighteen months old they had succeeded! Fro then on, it was all downhill. The more Edna and Harold tried to keep them in order, the more they did the opposite!

Your Aquarian infant has no interest in convention and dislikes it if it restricts his freedom or the freedom of others. If you are standing in line with your two-year-old in a store, and he wants to go to the bathroom, don't expect him to wait. He is not inhibited, so you might just as well suspend your inhibitions for the rest of this lifetime! This Aquarian baby enjoys shocking people. The more narrow-minded or orthodox people are, the more he loves to shock them. Unless his birth chart is heavily weighted with other more traditional aspects, he enjoys shaking people out of their ruts. This is not an unkind thing, but a deep-seated urge to help people become better. This is one of his greatest talents.

Please don't hold your head in your hands and despair. I am now going to tell you that given the right kind of support from you, your Aquarian child can grow into one of the best people you could ever hope to meet. The conscious Aquarian adult is a visionary, ahead of his time, independent in thought and action, courageous, outspoken, fair, humanitarian, logical, alive, fascinating, visionary, and with a touch of genius. Why would you expect your little baby to be "normal" with all that potential inside?

Despite his independence, you should teach him early on the value of certain constraints and why there is nothing wrong with relying upon others. There is an innate fear that if he does so, he may compromise his freedom, which does not have to happen.

An Aquarian friend, Michael, told me that when he was about three-years-old, he would create a scene every day when his mother drove him to school. She never understood why this annoyed him so much. Later, he revealed that he had felt embarrassed being driven to school by his mother. Even as a small child, this act made him feel helpless! These are intelligent children. Be careful to explain the reasons for things. Michael said that had his mother explained that she didn't feel safe having him walk to school alone (and she didn't have the time to walk with him), he would have appreciated the ride instead of resenting it. In other words, had she made him feel that she was driving him for her benefit, he would have felt better about it!

If you go through life not really noticing things or people, be prepared. Your Aquarian infant will wake you up! He is an eternal student of human nature and just as soon as he can communicate, he will be mimicking the mailman's funny walk or your best friend's high-pitched voice. If you're lucky... he'll only do this behind their backs!

Although not the most easy child to manage, he is certainly one of the most unique and creative. Ethan was only nine months when he discovered how to prevent his yellow Labrador from eating his food when it dropped from the edge of his tray to the floor. He watched for a while, then, like a light bulb turning on in his head, he scooped the squishy banana pieces and moved them to the edge of the tray. Next, to stop them from dropping off into his doggie's mouth, he bent down, brought his own mouth to the edge of the tray, and gobbled the banana from there!

Although one-of-a-kind, he is not a loner and will be happiest with playmates all around him. This infant will always be group-oriented. His nature is geared toward the world at large and he may, at a very early age, show signs of wanting to improve the group he is in.

Don't be surprised if your little Aquarian comes home from playschool ranting about how Suzie was told off by the teacher. He cares deeply about the plight of others and likes to see social justice. Encourage this trait, for your Aquarian baby can become one of the most tolerant human beings you could hope to meet and will probably teach adults a lesson or two in this area. His acceptance and enjoyment of everyone – despite their different backgrounds, beliefs, colors, religions, and creeds – will not diminish with age. Because of this, although he may typically be a quiet, rather aloof child with a cranky, zany, obstinate streak, he will always have plenty of friends. He will understand their abilities and their weaknesses and will delight in their success as much as his own. He will generously share his toys (unless he has a more possessive Moon sign or Rising sign), and sharing comes easily and naturally to him.

You may be thinking that your Aquarian baby will grow into a perfect genius, compassionate and caring. Well, that is almost true. He can grow into a fine person of high ideals and a deep sense of fairness and equality for all. Don't be surprised to find him giving support to his baby sister or friend from a very young age. Although sometimes innocent about the ways of society, as far as humanity is concerned, he has an innate maturity from Day One. One area where you can really help him, however, is in the area of human emotions. Although deeply sensitive, he has a detachment from his emotions that is awesome. He can suffer tremendous disappointment, yet switch off his emotions like turning off a faucet. This detachment can be good and bad. On the negative side, he can switch off and bury his feelings. On the positive side, this ability can help him on his journey toward unconditional love.

A friend's niece, Tessa, lost her beloved cat when she was three-years-old. The cat had been born two days after the child, and they were inseparable. Sadly, the cat had been run over on the busy road outside their house. Tessa refused to cry but instead started causing a rumpus, laughing and playing games around the house. Her mother was shocked until I explained Tessa's ability to detach from her emotions. I suggested that she spend time discussing this with her child so that Tessa could better understand her own emotional nature and how to handle it.

YOUR AQUARIAN BABY SURVIVAL GUIDE

Birth to One Year

Eating – Just remember your Aquarian baby was born unpredictable. Don't expect regular on-the-clock feeding times, like Capricorn or Taurus. Just expect irregularity, and you will feel at peace. Don't be surprised if your tiny Aquarian doesn't eat for several hours and then demands to be fed twice within the space of an hour. At first, go along with his erratic routines and then, in time, gradually and gently try to regularize his dining habits.

Sleeping – All I can say is that sleep patterns will follow a similar erratic course, unless this baby has a steady Taurus Moon or similar. You may even be used to this, finding that even before he was born you were yourself prone to out-or-character erratic behavior! It is the same with his feeding habits. Don't force, just gently try and regularize habits over time.

Motor Skills – This little genius can be pretty smart. Ethan has the Moon in Aquarius, and he loves to pass a ball back and forth with a willing partner, while sitting upright on the floor. Sometimes he becomes so excited that he falls backward, unable to get up again from his supine position. He doesn't let this stop his game, though. He continues to play by catching the ball with his feet, then transferring it to his hands, so that he can then throw it back again!

Language – With most babies, you will see signs that he understands your words from about eight to ten months, but don't be surprised if your Aquarian shows understanding even earlier than that. Don't be surprised about anything he does, actually. When you see him looking over at your puppy when you talk about Fido, realize that understanding is dawning. He may not yet understand the words, but he gets the gist of what you are saying.

Learning – He is bright as a button. He may not be particularly dexterous, unless he has a Virgo Moon or similar, but he has a good mind. You will notice how he learns things quickly and with understanding, even at this young age.

Socialization – His innate brightness shines through when he is with people. He is fascinated by them and at home in groups of friends or family. Don't be surprised if he tries to participate in your grown-up conversations by interrupting with his own comments. He is just enjoying the social interaction.

One to Two Years

Eating – Like those born under the other air signs, he is not really in touch with his body or his physical needs. Eating is not his main concern, and you will have to establish eating patterns for him. Ask him to tell you when he's feeling hungry. He probably won't know, but it will encourage him to tune in to his bodily needs and at least think about it.

Sleeping – Do not expect quiet nights, and you won't be disappointed. He is attuned to the mental world and needs rest to recuperate his busy mind. However, he may be a restless sleeper.

Motor Skills – Your Aquarius baby is fast-wired himself, and it is probably not by chance that he is attracted to things electrical and technical. They appeal to his techno-brain. Watch him when he starts toddling around, as he will probably make a beeline for the wires on the telephone, television set, or computer. Instead, supply him with some other equally interesting, but safe, object.

Language – This little one knows how to communicate what he is feeling. He is strong-willed and doesn't like to be pressured by your or anyone. You may be delighted that he cooed over his dinner and asked for more. However, don't expect that giving him the same dish every Tuesday will work. He doesn't like to be predicted. I knew an Aquarian two-year-old, Yanni, who would eat nothing but boiled eggs for days at a time, until he suddenly decided he hated them and transferred to baked beans on toast. His poor mother had a fit trying to keep up with his complete switches, until she learned to treat Yanni like an adult. She would sit down and explain to him the dos and don'ts of diet and suggest alternatives. He would nod his head wisely like a little sage and allow his mom the privilege of choosing a balanced diet. He might not like to be coerced but is intelligent enough to accept advice.

Learning – Aquarius toddlers are even more curious than most of their "into everything" contemporaries. When your Aquarius child pulls electrical cords out of sockets or investigates the computer connections, physically remove him while you say your "no" and supply him with a roll of Scotch tape or some other safe "adult" object he's never played with before.

Socialization – He's not born to be a loner. He is part of society and knows it. If he is an only child, make sure you have plenty of family gatherings or invite your friends round on a regular basis. Even if he is a shy Aquarian with a Cancer Moon, he will still, underneath his shyness, feel at home in a group of people. It is good for his soul.

Two to Three Years

Eating – He will have more important things to do than eating, such as wondering if his new playmate is going to play with him tomorrow. He will sit happily in front of the television set with a sandwich. Not ideal, but it can be a blessing at times for the harried parent.

Sleeping – Don't worry about rushing to get him to bed on time. He won't even notice if you are an hour or two later or earlier than normal! He may find it difficult to get up in the morning and would happily stay in bed half the day, dreaming his dreams. Explain why it is important to get up. He is always interested in intelligent explanations, though he may not agree.

Motor Skills – His development of motor skills, such as teeth cleaning, dressing, and lacing shoes, will be – like everything else – erratic. At times, he will insist on doing everything himself and will emerge with his shoes laced up the wrong way and his mouth smeared with toothpaste. Just tolerate it or assist him without making a big deal. If he doesn't feel that his newfound autonomy is threatened, he will no doubt ask you to do it the following day.

Language – Once you get used to his contradictory nature, you will not be surprised by his sweet comments one minute and his temper tantrums the next. The best way to deal with them is to establish honest and open communication. He is never too young for this. The world will not tolerate a prima donna, but it will admire and respect a budding genius. A lot of it boils down to your influence. He does not naturally respect authority, but he will respect you forever if you earn his respect. Once you have done that, he will become one of the most helpful and loyal of all children.

Learning – He is learning about the world and where he fits into it. Because of this, he tests his limits constantly. He may push your buttons, but remember, he is just learning about what he can and cannot do. He will want to stay up late to watch a television program or be with his elder brother. He will want to go with you to the theater and so on. One thing you don't want to do is keep saying no. Explanations are needed, and the more you explain, the better he will understand how the world works.

Socialization – By the age of three, he will probably be quite socially sophisticated. He may bring a group he is in together in some way by acting in some leadership capacity. When Tommy, the son of my friend, Irma, first went to playschool, he would resolve arguments over who was to have the best crayons by appointing himself the crayon monitor. When it was time to draw, he would hand out one yellow one to everyone first, then a blue one, then a red, and so on, until everyone had their fair share. He even managed to get a couple of willing assistants to help him in this task!

Aquarius Lessons Growing Up: The best way you can help your tiny Aquarian to develop into the wonderful human being he really is? First, learn to know your place as parents. Realize that your son or daughter will accept you as a companion far more readily than as a parent. When you tie his shoelaces, expect that he will know how to do it better than you (with all your thirty years' shoelace-tying experience). "Let me do it!" is his constant refrain, followed by "That's not right!" Companionship is permissible; guidance is not.

"That's not so" is another favorite retort to simple parental statements. Although one more or less expects this kind of stubborn rejection of authority from young children, with Aquarians, it is pretty much a lifelong habit of mind. And though it can pose problems for them when they try to function within the established order, it is also one of their strengths. His role in life is to open all of us up to new never-before-thought-of ways of being.

YOUR AQUARIUS BABY JOURNAL

Baby Pisces

February 20 – March 20

Your Pisces baby is a magical mystical child who is happier in her world of daydreams and moonbeams than the rough-and-tumble of early life. She is unpredictable, but not in the kooky way of an Aquarian baby. She is responsive and impressionable and soaks in the vibrations around her, reflecting them back. She is vulnerable, shy, and sensitive to every mood and nuance. She may at times retreat into her own world. At other times, she will dance and frolic with exuberance.

She has as many sides to her complex emotional nature as a diamond has facets. Always remember that the reason for this is her extreme sensitivity to all the undercurrents and unseen vibrations of life. If reality is too harsh, she will retreat into her make-believe world, where she can remain for hours, days, or even a whole lifetime. It is especially important for this child to be surrounded by love, peace, and harmony. She will need plenty of this all her life, and if she doesn't find it in the world around her, she will create it in a world of daydreams.

As you might imagine, this child is a natural actress. Like a chameleon, she can change her facial expression, her mood, and her posture from second to second. She has innate empathy, which means that the vibrations of the people she is surrounded by rub off on her. Although she can be as lively as the best, she does need big doses of peace. If she is born into a lively extrovert family, you may find this little infant wanting more sleep than other children. If daytime reality jars her sensitive nature, she will just switch off and retreat into her dream world of sleep.

I knew a Pisces child, Carmen, who loved to go to bed. If her parents went out to spend the day with relatives or friends, right after dinner, Carmen would tug on her mum's sleeve and whine that she was tired and wanted to go home to bed. Even if it was only 5:00 or 6:00 P.M., she knew her delicate constitution needed rest, and she didn't fight it like other children.

This is a child who may literally cling and hide behind your skirt hem, with thumb in mouth. Try not to be irritated by her behavior but understand that she is a magical child with depths of emotion that confuse her. She does not know how to set her own boundaries (unless she has a more practical Moon or Rising sign), and so her vulnerability is very real. It is especially important that you understand this side of your Piscean baby's nature and give her plenty of nurturing and scope for her wonderful artistic and loving nature.

The slightest unkind remark from another child, teacher, or parent can hurt this child. She responds to the world emotionally, as do those born under the other water signs, Cancer and Scorpio. However, little Pisces does not have the toughness of the Scorpio or the protective shell of the Cancer. Because of this, tears are her way of expressing her hurt. Don't be too alarmed by her constant weeping at the slightest thing. It is her way of coping.

Stephanie, the Pisces baby of a work associate, would burst into tears every single day of her young life. The slightest thing would upset her. When she stepped on a snail by mistake, she sobbed uncontrollably. When she spilled ketchup on her mum's new dress, it broke her little heart. When her dad yelled at Spot, their dog, she ran away in floods of tears. Kindness is like a tonic for this one, and she can dole it out better than anyone.

In the harsh fast-moving world in which we live, your Pisces baby is in danger of being overwhelmed, and it's important you get her to share with you her feelings. Instead of asking her what she did, ask her what she felt today. It is very therapeutic for this child to understand her diverse feelings so that she can gradually learn to control them.

A client of mine started a ritual of "feeling tales" with her daughter as an extension of her nightly readings of fairy tales. Elisa would look forward to sharing with her mommy her magical world of feeling and would act out the day's emotions with real tears, laughter, and looks of sadness and joy. When Elisa grew up, she decided that she would become a nurse. Almost twenty years later, she is now a wonderful caring nurse, a talented artist and musician, a healer, and a volunteer in her local community. She is soon to be married to a wonderful loving man who adores her gentle, kind, soft-spoken charm and romantic ways.

Don't be surprised if your Pisces baby shares her affection with every living thing, including pets, birds, and even insects. She will lavish kisses on your pet turtle and spend countless hours playing with what would appear to be a fairly boring creature. One little Pisces toddler, Scott, was distraught when he saw a fisherman catching fish. He toddled over, shouting, "Bad man! Bad man!" and howled with tears, until his parents explained to the embarrassed fisherman that Scott didn't like to see any living thing being hurt in any way.

Despite her affinity for pets, don't make the mistake of giving little Pisces the responsibility of feeding your family pet. She may start out with good intentions but is not yet organized enough to maintain any kind of routine. She may be the sweetest baby and the kindest kid on the block, but routine is not usually her strong point.

One of her greatest talents is her imagination. Don't ever tell her that imagination isn't real. She knows you're wrong on this one. Your child can, however, become so immersed in her fantasy world, especially if she perceives the world around her as harsh, that she needs to understand it's not the reality she should inhabit all the time.

When she runs to you to tell you about the fairies in the garden, do not insist on telling her that fairies do not exist. They certainly do and, as a psychic child, she may well see them. The worst thing you can do with a natural psychic is to force her to believe that what she is experiencing isn't real. If this is the case, then perhaps you need to open up to the unseen worlds around you. Encourage your toddler to explain what she saw and be open enough to believe her. Study the unseen worlds yourself so that you can guide her with wisdom. Encourage her to express and use her natural psychic talents in positive constructive ways, rather than suppress them. With your wise counsel, your Pisces infant can be among the most intuitive and perceptive of all.

Other ways to channel her imagination are through visual art, music, and dance. Encourage her with all these art forms. Keep her supplied with plenty of paper and crayons, and don't be surprised if she displays real talent just as soon as she can scrawl a pencil across the page. She may have enhanced visual abilities that enable her to create through artistic mediums such as painting, and, later, photography. Take her to music and dance classes. Make the most of her natural talents, and she could become a talented performer or artist. Although innately shy, she can blossom when performing in front of other people.

Julian, who had a Pisces Moon, was so shy as a baby that he would avert his eyes and hide behind his mother's dress at every opportunity. He dreaded playschool and the attention of the teacher and even his peers. His parents worried about this excessive shyness – until the wise teacher gave him a leading role in the playschool drama. Julian practiced his words like an acting veteran and performed around the house for weeks. When finally the production took place, he shone. His latent talent for drama and self-expression was evident. While the other children giggled and stumbled over their words, Julian was masterful and confident. At three-years-old, he had found his vocation!

Your Pisces baby will be a good test for you. Remember that she is aware of not only your words, but also your vibrations. However upset you may be, try to remain positive, calm, and centered around your child, especially when she is preverbal and cannot understand what is going on. Keep your comments about others positive and loving. If you are going through difficult times in your personal life, remember that she will soak up your difficulties as her own. Although it is impossible to wrap your children in cotton wool, you should defend them as much as possible from bad attitudes and pettiness. Feeding your little Pisces' soul with positive nourishment is just as important as feeding her body with good nourishing food. If you emphasize the positive, your child will grow strong and healthy.

You will soon learn that, although she is quite compliant by nature, she is as willful as any other child at this age and can stomp and scream with the best of them when she wants her own way. Give her lots of security, hugs, and kisses – but not her own way. She needs to learn that she can't "play" you.

YOUR PISCES BABY SURVIVAL GUIDE

Birth to One Year

Eating – These tiny delicate souls have enjoyed the peace and tranquility of the past nine months and are now thrust into the harsh world of form. It is hard for them, and they need lots of soothing in the form of breastfeeding, calm music, and gentle strokes. Be warned, she likes to nurse for long periods. You will soon learn that patience is indeed a virtue.

Sleeping – Although she may have objected forcibly to being ejected into the harsh brightly lit world, you may be relieved to hear that this high-strung infant does like to sleep. Unlike Aquarian babies, she enjoys a cuddle as much as you do (unless, of course, she is tired or hungry, which is most of the time!). Try and play soothing music at home instead of your favorite rock band. Boisterous music or loud noises can easily upset this sensitive little soul.

Motor Skills – Like those born under the other water signs,

Cancer and Scorpio, she loves the element of water. She will enjoy her bathing ritual and splash around with delight, as long as she feels safe and the environment is peaceful and calm, rather than harried and stressful. A colleague made her baby Annalisa's bath time into a personal meditation for herself. She would light a candle in the bathroom, play gentle soothing music, and even say a little prayer. Not only would Annalisa love the serenity and slip off to sleep afterward, but the mother would also feel calmed after a hectic day. She would take time out in the middle of her hectic day as well to take her for long walks in the stroller down by the local lake, and they would sit gazing at the ducks together, both of them dreamy and bonded.

Language – Your Pisces baby can learn quickly, as she is extremely empathetic and, because of this, quite a mimic. Spend time talking to her; although she may not understand you, she will chuckle when you do and have a great time. Also, read her plenty of fairy tales. She will never quite get used to the harshness of everyday life and will maintain a rich imagination all her life.

Learning – She also learns by mimicry. If you want to teach her language, just repeat words to her and ask her to repeat them. You may be surprised at her learning skills. She will also learn to copy other people's habits and even laughter. As her world of imagination is so rich and so real to her, you need to teach her the difference between her stuffed tigger and the real tiger at the zoo. This helps her distinguish between the world of form and the world of imagination early on (I am not saying that the world of imagination is any less real than the world of form, only that it is different).

Socialization – Like those born under the other water signs, she becomes very attached to what she knows and loves, and it is particularly true at this young age. Pisceans have a strongly developed feeling nature. Isaac is jealous if his little sister gets more attention than him. Even at eight months, he would make angry noises and push his sister away with both hands. Also, when Mom and Dad kiss and hug her, he gets angry and concerned.

One to Two Years

Eating – She is highly sensitive and attuned to the unseen world of vibrations and atmospheres. Of all the water signs, Pisces is the most vulnerable and sensitive of all. Make a point of creating a soothing atmosphere at mealtimes and play gentle healing music.

Sleeping – She needs more rest and recuperation than those born under any of the other signs, unless she has a more boisterous Moon sign or other factor in her chart. She enjoys cuddling up in bed and being tucked in, away from the cares and worries of the day.

Motor Skills – You will soon see that she is quite artistic, with a strong sense of rhythm. Two-year-old Russell listens to the leaves rattling on the window and rustling outside and waves his arms in rhythm with the sound. He toddles out to the garden in the rain if you let him and dances around gleefully as he tries to catch the raindrops.

Language – Encourage her to share stories and fantasies with you. She can be so good at explaining about her imaginary friends that it may be difficult for you to distinguish between what is real and what is make-believe. Young David used to talk about his "garnomes" (garden gnomes). For a long time, his parents thought he was making up stories until one day, almost fifteen years later, David told his mother that he really had seen gnomes and elves in the garden. He was a natural psychic, and the world of devas and nature spirits was a part of life to him. He also used to see auras around people and would describe people as being of different colors. You will need to use your discretion with this sensitive child.

Learning – Give her lots of toys to encourage her imagination and creativity and lots of reassurance. Your Pisces toddler may feel insecure once she learns how to walk and may even resort to crawling at times. As she is so sensitive, she doesn't like loud noises and scurries away when you use the vacuum cleaner or blender. She is rapidly learning that the world is big place, and she prefers to retreat in the face of unpleasant situations. She has a distaste for fighting back when the next-door neighbor's boy tries to pull her favorite toy away from her. Instead, she may shed a few tears or whimper a little. At other times, she will throw a tantrum, and you may find this is as a result of her feeling insecure or dismayed about someone else's actions.

Socialization – She is not the most sociable of children, but is adaptable by nature and so can adjust to new situations or people quite readily. However, if she withdraws into herself, you will know that on some level she is fearful and needs to feel secure again. Her moods are not always easy to understand, but do take notice of them because she has a type of psychic antenna around people and situations. She is very affectionate with people she loves and loves closeness and hugs and expressed affection. The Pisces toddler of a client would plead to go to bed as soon as dinner was finished, as she so enjoyed the coziness of being tucked up in bed and kissed and cuddling with her growing number of stuffed toys.

Two to Three Years

Eating – She is just as attuned to your moods as to her own, so it will be in everyone's interest if you calm yourself down before mealtimes, or she may have problems eating. Give her simple healthy food. She loves to indulge in sugar and all the bad things that will take their toll later on in life and are particularly bad for her sensitive disposition.

Sleeping – She loves being cozy and enjoys bedtime. Gently stroke her brow and head as you read to her at night. She will love that. In the hustle and bustle of daily life, she gets all messed up and needs smoothing down and calming down before she goes to sleep.

Motor Skills – You may often catch her dancing all by herself to music that you are not even aware of, such as the sounds of nature outside or music playing across the street. Conversely, her sensitive ears are sometimes bothered by obscure sounds that you don't notice, which is another indication of a natural talent for music. Encourage her to dance and to enjoy water sports, such as swimming or aquatics. Also keep her well stocked with crayons and paints, as she may have a talent for art.

Language – Remember that she is impressionable. While she is learning language, keep her away from too much television, or she will readily pick up swear words and slang and happily use them. She will have long conversations with her stuffed animals and toys, which have names and are real to her. She may even argue with them at times, telling them off in her voice and answering in an even squeakier voice (theirs!). If she doesn't have any siblings, it is a good way for her to learn to communicate, and you may even want to include her guests at the dinner table from time to time.

Learning – Your Pisces child has her own unique way of learning. Her style is to tune in to people and information to learn things and sort of absorb herself in it, rather than learning by rote. For this reason, you should be careful not to plonk her down in front of the television set and leave her there. Schedule a set viewing time together, where you can explain things to her. She is not at her best in new situations and may be worried for weeks about going to pre-school. You should talk to her about it and even take her there in the car a few times beforehand. Talk to her about the teacher and children she will meet there. Because of her good imagination, she will be able to visualize the scenario and then, when it happens for real, she will have a head start.

Socialization – Give her lots of opportunity to play with other children her age because she has a tendency to escape into her inner world, preferring to play with her toys. Help develop the kindness and compassion that is such a motivating factor for the spiritual sign of Pisces by giving her a pet goldfish.

Pisces Lessons Growing Up: Like the sign of Gemini, the twins, Pisces is also a dual sign. You may see your Piscean baby growing up with one foot in this world and one foot in her magical world of dreams. Understand this complex child and give her all your love and wise guidance. Surround her with positivity and encourage her to express her many talents. If you do this, she will return your love a thousand times and will grow to be a loving adult with a heart full of compassion for all living things. Your tiny Pisces baby can, with your thoughtful care, grow to be a spiritual and creative giant, uplifting and inspiring all around her with her kindness, love, and wisdom.

YOUR PISCES BABY JOURNAL

PART II

THE BROADER PICTURE

CHAPTER THREE

Your Baby's Past

Our birth is but a sleep and a forgetting:
The Soul that rises with us, our life's star
Hath had elsewhere its setting,
And cometh from afar:
Not in entire forgetfulness
And not in utter nakedness,
But trailing clouds of glory do we come
From God who is our home:
Heaven lies about us in our infancy.

-William Wordsworth

So far we have delved into your baby's psychological patterns, emotional needs, personality, and growth patterns. Now, through the use of astrology, we will look at your baby as a soul – with a past as well as a future.

As parents you give the wonderful gift of a body, but you do not create the essential, unique "being" of your child. This human soul already exists, a living entity that enters the cell and grows and provides the physical body necessary to live and gain experience.

Astrologers believe that your birth chart outlines not only your present and future, but also your past lives. Although the subject of past lives is not the focus of this book, it must be mentioned as an essential part of the soul's evolution

Although the majority of people on Earth believe in past lives and reincarnation, and this belief is a central part of several world religions, many people in the Western world still do not accept this.[9] Whether you believe in reincarnation or not is entirely up to you. However, I must reiterate that, as an astrologer, I do take past lives into account. I would add that there is also now a massive body of proof for the reality of reincarnation, thanks in part to the work of the brilliant academic, physician, and psychiatrist, Dr. Ian Stevenson[10], who has devoted the last forty years to the scientific documentation of past-life memories of children from all over the world. He has over three thousand cases in his files. Many people, including skeptics and scholars, agree that these cases offer the best evidence yet for reincarnation.

Dr. Stevenson's remarkable and painstaking work with young children who speak of previous lives, provides detailed and accurate information about people who died before the children were even born, as well as detailed descriptions of places and homes they had never visited in their current lifetime. Incredibly, the amazing body of work he amassed has been, for the most part, ignored by his peers, despite Dr. Stevenson's own illustrious academic career and qualifications. However, anyone who studies his work with an open mind will see that he presents undeniable proof of reincarnation.

Another scholar, Dr. Brian Weiss[11], a traditional psychotherapist, was astonished when one of his patients began recalling past-life traumas. However, when she began to give Dr. Weiss information about his own family and his dead son that she had obtained from the other realms or "space between lives," his skepticism began to erode. This started him on the next remarkable phase of his career using past-life therapy, which is documented extensively in his book *Many Lives, Many Masters*, which went on to become an international bestseller.[12]

Preparing for Birth

If you accept that your baby has lived before, it will explain why you may have spent months trying to choose the right name for your child, then, just before he was born the right name suddenly popped into your mind.

This certainly happened with my own parents, who had prepared a long list of names (names, by the way, that I would not have enjoyed!). Just before I was born, the name *Christina* popped into my mother's mind very clearly and stayed there. It was not a name my parents had ever thought of or discussed before, and they were surprised by its appearance. In my mother's words: "The name was persistent and wouldn't go away. It felt to me as if the little soul about to be born was announcing her arrival in very definite terms!"

Your name is not a random thing. It constantly reaffirms who you are. According to numerology[13], which I have studied and practiced for over twenty years, all the letters of the alphabet have vibrations, and the total letters of your name broadcast to the Universe who and what you are, and attract back the appropriate experiences you need in order to fulfill your destiny.

Numerologists can tell a lot about your child just from his name, as each letter represents a certain value or property. For example, if you name your child Alexander, he will approach life head-on, with a mental, analytical approach, whereas if your child is named Irene, she will have a more emotional approach. The letter "A" in numerology has the qualities of initiative, independence, and mental creativity; the letter "I" is more emotional; it has a self-sacrificing universal approach to life.

This is just a superficial glimpse into the fascinating complex study of numerology, but for a numerologist, choosing a name can be a complex task! However, if your wise little soul gives you a "head's up" before she is even born, take it seriously. She will have worked out her name, perhaps in cooperation with guides or teachers in the other realms, in order to give her the lessons she needs in her current lifetime.

As parents will know, there are many types of preparation that need to be made for the incoming infant. Choosing a name is just one small part of this process. How active you choose to be before your baby's birth is another. I know several mothers who like to work right up to the last minute before the birth of their babies and consider this as a type of badge of honor, showing dedication to their jobs. Then when the baby is born, they disappear from work, never to return. Strangely enough, I have observed that it is often the mothers who take time off before the birth of their children and become oriented to home life who have the fewest problems after birth and may even make the transition back to the workplace if it feels appropriate.

Having a baby is a huge event, a huge change in one's life, and preparation is essential. As parents, you are not just preparing for the physical birth of your infant, but for the incarnating soul with all her lessons and challenges brought with her from the past. We have so far looked at how your infant may develop in her current lifetime. Now let us look farther back - into the experiences and challenges from the past of this incarnating soul.

In your baby's birth chart, the path of his or her soul is illustrated by what is known as the Lunar Nodes or Nodes of the Moon.[14] To find out where these Nodes were when your baby was born, turn to Appendix III on page 303. You will see that there are two Lunar Nodes: a South Node and a North Node, both represented by symbols. You will see that there are two Lunar Nodes: a South Node and a North Node. The South Node is represented by the symbol ☋ and the North Node is represented by the symbol ☊. These mathematical points (they are not physical bodies as are the planets) are extraordinarily important to the astrologer.

Very simply put, the South Node represents your baby's talents and abilities learned in the past; the North Node, her future challenges. By its location in her birth chart, the South Node represents the gifts that your baby's incarnating soul has brought with her to this current life. These gifts comprise your baby's experiences, talents, abilities, and memories. In other words, the lessons and skills your baby has struggled with and learned over many lifetimes are still available to her through the influence of the South Node.

When we die, all the valuable experience we have gathered is not suddenly erased, even though most of us do not have direct memory of these experiences. These experiences, and our response to them, form what is called our "karmic pattern."[15] Once we pass over, our Higher Self then decides upon our place and time of rebirth, our parents, etc., so that we will have the correct experiences we need to continue our path of evolution, according to the lessons required by our karma.

Think of the South Node as being like your baby's report card. It can illustrate to you, as her parents or guardians, what lessons she has already learned and which examinations she has passed.

Just like the Sun, Moon, and planets in your baby's chart, so will the Nodes be in different signs and in different areas of the birth chart. In this chapter, we will look at what your baby's South Node means in each of the signs of the Zodiac from Pisces to Aries. From this, you can glean quite a bit about your baby's past. It can also indicate to you her strengths and early predispositions.

SOUTH NODE OF THE MOON THROUGH THE SIGNS OF THE ZODIAC

South Node in Aries

She is born independent and feisty. She was forced to stand on her own two feet in previous lifetimes and is armed with the courage and competitiveness of a little warrior. She is naturally athletic and will enjoy the thrill and challenge of competitive sports. She is tough, smart, noble, courageous, and self-centered, with natural leadership abilities. She is the little girl who bites her tongue when she is nervous or afraid, as she doesn't like to show her feelings or appear vulnerable. She has an innate desire to be seen as strong and fearless, even if she is shaking inside. Even if she has a gentle artistic Sun or Moon sign, there will still be a streak of the military about this strong-willed child. She will appreciate rules and regulations and is punctual and hardworking. You can be proud of her strength, independence and ambition, but teach her that there are others in the world apart from her. This lifetime will lead her toward lessons of cooperation and teamwork, putting the needs of others before her own so that she can learn understanding, tolerance, and selflessness. Encourage her in this process of growth and give her all the love and affection she craves. Once she takes to this higher path, she will become a wise diplomat and upholder of social justice.

South Node in Taurus

One of his favorite playthings may be that little mesh pocket of golden chocolate coins. First, he was born to appreciate money and the material comfort that can buy; second, he has a love for food and things of the senses. In previous lifetimes, he learned about the value of things and comes complete with his own moral code. This makes him self-sufficient, fair-minded and reliable, with a streak of stubbornness. He loves routine and is inclined toward laziness, preferring to stay in bed as long as possible, rather than get up and face another day. He is loyal and steadfast, with pleasant charming manners and an artistic flair. He likes you to be there for him, and he will always be there for you. He is popular with playmates and adults alike; his perfect smile charms the birds out of the trees and gets him exactly what he wants! In this lifetime, he may seek risky speculative ventures. Encourage him, while helping him maintain a secure foundation. Although he needs security, there is a deeper part of him that knows it is an illusion and leads him to explore unknown untried paths of power, challenge, and adventure.

South Node in Gemini

She brings with her from her past a natural zest and joyfulness for life and all that it offers, making her a happy lively baby who gurgles and coos at every new experience. She loves to learn and is enthusiastic about the richness and diversity of life. At school age, she may excel at sports, cookery and academia. She may have a sneaking interest in many diverse subjects, from home economics and karate to Latin and Philosophy. She will dabble with various religious paths and doctrines and will love them all. She is a lively, inquisitive and eternal student of life, and as soon as she can talk, her sentences will always begin with "Why?" At some point in her life, she may be attracted to a foreign country. She will love to travel and may live in several different places, imbibing the different cultures and languages. She may see herself giving up her regular everyday life and living in some retreat, devoting herself to higher academia or ancient spiritual knowledge. Later, she may long for her eternal quest for knowledge to merge into a one-pointed journey toward higher truth. From there, she will share her knowledge with others and can become a brilliant and talented teacher.

South Node in Cancer

As soon as you get out the cooking pots, he will be there with wooden spoon in hand, ready to join you in the cooking and eating. He loves both. In past lifetimes, he learned to nurture, feed, and care for himself and his family, and to be sensitive and home-loving. He is devoted to his mother and will literally hang onto her apron strings as a baby wanting to feel close. He will always be ready for a hug and kiss, as he loves to feel close and needed. Equally, he will be there for you when you are tired and stressed. He will just sense that you are feeling down and will throw his arms around you, making everything suddenly seem better. His home is where his heart is, and he would like to stay there with you forever. When he is old enough for his first job, he may prefer to build a home business; however, at some point in this lifetime, he will feel the urge to break away from his home comforts. Encourage him in his determination and ambition to succeed and help him to understand the value of having high and noble goals from an early age. He can become the chief executive or company president who takes a personal and paternal interest in the lives, ambitions, and problems of all his employees. He can become the bishop who feeds and cares for his parishioners' souls.

South Node in Leo

She will love sparkly things and will be drawn to your jewelry and glamorous dresses. As soon as she can dress up in them, she will. She will stomp around the house in your shoes and evening dresses, drawing laughter and admiring remarks from all the family. This adoration is what she seeks, and she will light up your life with her antics. In her past life, she was the center of attention and the leader of the pack, generously dispensing love, laughter, and favors on all around her. She has incarnated with a regal air and easily commands an audience. Teach her the beauty of simplicity, modesty, and humility, and help her to appreciate other people. At school, she will soon be the captain of the class and the hockey team, as she loves to excel. She is a natural for amateur dramatics, and dramatics will become a part of your daily life with this little one around. Later on, she will be drawn to teamwork and learn to sublimate her defined ego in order to help build a team and benefit the group. Once she learns to do this, she will emerge as the popular leader of the group and become one who seeks to bring out the best in all the team members with generosity and love. As she seeks to understand those around her, she will learn the meaning of true friendship.

South Node in Virgo

He will be attracted to organization and structure and will particularly enjoy Lego and other toys where he can build and be organized. You can keep him quiet for hours by letting him play with pieces of paper, folders, and colored Post-It notes. There is an innate desire for order and a talent for meticulous work and craftsmanship, which he learned in his past. The unruly world in which we live can seem overwhelming for your tiny infant, but as he grows, he will excel in the material world and can achieve great success in school, college, and business. He is particularly adept with numbers, with detailed work that requires sustained concentration, or with any painstaking craft such as writing. He can be extremely clever, industrious, good at tests and examinations, and gifted with words. He may be a little shy and quite modest at heart. Give him lots of hugs and kisses and teach him about love and kindness. Later in life, he will seek a world beyond his clearly defined parameters and may yearn for spiritual retreat. He may use his many crafts and talents to further a noble charitable cause or artistic venture. At heart, he yearns to bring more love and understanding into the world and will work hard to make this happen.

South Node in Libra

Your little baby girl is sweet, graceful and sociable, and everybody loves her. As a baby she will follow you around, not liking to be alone. In past lives, she excelled as a team player and was supportive, loving, and understanding to all around her. Now these wonderful attributes come easily to her. She also has an innate talent for harmony, whether it is in music, art, or language. If you are a feisty person, with a loud explosive temper, try and control this around your daughter. When she feels her peace is threatened, she becomes fearful and will do all she can to appease you. Her gentle manner will attract people to her, and they will come to her to sort out their problems, attracted by her sense of fairness and justice. She is open to both sides of an issue and may find it difficult to make decisions. Instead of presenting her with endless choices, pull out the yellow dress; if she has an objection, she will definitely let you know. She may be sweet, but she is not weak. She is "the iron fist in the velvet glove," and you will be aware of her strong will from the moment she is born. Channel this into challenging pursuits, and teach her about strength and leadership. As she grows, she will strive for independence; don't be shocked if she breaks away from her friends and family in order to venture into the unknown. It means her soul is ready to show her the lessons of standing on her own two feet. Once she learns this, she can achieve anything she desires through her one-pointed focus and iron will.

South Node in Scorpio

This powerful little character will make his presence felt through the sheer force of his feelings. He may not say much, but his personal "vibes" will cut through the atmosphere of any room. He can charm you out of the trees with his delightful smile and magical eyes, or he can make you wish you were not in the same room. Power comes naturally to this little one, for he has wielded it easily, gracefully, or forcefully in many a lifetime. To him, power and magnetism are natural and innate. Beware: As soon as he discovers girls, they will be drawn to him. He may grow up to be weedy and spotty with buckteeth, but your little Johnny is the perennial "chick magnet." As a baby, the word *fascinating* springs to mind. Elderly ladies will coo over him and teenage girls will think him the coolest baby in the world. So, what are his talents? A laser-like penetration into your darkest secrets: As soon as he can talk, he will cut through your lame excuses and soon you will be following *him* around. His talent with people is renowned. He came into this life with talents as a mentor, teacher, and keeper of secrets. He is a shoulder to cry on and a wise listener. He can rise high and will enjoy being around powerful successful people. Later on, his soul will crave a path less challenging, and personal power may lose its luster. He will yearn for the peace of emotional, material, and spiritual security. Encourage him to learn about the serenity and joys of nature and to trim his passionate sails to find a more peaceful routine path.

South Node in Sagittarius

When you see this South Node, you will know that your baby is an adventurer. He loves to travel, so please keep the doors shut and cupboards closed. In the past, he may have been a fearless adventurer who hiked the Amazon jungles and scaled Mount Kilimanjaro just for the thrill of it. His courageous tendencies will soon become apparent. He doesn't like to be fenced in the playpen, and you may find that the covers on his cot are always pulled off, as he squirms and fidgets about, frustrated by the fact that life is as yet pretty dull and routine. All children ask questions, but this one will plague you with impossible ones. His approach to life is fearless, mentally as well as physically. Best not to tell him he can't do something. He will love the challenge. The mother of one little Sagittarian South Node I know keeps her darling daring infant in check by saying, "I bet you can't finish your spinach today… I'll give you a dime if you can stay here until I get back." As he grows older, don't try and indoctrinate him with your belief systems. Give him all the freedom in the world to find his own way in life, with plenty of wise guidance, and he will surprise you by staying close. The minute you try and hem him in, he will be off like a shot. As he matures, he may decide to write all his adventures as a screenplay or book or will send you lengthy letters from every corner of the globe.

South Node in Capricorn

Even when she is a baby, you will sense her seriousness. Unlike the rebellious Sagittarian, your baby will enjoy routine and structure. In past lives, she has learned the power of discipline and the fulfillment that hard work, ambition, and success can bring. Caution comes more naturally to her than adventure. She will learn slowly but surely, one baby step at a time. However, don't underestimate her innate love of achievement. Give her lots of encouragement when she speaks her first word, takes her first few steps, and switches to solid food. She does not take easily to change, and your encouragement will help her to overcome the daily traumas as she is forced to learn about life. While she loves to bounce around and play as well as the next baby, her favorite toys may well be ones that are useful rather than purely decorative. When she screams in the supermarket, remind her that this is not the accepted way to behave around other people. You will appeal to her innate conservatism and sense of responsibility. She will catch on quickly and, as along as you give her the correct and wise guidance, she will grow into a thoughtful child and caring human being. Later, when she has risen to the top of her career, she may long for comfort and security and have children later in life and enjoy the homely comforts that she once rejected. She may become a gourmet chef or take upon herself the role of caretaker, as she learns the lessons of sensitivity, feeling, and nurturing of the bodies, minds, and souls of all in her environment.

South Node in Aquarius

Rebellion is his middle name. Although this may be too difficult for you as a parent or guardian to understand, understand it you must. Above all, your infant will require understanding – and lots of it – if he is to become the genius that he has the potential to be. When he first starts to toddle around, you may wonder why he doesn't like to follow the rules like his siblings do. He's not worse than they are; it's just that he's not geared for conformity. He has spent lifetimes striving to make society a better place and has been faced with challenging authority and convention in the process. As a baby, you won't see much of that. But as you watch him gurgling and cooing, you may catch a glimpse of the keen perception and intelligence behind this child's eyes. Sometimes you may feel he is older than you are – and who knows? Like all infants, this one needs encouragement. But Aquarian South Nodes are not reliant upon lots of hugs and kisses (unless they have a Cancer Moon or similar); they need encouragement to express their crazy ideas and initiatives. As he grows, he will long for the spotlight and push to be the leader and to excel. It is just his soul pushing him to define his ego, when for many past lives he has put others' needs before his own. Encourage him to take up some creative pursuits, such as drawing, dance, or make-believe.

South Node in Pisces

A baby born with the Moon's South Node in the sign of Pisces will incarnate as a sensitive artistic baby, very open to feelings and impressions. With the proper nurturing and care, the child can learn to work in the world and bring the inspiration from the past forward into proper channels. You will need to shield this little one from excess noise, temper tantrums, and bad vibes in general. She will be forced to deal with them soon enough, but at this sensitive age, she needs more nurturing than most in order to blossom as the radiant caring soul that she is. She is very open to spirituality and harmony. Try sending her healing, and you will see that she seems to revel in the peaceful energies. She soaks them up, and this is food for her sensitive artistic soul. She is impressionable and empathetic. Be careful what you say around her and how you say it. All babies are learning from the world around them, but this little one *becomes* the world around her. As an artistic soul from the past, she is used to soaking up vibrations and channeling them through her. Ensure that she is surrounded by positive vibrations; this will help her reach her full potential. As she matures, she may become interested in the healing arts and would make a marvelous doctor, nurse, or healer, or work in another role in which she can channel her compassion to be of service to others.

CHAPTER FOUR

Your Baby's Present

Soul Nourishment

This chapter focuses on the importance of nurturing the little soul that is your baby physically, mentally, emotionally and spiritually, and understanding her as part of a generation of souls incarnating at this time around the world.

By nurturing your baby on all levels, you can assist her in adjusting to the trauma of birth and the adjustments she must make as she emerges from the gentle watery realm of the womb into the harsh concrete realm of Earth. Those babies with the Sun, Moon, Rising Sign, or other planets in Earth signs, i.e., Taurus, Virgo, and Capricorn, may adjust more quickly to life on the material plane. However, all babies, no matter how much of the earth element is present in their birth charts, will need a period of adjustment.

This little soul's incarnation into the material world can be quite a shock. Her first glimpse of this realm is often as a noisy sterile environment with masked doctors and helpers. She has spent nine months in a warm, soothing, comfortable environment and now is forced to come into this harsh, noisy, frantic world. It is little wonder that she yells! According to scientist and spiritual teacher, Rudolf Steiner, it is particularly important for parents to pay special attention to their babies during the first six weeks or forty days of life.[16]

The first six weeks is a huge period of adjustment for the parents as well as the baby. In some cultures, after birth, a branch was placed over the door of the house with the newborn baby for the first six weeks. This was a symbol that meant *Do Not Disturb*, and it was known and respected by everyone.

How many times have you visited the theater recently and seen parents with tiny babies? The extremely loud noises at movie theaters, along with the germ-infested environment, may be damaging for a young infant. Certainly for the first few weeks, it is wise to avoid taking your newborn out for trips to busy shopping centers or to large family gatherings, whenever it can be avoided.

Also, be aware of loud noises around the home, such as the food processor or the vacuum cleaner. These may be an essential part of everyday life, but just be aware of your newborn's sensitivity to all the intangible things around her – as well as the influence of the planets – such as sound and atmospheres. We know that the influence of the planets affects human behavior; we should also remember that sound is a vibration that affects all living things. It is also known that thoughts and feelings are real and physically influence not just adults, but babies – and indeed all life forms.

As long ago as the 1960s, Cleve Backster[17] conducted some of the most notable experiments with plants. He discovered they have a perception capability that he called "primary perception." This "primary perception" operated regardless of distance and extended down to the single-cell level. Backster obtained reactions from fruits and vegetables until they were completely rotten, various single-celled organisms, and even some minerals, metals, and distilled water. His experiments proved that this perception exists in the apparently "non-living" world[18] as well.

Backster's plants registered a clear experience of the events around them and demonstrated a rich inner life. In one of his experiments, Backster failed to get a response when he dipped a leaf into a scalding cup of coffee, so he then got a match to urn the plant leaf being tested. Before he could even do it, at the moment he made the decision, there was a dramatic change in the tracing pattern on the polygraph, suggesting that the tracing might have been triggered by the mere thought of burning the leaf! He had discovered that even plants respond physically to the thoughts and feelings of those around them.

In another experiment, Backster had live brine shrimp dumped into boiling water at random times that were determined by automated equipment, in order to remove any possibility of human interference. In a series of experiments with three philodendron plants each located in a separate room, polygraph readings showed that five to seven seconds after the dumping of the shrimp, the instruments registered a large burst of plant activity that Backster concluded could only have come from the shrimp. It was as if the plants were in sympathy with the death of the shrimps and registered a silent gesture of despair and empathy.

In subsequent experiments with many things from fresh fruit and vegetables to amoeba, Backster's experiments demonstrated the same sort of primary perception. The results demonstrated that besides some sort of telepathic communication system, plants also possess something closely akin to feelings or emotions.

We love our plants and know they enjoy being watered and cared for. Backster's scientific experiments proved that we are correct. Apparently, our poor plants even worry when a dog comes near them and when violence threatens their well-being. Since Backster's amazing work, many other experiments have been performed, all just as bizarre and exciting.

More recently, the fascinating book *Messages from Water* by Masaru Emoto[19] proves that even water responds to vibrations. Distilled water was placed between speakers that played various pieces of music ranging from classical to heavy metal. The water was then frozen and the crystals were photographed. Further experiments were performed with kind words and indifferent words and by sending emotions like love and appreciation. The results were amazing and prove that harmonious soothing vibrations and disharmonious negative vibrations all affect even drops of water.

If water and plants are so affected, how much more so is your little newborn baby, for these experiments illustrate the incredible sensitivity of all living things. Your baby has now been thrust into this harsh environment called life. Just as your plants and pets react to every sound and emotion, how much more will this sensitive – and as yet unconditioned – little soul react?

However, this is not for you to worry about but just to be aware. Your baby needs to be surrounded not by anxiety, but by an atmosphere of love, peace, and spirituality, in which she can truly flourish and blossom.

This is a wonderful time to bond with your child and to wrap her in uplifting vibrations. You can protect her physically by keeping her warm and cozy, you can massage her and cuddle her. The following are some spiritual exercises you can do that will sensitize you and the atmosphere in your home, in order to provide her with the nourishment she needs on the spiritual soul level.

The following simple exercises will provide soul nourishment for you and your baby.

A Place of Peace
Everyone needs a place of peace that they can retreat to, if only for a few minutes a day. This will give you peace and strength, as well as offer protection to you, your baby, your family, and your home.

• Find a suitable area of your home that you can reserve exclusively for your spiritual practices, so that in time it becomes imbued with the pleasant rejuvenating vibrations of your meditations and prayers.

• The more you visit this sacred space, the more you will light a spiritual flame that will nourish you and will spread outward toward the nourishment of your home, family, and the world as a whole. This does not have to be a whole room, but just a corner of a room. You do not have to spend hours of time there; just a few minutes a day. Make this your place where you can sit quietly and reflect on your life, giving thanks for the baby who is in your care and asking for inspiration to assist you in the precious task of parenthood or guardianship.

• Because this area of your home and of your life will become your spiritual retreat and the place where you can find love and peace, it is important that you select it carefully. Choose a space that feels good to you and where you can, if possible, face east. The direction east is associated with mystical power.

•You can select precious objects to have in your little retreat, ones that have meaning to you and can inspire and uplift you.

• You may also want to use color. All color is a mode of a vibration of light. Matter radiates light, and all matter has a color vibration. This can be soothing, energetic, uplifting, or disturbing, depending upon the quality of the vibration. A lovely soothing color to use that will bring you calm after the hectic life of parenthood is a vibrant green, like the green of nature. Introduce a rich green cloth or light to this area and bathe yourself in this color, through your eyes. This is the next best thing to getting out into nature. In your busy life, you may not have time to go into the country, but you can spare just a few minutes every day in your own little mystic retreat.

• Other colors to use are violet, magenta, or purple. These colors are spiritual in vibration and by gazing at these colors, in the form of a richly colored cloth, you can help yourself to rise above the irritations of everyday life into a calm centered place.

Natural Breathing

Correct breathing is vitally important for your health and for the health of your child.

• Sit comfortably, either in your retreat or in a chair with your baby. If you have a rocking chair, even better. Breathe deeply and evenly using your diaphragm, chest, and lungs.[20] First fill the lower, then the middle, and finally the upper part of your lungs. This is known as the complete breath, or natural breathing. Retain the breath in the body for a few seconds and exhale slowly. Hold your chest in a firm position and draw your abdomen in slightly and lift it slowly upward as the air leaves. When you have exhaled, relax your chest and abdomen. At the end of each complete breath, your abdomen should be slightly drawn in.

• By deepening your breathing, you will automatically become calmer and more centered. Your baby will feel this change, and this will also help her feel nurtured and calm. Watch yourself the next time you feel anxious or worried, and you will be aware that your breathing is also shallow. This is an illustration of the mind-body-spirit connection. The mind is by its nature unsteady, and it is affected by our senses, by what we see, hear, feel, etc., at every minute of every day. When we concentrate our minds, we find our breathing automatically becomes deeper and slower. When we have bad news that causes us to be sad or angry, our breathing becomes irregular, the opposite of the slow smooth flow of the breath when the mind is calm. This proves that our mind and breath are interdependent and are each unable to act independently of each other. Correct breathing gives us physiological and psychological balance.

• Breathe, using this natural breathing method, for a few minutes a day, and in time this will become automatic. Start to breathe correctly now, using natural breathing, and you will automatically teach your child the correct breathing methods, which will sustain her throughout her lifetime.

Creating Harmony
Thinking positive, joyful, and uplifting thoughts will create a loving environment for your baby.

• Spend a day saying only positive constructive things about yourself, as well as others. Extend the day into a week.

• Now, watch your thoughts. Be sure that your thoughts, as well as your words, are positive and loving as well, remembering that when you think, you are creating "thought forms" that can harm or heal.

• When you are sitting quietly with your baby, read her some inspirational words from your favorite holy work. Although she will not understand the words, truth has a powerful vibration that helps to open up intuition and inspiration. There is no such thing as being too young. We are born spiritual, and we are here to unlock our divine potential.

• Notice how peaceful your baby looks when you do this. It will not only help her, but it will also help you and create a harmonious atmosphere in your home. This may seem difficult with the stresses and strains of parenthood, but try it and see what happens.

The Violet Flame Practice
One of the simplest, yet most sacred, practices we can use is the practice of the Violet Flame. This is an ancient mystic practice that was originally introduced to mankind by the Spiritual Hierarchy of Earth in order to help us grow spiritually. This is the hierarchy of Adepts, Masters, and Ascended Masters who live in retreats

around the world and whose main task is the preservation and growth of spirituality on Earth. I learned this wonderful practice from my own Master, Dr. George King.[21] The Violet Flame Practice brings great benefits, including cleansing, purifying, and strengthening the aura, which will bring protection in many ways. A strong healthy aura will protect you and your baby from disease, as well as from the negative thoughts of others. Also, as previously stated, the color violet has the highest vibration of light and will help to open the pathway to the soul – the superconscious mind – so that inspiration and high intuition can dawn.

The Violet Flame is given freely and always upon our request from the Logos of the Mother Earth herself. This great living Goddess beneath our feet who sustains us and allows us continued experience is an extremely advanced life form, far more advanced than we are. This is a great gift taught in the ancient mystery schools and is now being made readily available to everyone. The Violet Flame Practice can be used anywhere, at any time, although, as it is a sacred practice, it should be used with respect. The more you use it, the better will be the effects. This really is a spiritual gift and should always be used with love and reverence.

• Close your eyes and be relaxed around the neck and shoulders. Practice the complete breath[22] and allow the thoughts of the day to come and go until you feel detached and centered in the present. Then, using your powers of visualization, or imagination, think down to the beautiful Mother Earth, living silently beneath your feet. Feel appreciation and thankfulness for this great Goddess.

• Now, with love in your heart, visualize flowing right up through and around you a beautiful vibrant violet flame. See and feel this flowing right up from the Earth, filling and purifying every aspect of your physical body and your aura. In your 'mind's eye,' take this about thirty to forty feet above your head, or as high as you can see it go. Hold this visualization for a few moments, feeling yourself bathed and cleansed in this beautiful blueish light – the violet flame.

• At first, you may find it difficult to visualize. Some people find color difficult to visualize; others may see it but be unable to feel it. The secret is to keep practicing and to have faith that when you request this cleansing flame, it is indeed there.

Sending Healing

We are all healers. My own Spiritual Master, Dr. George King, taught that healing is the natural birthright of every man, woman, and child on Earth.[23] I have been a healer for over twenty years and have had many remarkable results, as you can. In order to start healing, we must first develop a "healing consciousness." Try this simple practice. You can either do it in your own quiet time or when you are holding your baby.

• Close your eyes and remember a time in your life when you felt truly loved.

• Feel this as a warm sparkly feeling around your heart area and hold this visualization for a few moments.

• Now, using the power of your mind, move the feeling down your arms and into your hands. At this point, many people feel the "love energy" as a tingling sensation or warmth in their hands.

• You can use the same technique when your plant looks tired or your pet is sick. You can even use it with your child's grazed knee or your spouse's headache. You can perk them up with a dose of healing power. Obviously, if your baby has any health condition, first see a doctor.

Health Patterns

You will see by now that astrology is valuable in many ways. As well as helping you to understand and nurture your baby, it can be used to observe tendencies toward weakness in parts of the body and to apply antidotes before these may manifest as illness. Infant mortality could be avoided more if doctors would read natal birth charts.

The size and shape of your baby's body is genetically preconditioned. It is the entering soul that infuses the body with specific tendencies, habits, and patterns that make him unique. Astrologers regard the physical body as the "temple" of the soul; this Earth plane on which we live and grow and gain experience is like a foreign land, and the soul must have a vehicle in order to survive here. The incarnating soul chooses his parents and by doing so, his body. The actual birth process may be quite a shock, and you can help him with some simple techniques to adjust to life.

Astrology and health is a complex subject; here, we will look at one simple aspect of your baby's chart – his Rising sign – which can show health tendencies, and how you can help. To calculate your baby's Rising Sign turn to Appendix II on page 300.

RISING SIGNS

Aries Rising – Aries rules the head. Your Aries baby may be particularly vulnerable in this area, so make sure you cover him with a hat, and pay special attention to protecting his head. Also, his headstrong impulsive nature can get him into scrapes. He is not one for lots of hugs and kisses, but gentle healing to his body will help calm him.

Taurus Rising – A vulnerable area for your Taurus baby is her throat and neck. When the weather is chilly, muffle her up well. A child of this Venus-ruled Earth sign has a sensual nature, loves physical touch, and will find your gentle massage very soothing.

She will respond well to beautiful music, color, and natural perfumes, such as flowers and newly mown grass.

Gemini Rising – Gemini rules pairs in the body, i.e., the lungs, legs, kidneys, etc. Take precaution to cover his lungs with a warm sweater, and do not allow him to breathe in cold air or be in a smoke-filled environment. Talk to him; you may be surprised at how much he appears to understand. Communication is like a balm to his sensitive disposition.

Cancer Rising – A stressful birth process can leave her feeling abandoned at the time of birth, and she needs lots of early nurturing to counteract this. This sensitive emotional child holds her feelings in her stomach or solar plexus region, which can result in an upset tummy. Make sure that there is a pleasant harmonious atmosphere during mealtimes.

Leo Rising – Health problems with Leo Rising are associated with the chest and heart, and stress can settle there. In order for your baby to be happy and stress free, he desperately needs to feel loved and appreciated from Day One. Keep telling him how wonderful he is, and give him lots of hugs and kisses. All babies need lots of love, but for this little one, it is food for his soul.

Virgo Rising – This baby is born with a sharp intellect and is a good-natured soul. Her biggest health problem, however, may be a tendency to worry. Even as a child, anxiety can settle, causing a restriction or blockage in some part of the body. Give her lots of confidence-boosting soothing massage and gentle healing if she becomes overtired or anxious.

Libra Rising – Here, the physical manifestations of birth trauma can settle in the organs of assimilation and elimination. He particularly needs a home atmosphere of peace, harmony, and beauty.

Soft soothing music will be a delight to his ear and bring balance to his soul.

Scorpio Rising – Typically, a baby with Scorpio Rising has to struggle with early life. You may sometimes feel as if she didn't want to be born, reluctant to face the tests that life usually offers children of this dynamic powerful Rising sign. You can assist her by giving her a natural free childhood with lots of fun and play to stimulate her vivid imagination and calm her deep emotions. She will also respond particularly well to healing, as it will help her release pent-up feelings.

Sagittarius Rising – Humor is essential for your Saggie Rising baby. Surround him with laughter; it will nourish and uplift him. He may be difficult to get hold of or to hug and smother with kisses, but encourage his natural exuberance and he will stay happy and healthy. Don't pen him in! This baby can't tolerate restrictions.

Capricorn Rising – This little soul may have been reluctant to enter the earth plane and so she needs an extra special welcome and reassurance. Like the children of the other earth signs, Taurus and Virgo, she responds well to gentle loving massage. There is a predisposition to tension that can cause blocks to the whole system, and massage of the spine and tops of the shoulders is particularly helpful.

Aquarius Rising – This is a unique baby, high-strung, restless, and impulsive. Aquarius rules the nervous system, so your job is to bring calm into his life. He is extremely sensitive, and you may find he is allergic to things like dust and pollen. He sometimes forgets to breathe, so take him outside in the garden for doses of prana.[24] He is also sensitive to music, and the right sounds are healing to this sensitive soul, as are other healing techniques, including hands-on healing or color therapy.

Pisces Rising – Your Pisces Rising baby is extremely sensitive and may be prone to picking up infections and other ailments. She is very receptive to healing and to love, and these are essential foods for her soul. Wrap her up well; she will enjoy being in a cocoon of warmth and love, and this will be a good antidote to her sensitive immune system.

CHAPTER FIVE

Your Baby's Future

Let there pour strength
Into my feeling;
Let there flow warmth
Into my thinking;
Let there shine light
Into my being;
That I may nurture this child
With enlightened purpose,
Bringing wisdom, love, light, and joy.

-Chrissie Blaze

With the evolving spiritual consciousness in our world, a new holistic approach to baby care is needed. Your newborn baby may be tiny, but she is also complex, with a mind and soul, as well as a body, to care for.

As parents, you have accepted the wonderful precious gift and responsibility of raising and teaching a child. If you raise your child with compassion and instill in her spiritual values, you can not only help develop a wonderful soul, but also one who could inspire and help other people or move forward our civilization in some degree. You are an essential part of these possibilities.

The New Generation

Many people are now talking about the new generation of children being born that are widely known as the Super-Gifted Children, the Creative Children, or the Indigo Children.[25] Astrologers believe the common traits of each generation and sub-generation are revealed by the position and movement of the "outer" or "transpersonal" planets, namely Uranus, Neptune, and Pluto. It is these plants that move slowly around the zodiac. This means that babies who are born at roughly the same time throughout the world share many common characteristics, and their attitudes are formed by common experiences.

The particular configuration of outer planets at this time in our history is the cause of the sensitive and highly strung nervous systems displayed by many of these children, making them ideally suited for the extremely high-tech future ahead. Astrological analyses of these children have greatly helped many irate, harried parents of these unusual children to understand why they are as they are.

These extremely sensitive high-energy boys and girls display previously undocumented behavior. According to the National Foundation for Gifted and Creative Children,[26] some common characteristics are that they are self-possessed and sure of what they want and need. They bore easily, with a short attention span, and do not enjoy much of what goes on in school, such as rote learning or authority. They do not respond well to authority, unless it is democratically based. They demand respect and intelligent discussion and like to be treated as adults. They have their own preferred methods of learning and their own agendas, which are focused and purposeful. They are also very compassionate. On the downside, these children do not respond well to failure, and if they experience it, they may give up easily and develop permanent learning blocks. Also, they may withdraw if they feel threatened or alienated and sacrifice their own talents and creativity in order to "belong."

From this, you can see that more conventional parents and teachers may feel confused by the behavior of these unusual difficult-to-handle children. Because of this, many of them are being placed on medication to help them "fit in" and be more manageable, although when tested, they are very gifted academically. It is important you understand this to see whether your own baby fits the description of these special children. You can then help him avoid academic failure and the medication route, unless absolutely necessary.

Some of these Super-Gifted Children are diagnosed as having Attention Deficit Disorder (ADD) or Attention Deficit Hyperactivity Disorder (ADHD), and there are certainly genuine cases of these, but you should question whether this diagnosis is really accurate for your child. According to the Drug Enforcement Administration (DEA), prescriptions for the drug Ritalin, used for ADD and ADHD, have increased 600 percent this decade, and 20 percent of schoolchildren are medicated to make them more manageable.[27] According to Beverly Eakman, president of the National Education Consortium 2001, "these drugs make children more manageable, not necessarily better. ADHD is a phenomenon, not a brain disease. Because the diagnosis of ADHD is fraudulent, it doesn't matter whether a drug works. Children are being forced to take a drug that is stronger than cocaine for a disease that is yet to be proven."[28]

There is certainly controversy surrounding the extensive use of Ritalin for these children, who some believe are just wired differently and so are not yet understood by society at large. Many astrologers believe that it is not by chance that the Super-Gifted Children are incarnating and joining us on Earth at this crucial time in history, bringing talents and abilities that will be needed in our uncertain future on this planet.

Astrologers have found that many children in the sub-generation born from 1988-1995 and 1996-2003 have outstanding potential, with great talent and intellectual prowess, and I believe they will help to lay the foundations for the new age of enlightenment that must dawn. The first group is strong, intense, focused, and ambitious, and the latter group is more outgoing and exuberant, quick to question conventional norms and authority in general. These generations are likely to be reformers of society, inventors, and great intellectuals.

The characteristics of many children born in the next sub-generation, from 2003-2010, will display similar characteristics and be potential leaders for the future. If you have a baby who was born at this time, watch as he grows to see if he develops the more sensitive mystic nature that is also a part of this generation.

These high-energy children, born during this twenty-two-year time period, are destined, as a group, to develop tremendous compassion for mankind. They may become spiritual revolutionaries, highly intelligent and intuitive, bringing tremendous light and love into a world that so desperately needs it.

In studying the birth charts of babies and young children over many years, I believe these children are advanced or "old souls" who are being reborn at this crossroads in our evolution to help prepare mankind for the new age of peace and enlightenment that is dawning.

As you can see, these "old souls" are more sensitive and bright than average and so need more understanding from their parents and guardians. Being more enlightened, they also need more spiritual nurturing and exposure to spiritual vibrations. If they do not receive this, then they can be more difficult than more "average" babies and young children, as they are strong-willed, smart, and perceptive.

There are theories that there are more of these Super-Gifted Children being born now than ever before. I do not want to give the impression that all children diagnosed with ADD and ADHD are "old souls" or "Super-Gifted." However, as the new Aquarian Age dawns and as there is a global quickening of vibrations, it may be that advanced people are choosing to be reborn at this crucial crossroads in our history. These old souls want to be here on the material plane in order to help – through selfless service in many different ways – combat the potentially negative effects of these heightened vibrations we are feeling. Although these heightened vibrations are positive for the more spiritually-minded person, as they enhance intuition, compassion, and inspiration, they can be hard to handle for people who operate at a more basic level, desiring only to satisfy their own selfish desires.

This is not a new phenomenon. There are old souls in every generation, but they are now being highlighted, which is a good thing. This is partly due to the fact that more attention is now being paid to our babies and children than ever before; therefore, these gifted children are being noticed. There are stories of wonderful magical feats performed by these children, such as the ability to transfer healing energy from their fingertips. In the past, they may have been considered odd or strange. Sometimes, they have been regarded as learning impaired. Now, at last, their uniqueness is being acknowledged, and enlightened parents can help ensure that their young "old soul" babies find their rightful place in life.

Your Baby's Future Destiny

These babies are often born with an awareness of their past lives and future destiny. Also, there are children who, because of their spiritual maturity, are able to attune themselves more easily to the more refined spiritual energies radiating from the planets. This is why they have high-frequency nervous systems and also why a balanced diet of spiritual practices is so vital for their healthy growth.

These children also need stable, secure, and loving family lives because of their sensitivity and psychic awareness. The Super-Gifted Children I have met have strong intuitive faculties and also a degree of psychic awareness and an innate understanding of the basic laws of metaphysics. In other words, their understanding is global, and they think in terms of helping mankind rather than just about getting a good career and leading a "normal" life. These old souls are more enlightened than the average person, and this is why they are not so easily conditioned by society. Because of their enhanced spiritual awareness, they naturally utilize more of their right-brain creative characteristics, and so do not necessarily fit well into the current "left-brain" more regimented structure of mainstream society.

Since society will not – at least at the present time – adjust to their more spiritual outlook, it is essential not only to give them understanding and spiritual nourishment, but also to teach them the "how's" and "why's" of fitting into society. How to "render unto Caesar what is Caesar's," so to speak. They need to be taught left-brain activities in order to produce a good balance between the right and left-brains so that they can function and shine in society. If not, although they may become wonderful people, leaders, and innovators, they may not have the material means to fulfill their spiritual desires and unique destinies.

In other words, they need wise parents who themselves have a good understanding of metaphysical laws (the natural rhythm and harmony of life) and are open-minded enough to embrace worlds beyond their own comprehension. When your gifted child chats about the fairies she has been talking to, don't just laugh or dismiss her out of hand. She wants to be understood, and it is quite likely that she has experienced or seen angels or fairies. She may also be able to see auras around people and feel things that others do not feel. She may have a tremendous sensitivity to atmospheres and instantly like or dislike people for no apparent reason. This is where a wise astrologer can really help.

Not long ago, a friend of mine told me that her brilliant son, who had recently graduated from Yale, was offered an incredibly prestigious and well-paying position designing weaponry. He was thrilled at the offer, but my friend was deeply shocked. She explained to him that by doing so, he could be responsible for killing and maiming thousands of people. At first, he resisted and said that defense was important to the country and so forth. However, she just asked him to go away and think about it more deeply. He did so, out of respect for her, and came back to her and told her he realized that she was right and wanted to use his skill in service to the world in a positive way.

As parents, your thoughts, words, and actions really count. Not just when your children are teenagers, but ever since the time they are born. I remember my grandmother telling me at the age of three, "Thoughts are things." This affected me deeply, and I remember trying not to think anything bad, for fear of the nasty little "things" or thought forms I could create. It was hard for a three-year-old, but her wise advice later led me to a study of metaphysics. I learned at a very early age that we are all responsible for not only our actions, but also our thoughts.

Like the body, the soul also needs nourishment throughout life. The developing baby's world grows even more complex as she tries to balance physical, emotional, mental, and spiritual needs. By focusing on and catering to this balance during the first few years of life, the child will grow up with personal power in all areas. A new parent told me that raising her baby correctly was like a minefield. She had read dozens of books on childcare with conflicting advice. I suggested that, if she cared for her child with intuition, love, and common sense (a truly rare and spiritual virtue), and allowed herself just ten or fifteen minutes a day for her own spiritual practices,[29] the right methods would unfold.

Babies have a need to evolve, just as we do. We feed them because they are hungry, but they also hunger spiritually. They cannot meditate or pray, visualize or heal, but if we do these things, then they will feel secure, not only physically and emotionally but also spiritually.

We may feel that it is not important or that we don't have the time. However, if we look at our world honestly, we will see that the biggest problems are due to greed and selfishness, intolerance, and hatred – all a lack of spirituality. Many astrologers regard spirituality as a real part of life, but are not necessarily referring to religion. Religion can and should be spiritual; however, one does not have to adhere to a particular religious faith in order to be spiritual. Spirituality emanates from the soul; it is a desire to develop one's finer nature, to evolve and to be of loving service to others.

As mentioned in the chapter "Your Baby's Past," the path of the soul is illustrated by what is known as the Moon's Nodes. Just as the South Node represents our baby's talents and abilities learned in the past, the North Node represents her future challenges and destiny.

To find where your baby's North Node was when he was born, look at Appendix III on page 303, or at a copy of your baby's birth chart. The North Node in your baby's chart will appear as this symbol ☊.

In this chapter, we will look at what the North Node in each of the signs of the Zodiac from Pisces to Aries means. From this, you can glean quite a bit about your baby's future challenges.

NORTH NODE OF THE MOON THROUGH THE SIGNS OF THE ZODIAC

North Node in Aries

Your Aries North Node baby is good-looking, amiable, and peace-loving; he is the darling of the family, and everyone will love his sweet ways and dimpled smile. In his past lives, he was a team player and supporter of other people. He is kind and easily gives in to others in order to maintain peace and harmony. Now, in this life, his challenges will come in the area of learning to stand on his own two feet. The destiny of this child is to learn independence of thought and action. It is particularly important that this child learns about himself and his own limits from a very young age. He may be overly concerned with pleasing others and must learn that his own opinion and his own talents are valuable and need to be expressed. Respect him as well as love him, and teach him the value of self-love and having confidence in his own substantial abilities, as opposed to the limitations of egotism. In time, he will make a fine, fair, and just teacher if his challenges are overcome.

North Node in Taurus

This little baby will love to stay close to you and will never let you out of her sight if she can help it. In her past life, she enjoyed power and may have held high positions of authority, enabling her to gain the ear of important and powerful people. Her life was exciting and challenging. Now, she will face lessons involving money and security. In the past, others have looked after her security needs, but now she is here to learn the value and limitation of material existence. Teach her the importance of health and finances as soon as she is old enough. Also start her with her own savings account and savings plan that will mature when she is old enough to understand the value of money. Encourage her to understand the importance of values so that she will make wise decisions based on sound moral judgment, rather than selfish desire. Take her on frequent trips to the countryside to learn the value and beauty of Mother Nature. This will be a soothing balm to her passionate soul and enable her to become the healer that she is.

North Node in Gemini

This baby is a restless infant, always kicking off his covers and resisting your warm hugs and kisses. He's a wriggler and a squirmer. After lifetimes of adventure and travel, he is now here to learn that the Holy Grail can actually be found in everyday life. As he ages, he will slowly but surely learn that he does not have to travel to the ends of the Earth to find challenge and excitement. During his childhood, introduce him to the charm of viewpoints other than his own. One of his challenges is that he has a tendency to think his way is the right way and the only way, and you can encourage him to appreciate the richness and beauty of diversity. Talk to him constantly. Encourage dexterity, for he has a great talent for working with his hands, as well as his mind. Encourage him to smell the flowers and be prepared to explain why the roses are pink and the daffodils are yellow. Introduce him to the snail slowly sliding across your garden path. He will want to know its name and its destination, but it will help him to notice the small things and the joy that exists within everything around him. Teach him to bring love into the lives of others.

North Node in Cancer

Don't be surprised if this baby is born with a frown on her face and a quizzical look in her clear eyes. Has she fallen from grace? This tiny one spent time achieving the pinnacles of success in the material world. Ambition and responsibility went hand in hand for her, and she learned to work hard and never shirk her duties. Now she faces a world that does not yet recognize her talents, developed through many industrious years. She can be overly serious and not naturally demonstrative (unless there are other opposite tendencies in her birth chart), so encourage her to accept plenty of hugs and kisses while she's young. She needs to learn that life is not just about work and achievement. Don't be surprised if she becomes school captain, then goes on to become President of the Student Union before landing an excellent job. However, her highest attainment in this life will be nurturing other souls. Whether she is a mother, or the captain of a ship, she will have a growing desire to be responsible, not just for herself or for her work – but for other people. She aspires to become a sort of universal mother to whom all go with their problems, love, respect, and reverence.

North Node in Leo

In her past lives, this little one was somewhat of a revolutionary. He saw life differently from others and was open-minded enough to embrace new philosophies and ways of looking at the world. He was most at home as part of a group of people who thought the same way as he did. In this lifetime, he is here to develop his own unique sense of self and learn to shine as an individual and as a leader. In the past, he learned to understand the differences between people, and now he is here to put that understanding to good use as the one who draws people together for a common goal. There is a part of him that likes to merge into a group, so encourage him to find himself, as well as to develop his natural dramatic flair and secret yearning for the limelight. Realize that he tends to lack confidence in his real self. You can help with this by surrounding him with love and encouragement. He is here to develop his unique creativity and to use his talents to make a positive difference to our world.

North Node in Virgo

She has a shy quiet side, with a sweet kind nature and a spiritual approach to life. In the past, she may have been a musician, artist, or dreamer who longed for peace and love. However, one of her challenges in this lifetime is that sooner or later, she will be forced to use and hone her skills and put them to work. While she may prefer to cuddle up on the sofa and stare into space when she is young, do not fear; this baby will become a dynamite organizer and will always be on the go with anything from sawing wood to writing a novel to helping an old lady across the street. Encourage her to fulfill her destiny of service to giving her little tasks to do when she is a child. She will enjoy the challenge of categorizing all her jewelry into colors or researching something for you on the Internet, as long as it is fun and not too arduous. She may have been an artist in a past life, but this time around, she has the skill and intellectual capacity to become a model of efficiency and organization. While she will always need a foundation of love and spirituality, her highest growth comes when she puts her talents to work in service to a noble cause or to help others less fortunate than herself.

North Node in Libra

As a child, he may struggle to get along with his playmates. In past lives, he functioned as a leader or worked alone, and now he likes to do things his way and enjoys his own company. He is generally self-confident, athletic, disciplined, and strong-willed – and thinks all the world should be like him! His lesson in this life is to learn that there are other people in the world besides him and that partnership and teamwork are wonderful things. He will learn that these actually enhance his life and open him up to new possibilities and growth. When seeking his destiny, he may well seek roles such as mediator or judge – roles in which understanding justice and fair play are highlighted. You may even find him reading poetry books or listening to classical music. If you do, you will know that he is on his way. You can help him by encouraging him to enjoy artistic pursuits and organize parties and social gatherings and bring joy, love, and harmony into the lives of others.

North Node in Scorpio
She enjoys her food, loves to stop and smell the flowers, give you a hug, and stay late in bed. She is a creature of the senses and a little lazy to boot! She comes into this life craving the security that she achieved and enjoyed in the past. Now, in this lifetime, a certain element of risk is what will propel her forward. I am not talking about gambling, but about learning to let go of the routine existence that brings her comfort and also boredom, and to take a leap of faith into the unknown. She will seek close relationships with others and will fare well in careers where she can help others with her perception and keen understanding. This help may take many forms, depending on other factors in her chart, including counseling or healing. Teach her the value of self-love so that she does not seek risk in her relationships with others. Encourage her to turn her stubbornness into wise determination, and she can achieve whatever she desires. She understands values and will readily apply them to her life; encourage her toward self-mastery and high spiritual goals.

North Node in Sagittarius

As soon as he can talk, he will astonish you with his easy chatter and avid curiosity. His communication skills are above average, honed through lifetimes of intellectual debate. Now, in this lifetime, he has chosen to find one path out of the thousands of myriad avenues that constantly spark his interest. When he is a youngster, you may despair as he constantly starts new things and drops them like hot potatoes. There is so much for him to see and do. He may long to travel the world, always thinking that what he seeks is just around the next corner. However, finally he will settle down and seek a path that he can stick to. This can take many forms, such as higher education, an athletic career, a vocation, travel, or a spiritual path. His soul is urging him to expand his understanding, achieve his goals, and develop his higher mind through staying true and loyal to a chosen path, instead of constantly seeking stimulation. Do not expect to restrain or control him; just love and understand him, and he will always be yours.

North Node in Capricorn

She may fuss and cry a lot as a baby. She is highly sensitive and feels things very acutely. She has a psychic antenna around people and does not take readily to strangers or people who are too loud or abrasive. In previous lifetimes, she developed her feminine nurturing side and may have been a wonderful parent to hordes of children or a successful caretaker of some kind. In this life, she will choose to venture from the joys and intimacy of home out into the ruthless world of career and achievement. She may cling to your apron strings as a child; encourage her to take responsibility for things and teach her that her thoughts, words, and actions have consequences. If you do this, she can add thoughtfulness to the success that she will crave. She can then imbue her ambitions with wisdom and love. She can become a public figure who is respected and admired. With your support and guidance, there are no limits to her achievement in all areas of life – from the material world to a rich rewarding spiritual life.

North Node in Aquarius

This star will make his presence felt from Day One. He will be bolder, brighter, and more charismatic than the other children, for he has spent past lifetimes honing his ego to support his leadership roles. At school, don't be surprised if he is captain of the soccer team, has the lead role in amateur dramatics, and is voted most popular boy in his class. His highest aspirations come in the form of helping society to become a better place and inspiring others toward realizing their potential. His challenge is that he may be overly confident, with a touch of arrogance or superiority. Teach him about people who are wiser and stronger than he is, and he will be encouraged to grow and to improve. Encourage him to use the highly developed ego that he has brought with him wisely, as a teacher and inspirer of others. Encourage him to understand and care for others, the Earth, nature, and society at large. He has a genius about him that he will want to put to work for the good of mankind, if properly directed by those whom he respects.

North Node in Pisces

She will probably do very well at school, as she has incarnated with a quick mentality and "left-brain" consciousness. She may sail through her exams and excel in her career. She quickly learns new skills and has awesome organizational skills. One of her challenges is that she may get stuck in the endless routines and details of life and become frustrated. Realize that, until she allows her soul to speak through her, she will not really find fulfillment. Introduce artistic pursuits and spiritual practices into her life from an early age. They will be like food to her and will help her develop her inner spiritual riches, bringing her great joy and enriching the lives of all around her. Encourage her to perform acts of kindness to life in all its forms, and she will become the gentle loving soul she aspires to be. Teach her in the ways of service to others, and she can use her innate skills and capacity for work to help those less fortunate than herself. It is then that she will find true joy, as she tastes the meaning of compassion, her soul food.

AFTERWORD

Through the use of astrology in bringing up your baby, you can lay the correct foundations for her unique life and destiny. You will then help her to become the wonderful person her soul wants her to be. In life, we are constantly faced with choices, and we often make the wrong choices, based on fear, lack of understanding, or prejudice. We then waste the precious time we have to make life a joyful, fulfilling, enlightening experience for ourselves as well as others.

You can help your baby to make good choices by remembering that she is first and foremost a spiritual being, wrapped up in the confines of a physical body with a brain and senses to take her safely through experience. Encourage her to frame her choices in a spiritual context, with thoughtfulness and kindness to others always uppermost in her mind. Encourage her to be the best she can be in every area, without compromising her integrity. Explain to her the necessity of such values as truth, honor, justice, discrimination, loyalty, love, understanding, wisdom, and true freedom, so that these become ideals by which she lives, instead of dusty concepts remote from her life.

Understand that, however happy your child may be, she is not here just to traipse through life, enjoying a nice meal or gazing at a sunset. She is here to learn, grown, and blossom into the spiritual flower that she truly is. There are many things you must do in this noble task of parent or guardian that you have taken on; you must feed, clothe, educate, and nurture her. You must teach her the ways of life, as well as understanding and loving her. You must respect and care for her with intuition as well as intelligence. Listen to her and pay attention to her, and teach her the value of joy and enthusiasm. She will repay you a thousand times with her love and lighten your load with her understanding and help.

As well as nurturing your baby's spiritual essence, also remember to nurture the spiritual flame within you. This impregnable part of you can then sustain you through all the trials and challenges that parenthood brings. Through correct education on all levels, your baby can then sustain not only her highest principles, but also help sustain the future of our species.

May God bless and guide you toward wise and loving parenthood, and may this be a key toward your own becoming.

APPENDIX I

YOUR BABY'S MOON SIGN – YEARS 2000 – 2020

Check your baby's birthday in the Tables below to find the Sign of the Zodiac the Moon was in when she was born (her Moon Sign). If the date is not there, go to the nearest date **before** her birthday. For example, if she was born on February 5, 2000, at 10:00 P.M., you will see she has the Moon in Aquarius.

Note: All times are in GMT. Add or subtract hours according to your time zone, i.e., a baby born in London on January 5, 2000, at 11:00 A.M. GMT would have the Moon in Capricorn; a baby born at the same time and date in Los Angeles would have the Moon in Sagittarius (subtract 8 hours from Greenwich Mean Time to find Pacific Daylight Time).

Year 2000

DATE	TIME	SIGN OF ZODIAC
Jan 2	21:32	Sagittarius
Jan 5	10:24	Capricorn
Jan 7	22:53	Aquarius
Jan 10	09:59	Pisces
Jan 12	18:48	Aries
Jan 15	00:38	Taurus
Jan 17	03:25	Gemini
Jan 19	04:01	Cancer
Jan 21	03:58	Leo
Jan 23	05:07	Virgo
Jan 25	09:09	Libra
Jan 27	17:01	Scorpio
Jan 30	04:17	Sagittarius

Feb 1	17:10	Capricorn
Feb 4	05:31	Aquarius
Feb 6	16:02	Pisces
Feb 9	00:17	Aries
Feb 11	06:21	Taurus
Feb 13	10:23	Gemini
Feb 15	12:45	Cancer
Feb 17	14:11	Leo
Feb 19	15:53	Virgo
Feb 21	19:21	Libra
Feb 24	01:58	Scorpio
Feb 26	12:10	Sagittarius
Feb 29	00:45	Capricorn
Mar 2	13:14	Aquarius
Mar 4	23:30	Pisces
Mar 7	06:54	Aries
Mar 9	12:01	Taurus
Mar 11	15:46	Gemini
Mar 13	18:51	Cancer
Mar 15	21:43	Leo
Mar 18	00:48	Virgo
Mar 20	04:57	Libra
Mar 22	11:17	Scorpio
Mar 24	20:43	Sagittarius
Mar 27	08:51	Capricorn
Mar 29	21:34	Aquarius
Apr 1	08:12	Pisces
Apr 3	15:22	Aries
Apr 5	19:29	Taurus
Apr 7	21:58	Gemini
Apr 10	00:16	Cancer
Apr 12	03:16	Leo

Apr 14	07:19	Virgo
Apr 16	12:36	Libra
Apr 18	19:35	Scorpio
Apr 21	04:58	Sagittarius
Apr 23	16:47	Capricorn
Apr 26	05:42	Aquarius
Apr 28	17:06	Pisces
May 1	00:54	Aries
May 3	04:54	Taurus
May 5	06:23	Gemini
May 7	07:14	Cancer
May 9	09:01	Leo
May 11	12:41	Virgo
May 13	18:27	Libra
May 16	02:16	Scorpio
May 18	12:09	Sagittarius
May 21	00:01	Capricorn
May 23	13:00	Aquarius
May 26	01:07	Pisces
May 28	10:08	Aries
May 30	15:02	Taurus
Jun 1	16:34	Gemini
Jun 3	16:30	Cancer
Jun 5	16:45	Leo
Jun 7	18:57	Virgo
Jun 9	23:58	Libra
Jun 12	07:55	Scorpio
Jun 14	18:18	Sagittarius
Jun 17	06:26	Capricorn
Jun 19	19:26	Aquarius
Jun 22	07:52	Pisces
Jun 24	17:55	Aries

Jun 27	00:19	Taurus
Jun 29	02:59	Gemini
Jul 1	03:09	Cancer
Jul 3	02:38	Leo
Jul 5	03:19	Virgo
Jul 7	06:47	Libra
Jul 9	13:48	Scorpio
Jul 12	00:06	Sagittarius
Jul 14	12:28	Capricorn
Jul 17	01:27	Aquarius
Jul 19	13:44	Pisces
Jul 22	00:09	Aries
Jul 24	07:44	Taurus
Jul 26	12:01	Gemini
Jul 28	13:30	Cancer
Jul 30	13:23	Leo
Aug 3	15:31	Libra
Aug 5	21:04	Scorpio
Aug 8	06:30	Sagittarius
Aug 10	18:44	Capricorn
Aug 13	07:43	Aquarius
Aug 15	19:41	Pisces
Aug 18	05:44	Aries
Aug 20	13:31	Taurus
Aug 22	18:55	Gemini
Aug 24	22:00	Cancer
Aug 26	23:17	Leo
Aug 28	23:55	Virgo
Aug 31	01:33	Libra
Sep 2	05:55	Scorpio
Sep 4	14:08	Sagittarius

Sep 7	01:47	Capricorn
Sep 9	14:44	Aquarius
Sep 12	02:34	Pisces
Sep 14	12:00	Aries
Sep 16	19:05	Taurus
Sep 19	00:22	Gemini
Sep 21	04:16	Cancer
Sep 23	07:00	Leo
Sep 25	09:02	Virgo
Sep 27	11:22	Libra
Sep 29	15:29	Scorpio
Oct 1	22:50	Sagittarius
Oct 4	09:42	Capricorn
Oct 6	22:33	Aquarius
Oct 9	10:36	Pisces
Oct 11	19:51	Aries
Oct 14	02:06	Taurus
Oct 16	06:19	Gemini
Oct 18	09:37	Cancer
Oct 20	12:42	Leo
Oct 22	15:52	Virgo
Oct 24	19:30	Libra
Oct 27	00:23	Scorpio
Oct 29	07:40	Sagittarius
Oct 31	18:01	Capricorn
Nov 3	06:41	Aquarius
Nov 5	19:13	Pisces
Nov 8	05:02	Aries
Nov 10	11:12	Taurus
Nov 12	14:27	Gemini
Nov 14	16:21	Cancer
Nov 16	18:19	Leo

Nov 18	21:15	Virgo
Nov 21	01:35	Libra
Nov 23	07:33	Scorpio
Nov 25	15:33	Sagittarius
Nov 28	01:57	Capricorn
Nov 30	14:26	Aquarius
Dec 3	03:23	Pisces
Dec 5	14:17	Aries
Dec 7	21:27	Taurus
Dec 10	00:50	Gemini
Dec 12	01:48	Cancer
Dec 14	02:08	Leo
Dec 16	03:30	Virgo
Dec 18	07:01	Libra
Dec 20	13:12	Scorpio
Dec 22	21:57	Sagittarius
Dec 25	08:54	Capricorn
Dec 27	21:25	Aquarius
Dec 30	10:27	Pisces

Year 2001

DATE	TIME	SIGN OF ZODIAC
Jan 1	22:14	Aries
Jan 4	06:57	Taurus
Jan 6	11:44	Gemini
Jan 8	13:09	Cancer
Jan 10	12:44	Leo
Jan 12	12:26	Virgo
Jan 14	14:05	Libra
Jan 16	19:02	Scorpio
Jan 19	03:35	Sagittarius
Jan 21	14:57	Capricorn

Jan 24	03:43	Aquarius
Jan 26	16:39	Pisces
Jan 29	04:35	Aries
Jan 31	14:21	Taurus
Feb 2	20:56	Gemini
Feb 5	00:00	Cancer
Feb 7	00:21	Leo
Feb 8	23:35	Virgo
Feb 10	23:46	Libra
Feb 13	02:51	Scorpio
Feb 15	10:02	Sagittarius
Feb 17	20:59	Capricorn
Feb 20	09:53	Aquarius
Feb 22	22:45	Pisces
Feb 25	10:20	Aries
Feb 27	20:06	Taurus
Mar 2	03:36	Gemini
Mar 4	08:24	Cancer
Mar 6	10:30	Leo
Mar 8	10:44	Virgo
Mar 10	10:47	Libra
Mar 12	12:42	Scorpio
Mar 14	18:16	Sagittarius
Mar 17	04:02	Capricorn
Mar 19	16:36	Aquarius
Mar 22	05:28	Pisces
Mar 24	16:44	Aries
Mar 27	01:50	Taurus
Mar 29	09:01	Gemini
Mar 31	14:23	Cancer
Apr 2	17:54	Leo

Apr 4	19:46	Virgo
Apr 6	20:57	Libra
Apr 8	23:01	Scorpio
Apr 11	03:47	Sagittarius
Apr 13	12:21	Capricorn
Apr 16	00:11	Aquarius
Apr 18	13:00	Pisces
Apr 21	00:18	Aries
Apr 23	08:56	Taurus
Apr 23	15:11	Gemini
Apr 27	19:49	Cancer
Apr 29	23:25	Leo
May 2	02:16	Virgo
May 4	04:50	Libra
May 6	08:00	Scorpio
May 8	13:05	Sagittarius
May 10	21:10	Capricorn
May 13	08:20	Aquarius
May 15	21:01	Pisces
May 18	08:41	Aries
May 20	17:29	Taurus
May 22	23:12	Gemini
May 25	02:42	Cancer
May 27	05:12	Leo
May 29	07:38	Virgo
May 31	10:41	Libra
Jun 2	14:56	Scorpio
Jun 4	20:58	Sagittarius
Jun 7	05:23	Capricorn
Jun 9	16:19	Aquarius
Jun 12	04:53	Pisces
Jun 14	17:03	Aries

Jun 17	02:39	Taurus
Jun 19	08:42	Gemini
Jun 21	11:41	Cancer
Jun 23	12:55	Leo
Jun 25	13:57	Virgo
Jun 27	16:11	Libra
Jun 29	20:28	Scorpio
Jul 2	03:13	Sagittarius
Jul 4	12:21	Capricorn
Jul 6	23:33	Aquarius
Jul 9	12:05	Pisces
Jul 12	00:36	Aries
Jul 14	11:13	Taurus
Jul 16	18:26	Gemini
Jul 18	21:56	Cancer
Jul 20	22:43	Leo
Jul 22	22:28	Virgo
Jul 24	23:08	Libra
Jul 27	02:17	Scorpio
Jul 29	08:44	Sagittarius
Jul 31	18:16	Capricorn
Aug 3	05:53	Aquarius
Aug 5	18:30	Pisces
Aug 8	07:05	Aries
Aug 10	18:23	Taurus
Aug 13	02:59	Gemini
Aug 15	07:55	Cancer
Aug 17	09:25	Leo
Aug 19	08:53	Virgo
Aug 21	08:19	Libra
Aug 23	09:50	Scorpio
Aug 25	14:59	Sagittarius

Aug 28	00:02	Capricorn
Aug 30	11:48	Aquarius
Sep 2	00:32	Pisces
Sep 4	12:58	Aries
Sep 7	00:18	Taurus
Sep 9	09:41	Gemini
Sep 11	16:09	Cancer
Sep 13	19:16	Leo
Sep 15	19:39	Virgo
Sep 17	19:00	Libra
Sep 19	19:27	Scorpio
Sep 21	23:02	Sagittarius
Sep 24	06:48	Capricorn
Sep 26	18:05	Aquarius
Sep 29	06:50	Pisces
Oct 1	19:08	Aries
Oct 4	06:01	Taurus
Oct 6	15:12	Gemini
Oct 8	22:19	Cancer
Oct 11	02:54	Leo
Oct 13	04:58	Virgo
Oct 15	05:26	Libra
Oct 17	06:02	Scorpio
Oct 19	08:47	Sagittarius
Oct 21	15:11	Capricorn
Oct 24	01:26	Aquarius
Oct 26	13:56	Pisces
Oct 29	02:15	Aries
Oct 31	12:48	Taurus
Nov 2	21:12	Gemini
Nov 5	03:44	Cancer

Nov 7	08:34	Leo
Nov 9	11:49	Virgo
Nov 11	13:53	Libra
Nov 13	15:44	Scorpio
Nov 15	18:51	Sagittarius
Nov 18	00:40	Capricorn
Nov 20	09:55	Aquarius
Nov 22	21:52	Pisces
Nov 25	10:21	Aries
Nov 27	21:06	Taurus
Nov 30	05:04	Gemini
Dec 2	10:30	Cancer
Dec 4	14:15	Leo
Dec 6	17:11	Virgo
Dec 8	19:57	Libra
Dec 10	23:09	Scorpio
Dec 13	03:30	Sagittarius
Dec 15	09:48	Capricorn
Dec 17	18:43	Aquarius
Dec 20	06:09	Pisces
Dec 22	18:45	Aries
Dec 25	06:12	Taurus
Dec 27	14:39	Gemini
Dec 29	19:40	Cancer
Dec 31	22:09	Leo

Year 2002

DATE	TIME	SIGN OF ZODIAC
Jan 2	23:34	Virgo
Jan 5	01:23	Libra
Jan 7	04:41	Scorpio
Jan 9	09:57	Sagittarius

Jan 11	17:18	Capricorn
Jan 14	02:41	Aquarius
Jan 16	14:00	Pisces
Jan 19	02:35	Aries
Jan 21	14:47	Taurus
Jan 24	00:28	Gemini
Jan 26	06:17	Cancer
Jan 28	08:31	Leo
Jan 30	08:40	Virgo
Feb 1	08:44	Libra
Feb 3	10:35	Scorpio
Feb 5	15:21	Sagittarius
Feb 7	23:08	Capricorn
Feb 10	09:15	Aquarius
Feb 12	20:53	Pisces
Feb 15	09:26	Aries
Feb 17	21:58	Taurus
Feb 20	08:50	Gemini
Feb 22	16:16	Cancer
Feb 24	19:36	Leo
Feb 26	19:47	Virgo
Feb 28	18:47	Libra
Mar 2	18:51	Scorpio
Mar 4	21:55	Sagittarius
Mar 7	04:48	Capricorn
Mar 9	14:56	Aquarius
Mar 12	02:56	Pisces
Mar 14	15:34	Aries
Mar 17	04:01	Taurus
Mar 19	15:20	Gemini
Mar 22	00:06	Cancer
Mar 24	05:13	Leo

Mar 26	06:44	Virgo
Mar 28	06:04	Libra
Mar 30	05:21	Scorpio
Apr 1	06:48	Sagittarius
Apr 3	11:58	Capricorn
Apr 5	21:07	Aquarius
Apr 8	08:57	Pisces
Apr 10	21:40	Aries
Apr 13	09:55	Taurus
Apr 15	20:56	Gemini
Apr 18	06:01	Cancer
Apr 20	12:21	Leo
Apr 22	15:35	Virgo
Apr 24	16:22	Libra
Apr 26	16:15	Scorpio
Apr 28	17:12	Sagittarius
Apr 30	21:02	Capricorn
May 3	04:43	Aquarius
May 5	15:46	Pisces
May 8	04:22	Aries
May 10	16:32	Taurus
May 13	03:04	Gemini
May 15	11:33	Cancer
May 17	17:52	Leo
May 19	22:01	Virgo
May 22	00:19	Libra
May 24	01:38	Scorpio
May 26	03:20	Sagittarius
May 28	06:54	Capricorn
May 30	13:35	Aquarius
Jun 1	23:37	Pisces

Jun 4	11:51	Aries
Jun 7	00:06	Taurus
Jun 9	10:29	Gemini
Jun 11	18:15	Cancer
Jun 13	23:39	Leo
Jun 16	03:23	Virgo
Jun 18	06:11	Libra
Jun 20	08:42	Scorpio
Jun 22	11:42	Sagittarius
Jun 24	16:01	Capricorn
Jun 26	22:36	Aquarius
Jun 29	08:00	Pisces
Jul 1	19:49	Aries
Jul 4	08:16	Taurus
Jul 6	19:01	Gemini
Jul 9	02:36	Cancer
Jul 11	07:08	Leo
Jul 13	09:41	Virgo
Jul 15	11:39	Libra
Jul 17	14:13	Scorpio
Jul 19	18:02	Sagittarius
Jul 21	23:26	Capricorn
Jul 24	06:40	Aquarius
Jul 26	16:04	Pisces
Jul 29	03:38	Aries
Jul 31	16:17	Taurus
Aug 3	03:46	Gemini
Aug 5	12:02	Cancer
Aug 7	16:27	Leo
Aug 9	18:03	Virgo
Aug 11	18:38	Libra
Aug 13	20:00	Scorpio

Aug 15	23:25	Sagittarius
Aug 18	05:15	Capricorn
Aug 20	13:16	Aquarius
Aug 22	23:11	Pisces
Aug 25	10:47	Aries
Aug 27	23:31	Taurus
Aug 30	11:45	Gemini
Sep 1	21:14	Cancer
Sep 4	02:36	Leo
Sep 6	04:16	Virgo
Sep 8	03:57	Libra
Sep 10	03:48	Scorpio
Sep 12	05:44	Sagittarius
Sep 14	10:47	Capricorn
Sep 16	18:54	Aquarius
Sep 19	05:18	Pisces
Sep 21	17:11	Aries
Sep 24	05:54	Taurus
Sep 26	18:26	Gemini
Sep 29	05:01	Cancer
Oct 1	11:58	Leo
Oct 3	14:52	Virgo
Oct 5	14:51	Libra
Oct 7	13:57	Scorpio
Oct 9	14:21	Sagittarius
Oct 11	17:45	Capricorn
Oct 14	00:51	Aquarius
Oct 16	11:07	Pisces
Oct 18	23:13	Aries
Oct 21	11:57	Taurus
Oct 24	00:17	Gemini
Oct 26	11:10	Cancer

Oct 28	19:20	Leo
Oct 30	23:59	Virgo
Nov 2	01:28	Libra
Nov 4	01:10	Scorpio
Nov 6	01:01	Sagittarius
Nov 8	02:59	Capricorn
Nov 10	08:27	Aquarius
Nov 12	17:42	Pisces
Nov 15	05:38	Aries
Nov 17	18:23	Taurus
Nov 20	06:25	Gemini
Nov 22	16:47	Cancer
Nov 25	01:00	Leo
Nov 27	06:42	Virgo
Nov 29	09:54	Libra
Dec 1	11:15	Scorpio
Dec 3	11:58	Sagittarius
Dec 5	13:39	Capricorn
Dec 7	17:54	Aquarius
Dec 10	01:46	Pisces
Dec 12	12:58	Aries
Dec 15	01:43	Taurus
Dec 17	13:43	Gemini
Dec 19	23:30	Cancer
Dec 22	06:48	Leo
Dec 24	12:05	Virgo
Dec 26	15:53	Libra
Dec 28	18:41	Scorpio
Dec 30	21:01	Sagittarius

Year 2003

DATE	TIME	SIGN OF ZODIAC
Jan 1	23:42	Capricorn
Jan 4	03:56	Aquarius
Jan 6	10:57	Pisces
Jan 8	21:15	Aries
Jan 11	09:48	Taurus
Jan 13	22:08	Gemini
Jan 16	07:56	Cancer
Jan 18	14:29	Leo
Jan 20	18:32	Virgo
Jan 22	21:23	Libra
Jan 25	00:09	Scorpio
Jan 27	03:26	Sagittarius
Jan 29	07:30	Capricorn
Jan 31	12:44	Aquarius
Feb 2	19:54	Pisces
Feb 5	05:44	Aries
Feb 7	17:59	Taurus
Feb 10	06:45	Gemini
Feb 12	17:19	Cancer
Feb 15	00:04	Leo
Feb 17	03:22	Virgo
Feb 19	04:48	Libra
Feb 21	06:09	Scorpio
Feb 23	08:46	Sagittarius
Feb 25	13:11	Capricorn
Feb 27	19:24	Aquarius
Mar 2	03:26	Pisces
Mar 4	13:30	Aries
Mar 7	01:36	Taurus

Mar 9	14:37	Gemini
Mar 12	02:12	Cancer
Mar 14	10:06	Leo
Mar 16	13:52	Virgo
Mar 18	14:43	Libra
Mar 20	14:38	Scorpio
Mar 22	15:33	Sagittarius
Mar 24	18:48	Capricorn
Mar 27	00:51	Aquarius
Mar 29	09:26	Pisces
Mar 31	20:04	Aries
Apr 3	08:20	Taurus
Apr 5	21:24	Gemini
Apr 8	09:36	Cancer
Apr 10	18:54	Leo
Apr 13	00:07	Virgo
Apr 15	01:42	Libra
Apr 17	01:16	Scorpio
Apr 19	00:51	Sagittarius
Apr 21	02:20	Capricorn
Apr 23	06:58	Aquarius
Apr 25	15:02	Pisces
Apr 28	01:54	Aries
Apr 30	14:26	Taurus
May 3	03:27	Gemini
May 5	15:42	Cancer
May 8	01:46	Leo
May 10	08:31	Virgo
May 12	11:42	Libra
May 14	12:14	Scorpio
May 16	11:43	Sagittarius
May 18	12:03	Capricorn

May 20	15:01	Aquarius
May 22	21:41	Pisces
May 25	07:59	Aries
May 27	20:32	Taurus
May 30	09:32	Gemini

Jun 1	21:27	Cancer
Jun 4	07:25	Leo
Jun 6	14:51	Virgo
Jun 8	19:30	Libra
Jun 10	21:39	Scorpio
Jun 12	22:12	Sagittarius
Jun 14	22:38	Capricorn
Jun 17	00:41	Aquarius
Jun 19	05:57	Pisces
Jun 21	15:06	Aries
Jun 24	03:15	Taurus
Jun 26	16:13	Gemini
Jun 29	03:52	Cancer

Jul 1	13:13	Leo
Jul 3	20:16	Virgo
Jul 6	01:20	Libra
Jul 8	04:43	Scorpio
Jul 10	06:48	Sagittarius
Jul 12	08:21	Capricorn
Jul 14	10:38	Aquarius
Jul 16	15:13	Pisces
Jul 18	23:20	Aries
Jul 21	10:48	Taurus
Jul 23	23:42	Gemini
Jul 26	11:23	Cancer
Jul 28	20:17	Leo
Jul 31	02:27	Virgo

Aug 2	06:48	Libra
Aug 4	10:12	Scorpio
Aug 6	13:11	Sagittarius
Aug 8	16:02	Capricorn
Aug 10	19:23	Aquarius
Aug 13	00:19	Pisces
Aug 15	08:00	Aries
Aug 17	18:52	Taurus
Aug 20	07:41	Gemini
Aug 22	19:44	Cancer
Aug 25	04:48	Leo
Aug 27	10:27	Virgo
Aug 29	13:41	Libra
Aug 31	16:00	Scorpio
Sep 2	18:32	Sagittarius
Sep 4	21:51	Capricorn
Sep 7	02:15	Aquarius
Sep 9	08:07	Pisces
Sep 11	16:09	Aries
Sep 14	02:50	Taurus
Sep 16	15:32	Gemini
Sep 19	04:07	Cancer
Sep 21	14:03	Leo
Sep 23	20:04	Virgo
Sep 25	22:49	Libra
Sep 27	23:52	Scorpio
Sep 30	00:57	Sagittarius
Oct 2	03:21	Capricorn
Oct 4	07:45	Aquarius
Oct 6	14:20	Pisces
Oct 8	23:07	Aries
Oct 11	10:05	Taurus

Oct 13	22:45	Gemini
Oct 16	11:41	Cancer
Oct 18	22:41	Leo
Oct 21	06:01	Virgo
Oct 23	09:27	Libra
Oct 25	10:08	Scorpio
Oct 27	09:55	Sagittarius
Oct 29	10:37	Capricorn
Oct 31	13:41	Aquarius
Nov 2	19:52	Pisces
Nov 5	05:02	Aries
Nov 7	16:29	Taurus
Nov 10	05:14	Gemini
Nov 12	18:10	Cancer
Nov 15	05:48	Leo
Nov 17	14:36	Virgo
Nov 19	19:42	Libra
Nov 21	21:24	Scorpio
Nov 23	21:02	Sagittarius
Nov 25	20:31	Capricorn
Nov 27	21:48	Aquarius
Nov 30	02:25	Pisces
Dec 2	10:56	Aries
Dec 4	22:30	Taurus
Dec 7	11:26	Gemini
Dec 10	00:11	Cancer
Dec 12	11:40	Leo
Dec 14	21:07	Virgo
Dec 17	03:46	Libra
Dec 19	07:20	Scorpio
Dec 21	08:16	Sagittarius
Dec 23	07:55	Capricorn

Dec 25	08:13	Aquarius
Dec 27	11:10	Pisces
Dec 29	18:08	Aries

Year 2004

DATE	TIME	SIGN OF ZODIAC
Jan 1	05:01	Taurus
Jan 3	17:58	Gemini
Jan 6	06:38	Cancer
Jan 8	17:38	Leo
Jan 11	02:37	Virgo
Jan 13	09:38	Libra
Jan 15	14:32	Scorpio
Jan 17	17:18	Sagittarius
Jan 19	18:24	Capricorn
Jan 21	19:10	Aquarius
Jan 23	21:29	Pisces
Jan 26	03:06	Aries
Jan 28	12:46	Taurus
Jan 31	01:18	Gemini
Feb 2	14:03	Cancer
Feb 5	00:50	Leo
Feb 7	09:03	Virgo
Feb 9	15:12	Libra
Feb 11	19:57	Scorpio
Feb 13	23:35	Sagittarius
Feb 16	02:14	Capricorn
Feb 18	04:27	Aquarius
Feb 20	07:26	Pisces
Feb 22	12:45	Aries
Feb 24	21:30	Taurus
Feb 27	09:22	Gemini

Feb 29	22:12	Cancer
Mar 3	09:18	Leo
Mar 5	17:18	Virgo
Mar 7	22:31	Libra
Mar 10	02:03	Scorpio
Mar 12	04:57	Sagittarius
Mar 14	07:51	Capricorn
Mar 16	11:10	Aquarius
Mar 18	15:26	Pisces
Mar 20	21:29	Aries
Mar 23	06:09	Taurus
Mar 25	17:34	Gemini
Mar 28	06:23	Cancer
Mar 30	18:07	Leo
Apr 1	02:45	Virgo
Apr 4	07:52	Libra
Apr 6	10:24	Scorpio
Apr 8	11:50	Sagittarius
Apr 10	13:33	Capricorn
Apr 12	16:33	Aquarius
Apr 14	21:24	Pisces
Apr 17	04:24	Aries
Apr 19	13:42	Taurus
Apr 22	01:10	Gemini
Apr 24	13:56	Cancer
Apr 27	02:14	Leo
Apr 29	12:00	Virgo
May 1	18:03	Libra
May 3	20:38	Scorpio
May 5	21:08	Sagittarius
May 7	21:16	Capricorn

May 9	22:46	Aquarius
May 12	02:52	Pisces
May 14	10:02	Aries
May 16	19:57	Taurus
May 19	07:47	Gemini
May 21	20:35	Cancer
May 24	09:07	Leo
May 26	19:52	Virgo
May 29	03:22	Libra
May 31	07:08	Scorpio
Jun 2	07:52	Sagittarius
Jun 4	07:12	Capricorn
Jun 6	07:09	Aquarius
Jun 8	09:38	Pisces
Jun 10	15:49	Aries
Jun 13	01:37	Taurus
Jun 15	13:44	Gemini
Jun 18	02:37	Cancer
Jun 20	15:05	Leo
Jun 23	02:10	Virgo
Jun 25	10:50	Libra
Jun 27	16:13	Scorpio
Jun 29	18:15	Sagittarius
Jul 3	17:22	Aquarius
Jul 5	18:26	Pisces
Jul 7	23:03	Aries
Jul 10	07:50	Taurus
Jul 12	19:45	Gemini
Jul 15	08:40	Cancer
Jul 17	20:56	Leo
Jul 20	07:44	Virgo
Jul 22	16:39	Libra

Jul 24	23:08	Scorpio
Jul 27	02:48	Sagittarius
Jul 29	03:57	Capricorn
Jul 31	03:54	Aquarius

Aug 2	04:34	Pisces
Aug 4	07:59	Aries
Aug 6	15:26	Taurus
Aug 9	02:33	Gemini
Aug 11	15:20	Cancer
Aug 14	03:30	Leo
Aug 16	13:49	Virgo
Aug 18	22:09	Libra
Aug 21	04:37	Scorpio
Aug 23	09:08	Sagittarius
Aug 25	11:46	Capricorn
Aug 27	13:08	Aquarius
Aug 29	14:33	Pisces
Aug 32	17:46	Aries

Sep 3	00:16	Taurus
Sep 5	10:24	Gemini
Sep 7	22:50	Cancer
Sep 10	11:06	Leo
Sep 12	21:16	Virgo
Sep 15	04:53	Libra
Sep 17	10:25	Scorpio
Sep 19	14:29	Sagittarius
Sep 21	17:35	Capricorn
Sep 23	20:10	Aquarius
Sep 25	22:55	Pisces
Sep 28	02:57	Aries
Sep 30	09:24	Taurus

Oct 2	18:55	Gemini
Oct 5	06:54	Cancer
Oct 7	19:23	Leo
Oct 10	06:00	Virgo
Oct 12	13:32	Libra
Oct 14	18:10	Scorpio
Oct 16	20:58	Sagittarius
Oct 18	23:07	Capricorn
Oct 21	01:37	Aquarius
Oct 23	05:13	Pisces
Oct 25	10:24	Aries
Oct 27	17:37	Taurus
Oct 30	03:11	Gemini
Nov 1	14:53	Cancer
Nov 4	03:32	Leo
Nov 6	15:00	Virgo
Nov 8	23:23	Libra
Nov 11	04:05	Scorpio
Nov 13	05:56	Sagittarius
Nov 15	06:33	Capricorn
Nov 17	07:39	Aquarius
Nov 19	10:38	Pisces
Nov 21	16:11	Aries
Nov 24	00:16	Taurus
Nov 26	10:25	Gemini
Nov 28	22:10	Cancer
Dec 1	10:50	Leo
Dec 3	23:00	Virgo
Dec 6	08:46	Libra
Dec 8	14:43	Scorpio
Dec 10	16:54	Sagittarius
Dec 12	16:41	Capricorn

Dec 14	16:10	Aquarius
Dec 16	17:24	Pisces
Dec 18	21:52	Aries
Dec 21	05:52	Taurus
Dec 23	16:32	Gemini
Dec 26	04:38	Cancer
Dec 28	17:14	Leo
Dec 31	05:33	Virgo

Year 2005

DATE	TIME	SIGN OF ZODIAC
Jan 2	16:19	Libra
Jan 4	23:59	Scorpio
Jan 7	03:44	Sagittarius
Jan 9	04:11	Capricorn
Jan 11	03:07	Aquarius
Jan 13	02:50	Pisces
Jan 15	05:27	Aries
Jan 17	12:06	Taurus
Jan 19	22:24	Gemini
Jan 22	10:42	Cancer
Jan 24	23:21	Leo
Jan 27	11:24	Virgo
Jan 29	22:13	Libra
Feb 1	06:51	Scorpio
Feb 3	12:21	Sagittarius
Feb 5	14:32	Capricorn
Feb 7	14:26	Aquarius
Feb 9	13:59	Pisces
Feb 11	15:21	Aries
Feb 13	20:17	Taurus
Feb 16	05:18	Gemini

Feb 18	17:13	Cancer
Feb 21	05:54	Leo
Feb 23	17:44	Virgo
Feb 26	03:59	Libra
Feb 28	12:20	Scorpio
Mar 2	18:29	Sagittarius
Mar 4	22:11	Capricorn
Mar 6	23:49	Aquarius
Mar 9	00:32	Pisces
Mar 11	02:03	Aries
Mar 13	06:05	Taurus
Mar 15	13:44	Gemini
Mar 18	00:44	Cancer
Mar 20	13:17	Leo
Mar 23	01:10	Virgo
Mar 25	11:00	Libra
Mar 27	18:29	Scorpio
Mar 29	23:56	Sagittarius
Apr 1	03:48	Capricorn
Apr 3	06:31	Aquarius
Apr 5	08:45	Pisces
Apr 7	11:28	Aries
Apr 9	15:50	Taurus
Apr 11	22:54	Gemini
Apr 14	09:03	Cancer
Apr 16	21:17	Leo
Apr 19	09:27	Virgo
Apr 21	19:27	Libra
Apr 24	02:25	Scorpio
Apr 26	06:46	Sagittarius
Apr 28	09:32	Capricorn
Apr 30	11:54	Aquarius

May 2	14:43	Pisces
May 4	18:36	Aries
May 7	00:01	Taurus
May 9	07:28	Gemini
May 11	17:20	Cancer
May 14	05:17	Leo
May 16	17:46	Virgo
May 19	04:30	Libra
May 21	11:49	Scorpio
May 23	15:38	Sagittarius
May 25	17:11	Capricorn
May 27	18:09	Aquarius
May 29	20:09	Pisces
Jun 1	00:07	Aries
Jun 3	06:20	Taurus
Jun 5	14:35	Gemini
Jun 8	00:46	Cancer
Jun 10	12:39	Leo
Jun 13	01:22	Virgo
Jun 15	12:59	Libra
Jun 17	21:23	Scorpio
Jun 20	01:45	Sagittarius
Jun 22	02:52	Capricorn
Jun 24	02:36	Aquarius
Jun 26	03:03	Pisces
Jun 28	05:51	Aries
Jun 30	11:45	Taurus
Jul 2	20:26	Gemini
Jul 5	07:07	Cancer
Jul 7	19:11	Leo
Jul 10	07:57	Virgo
Jul 12	20:09	Libra

Jul 15	05:51	Scorpio
Jul 17	11:35	Sagittarius
Jul 19	13:26	Capricorn
Jul 21	12:55	Aquarius
Jul 23	12:11	Pisces
Jul 25	13:22	Aries
Jul 27	17:54	Taurus
Jul 30	02:02	Gemini
Aug 1	12:52	Cancer
Aug 4	01:10	Leo
Aug 6	13:54	Virgo
Aug 9	02:08	Libra
Aug 11	12:35	Scorpio
Aug 13	19:47	Sagittarius
Aug 15	23:13	Capricorn
Aug 17	23:39	Aquarius
Aug 19	22:52	Pisces
Aug 21	23:01	Aries
Aug 24	01:57	Taurus
Aug 26	08:42	Gemini
Aug 28	18:57	Cancer
Aug 31	07:14	Leo
Sep 2	19:56	Virgo
Sep 5	07:52	Libra
Sep 7	18:10	Scorpio
Sep 10	02:03	Sagittarius
Sep 12	06:56	Capricorn
Sep 14	09:02	Aquarius
Sep 16	09:24	Pisces
Sep 18	09:43	Aries
Sep 20	11:47	Taurus
Sep 22	17:06	Gemini

Sep 25	02:10	Cancer
Sep 27	14:02	Leo
Sept 30	02:44	Virgo
Oct 2	14:24	Libra
Oct 5	00:03	Scorpio
Oct 7	07:28	Sagittarius
Oct 9	12:43	Capricorn
Oct 11	16:05	Aquarius
Oct 13	18:05	Pisces
Oct 15	19:39	Aries
Oct 17	22:04	Taurus
Oct 20	02:44	Gemini
Oct 22	10:41	Cancer
Oct 24	21:48	Leo
Oct 27	10:28	Virgo
Oct 29	22:15	Libra
Nov 1	07:29	Scorpio
Nov 3	13:55	Sagittarius
Nov 5	18:17	Capricorn
Nov 7	21:31	Aquarius
Nov 10	00:22	Pisces
Nov 12	03:22	Aries
Nov 14	07:02	Taurus
Nov 16	12:10	Gemini
Nov 18 e	19:42	Cancer
Nov 21	06:10	Leo
Nov 23	18:41	Virgo
Nov 26	06:58	Libra
Nov 28	16:33	Scorpio
Nov 30	22:32	Sagittarius
Dec 3	01:42	Capricorn

Dec 5	03:36	Aquarius
Dec 7	05:44	Pisces
Dec 9	09:02	Aries
Dec 11	13:46	Taurus
Dec 13	19:59	Gemini
Dec 16	04:01	Cancer
Dec 18	14:18	Leo
Dec 21	02:39	Virgo
Dec 23	15:26	Libra
Dec 26	02:04	Scorpio
Dec 28	08:43	Sagittarius
Dec 30	11:35	Capricorn

Year 2006

DATE	TIME	SIGN OF ZODIAC
Jan 1	12:14	Aquarius
Jan 3	12:43	Pisces
Jan 5	14:44	Aries
Jan 7	19:09	Taurus
Jan 10	01:58	Gemini
Jan 12	10:50	Cancer
Jan 14	21:31	Leo
Jan 17	09:49	Virgo
Jan 19	22:49	Libra
Jan 22	10:28	Scorpio
Jan 24	18:38	Sagittarius
Jan 26	22:31	Capricorn
Jan 28	23:09	Aquarius
Jan 30	22:32	Pisces
Feb 1	22:46	Aries
Feb 4	01:31	Taurus
Feb 6	07:32	Gemini

Feb 8	16:33	Cancer
Feb 11	03:44	Leo
Feb 13	16:13	Virgo
Feb 16	05:09	Libra
Feb 18	17:11	Scorpio
Feb 21	02:38	Sagittarius
Feb 23	08:16	Capricorn
Feb 25	10:14	Aquarius
Feb 27	09:56	Pisces
Mar 1	09:18	Aries
Mar 3	10:22	Taurus
Mar 5	14:37	Gemini
Mar 7	22:38	Cancer
Mar 10	09:42	Leo
Mar 12	22:23	Virgo
Mar 15	11:12	Libra
Mar 17	22:59	Scorpio
Mar 20	08:43	Sagittarius
Mar 22	15:36	Capricorn
Mar 24	19:21	Aquarius
Mar 26	20:33	Pisces
Mar 28	20:31	Aries
Mar 30	21:00	Taurus
Apr 1	23:49	Gemini
Apr 4	06:15	Cancer
Apr 6	16:25	Leo
Apr 9	04:58	Virgo
Apr 11	17:46	Libra
Apr 14	05:08	Scorpio
Apr 16	14:19	Sagittarius
Apr 18	21:13	Capricorn
Apr 21	01:56	Aquarius

Apr 23	04:43	Pisces
Apr 25	06:12	Aries
Apr 27	07:27	Taurus
Apr 29	09:58	Gemini
May 1	15:17	Cancer
May 4	00:18	Leo
May 6	12:20	Virgo
May 9	01:10	Libra
May 11	12:24	Scorpio
May 13	20:56	Sagittarius
May 16	02:59	Capricorn
May 18	07:19	Aquarius
May 20	10:39	Pisces
May 22	13:24	Aries
May 24	16:00	Taurus
May 26	19:19	Gemini
May 29	00:33	Cancer
May 31	08:51	Leo
Jun 2	20:17	Virgo
Jun 5	09:08	Libra
Jun 7	20:41	Scorpio
Jun 10	05:05	Sagittarius
Jun 12	10:19	Capricorn
Jun 14	13:32	Aquarius
Jun 16	16:05	Pisces
Jun 18	18:54	Aries
Jun 20	22:23	Taurus
Jun 23	02:49	Gemini
Jun 25	08:48	Cancer
Jun 27	17:09	Leo
Jun 30	04:15	Virgo

Jul 2	17:06	Libra
Jul 5	05:13	Scorpio
Jul 7	14:13	Sagittarius
Jul 9	19:25	Capricorn
Jul 11	21:46	Aquarius
Jul 13	22:59	Pisces
Jul 16	00:39	Aries
Jul 18	03:44	Taurus
Jul 20	08:38	Gemini
Jul 22	15:28	Cancer
Jul 25	00:24	Leo
Jul 27	11:36	Virgo
Jul 30	00:27	Libra
Aug 1	13:08	Scorpio
Aug 3	23:13	Sagittarius
Aug 6	05:19	Capricorn
Aug 8	07:47	Aquarius
Aug 10	08:10	Pisces
Aug 12	08:22	Aries
Aug 14	10:00	Taurus
Aug 16	14:07	Gemini
Aug 18	21:03	Cancer
Aug 21	06:33	Leo
Aug 23	18:08	Virgo
Aug 26	07:01	Libra
Aug 28	19:56	Scorpio
Aug 31	07:00	Sagittarius
Sep 2	14:34	Capricorn
Sep 4	18:15	Aquarius
Sep 6	18:56	Pisces
Sep 8	18:23	Aries
Sep 10	18:30	Taurus

Sep 12	20:59	Gemini
Sep 15	02:53	Cancer
Sep 17	12:15	Leo
Sep 20	00:07	Virgo
Sep 22	13:06	Libra
Sep 25	01:54	Scorpio
Sep 27	13:16	Sagittarius
Sep 29	22:01	Capricorn
Oct 2	03:24	Aquarius
Oct 4	05:33	Pisces
Oct 6	05:32	Aries
Oct 8	05:04	Taurus
Oct 10	06:06	Gemini
Oct 12	10:21	Cancer
Oct 14	18:38	Leo
Oct 17	06:15	Virgo
Oct 19	19:19	Libra
Oct 22	07:54	Scorpio
Oct 24	18:53	Sagittarius
Oct 27	03:47	Capricorn
Oct 29	10:17	Aquarius
Oct 31	14:10	Pisces
Nov 2	15:46	Aries
Nov 4	16:05	Taurus
Nov 6	16:46	Gemini
Nov 8	19:46	Cancer
Nov 11	02:34	Leo
Nov 13	13:18	Virgo
Nov 16	02:14	Libra
Nov 18	14:46	Scorpio
Nov 21	01:15	Sagittarius
Nov 23	09:25	Capricorn

Nov 25	15:41	Aquarius
Nov 27	20:20	Pisces
Nov 29	23:30	Aries
Dec 2	01:26	Taurus
Dec 4	03:05	Gemini
Dec 6	06:00	Cancer
Dec 8	11:52	Leo
Dec 10	21:31	Virgo
Dec 13	10:00	Libra
Dec 15	22:42	Scorpio
Dec 18	09:10	Sagittarius
Dec 20	16:39	Capricorn
Dec 22	21:49	Aquarius
Dec 25	01:43	Pisces
Dec 27	05:04	Aries
Dec 29	08:08	Taurus
Dec 31	11:16	Gemini

Year 2007

DATE	TIME	SIGN OF ZODIAC
Jan 2	15:14	Cancer
Jan 4	21:14	Leo
Jan 7	06:18	Virgo
Jan 9	18:15	Libra
Jan 12	07:08	Scorpio
Jan 14	18:11	Sagittarius
Jan 17	01:49	Capricorn
Jan 19	06:15	Aquarius
Jan 21	08:48	Pisces
Jan 23	10:52	Aries
Jan 25	13:28	Taurus
Jan 27	17:10	Gemini

Jan 29	22:16	Cancer
Feb 1	5:14	Leo
Feb 3	14:34	Virgo
Feb 6	02:15	Libra
Feb 8	15:09	Scorpio
Feb 11	03:01	Sagittarius
Feb 13	11:42	Capricorn
Feb 15	16:34	Aquarius
Feb 17	18:30	Pisces
Feb 19	19:06	Aries
Feb 21	20:03	Taurus
Feb 23	22:42	Gemini
Feb 26	03:47	Cancer
Feb 28	11:29	Leo
Mar 2	21:32	Virgo
Mar 5	09:25	Libra
Mar 7	22:16	Scorpio
Mar 10	10:37	Sagittarius
Mar 12	20:34	Capricorn
Mar 15	02:52	Aquarius
Mar 17	05:30	Pisces
Mar 19	05:41	Aries
Mar 21	05:15	Taurus
Mar 23	06:06	Gemini
Mar 25	09:49	Cancer
Mar 27	17:04	Leo
Mar 30	03:27	Virgo
Apr 1	15:43	Libra
Apr 4	04:35	Scorpio
Apr 6	16:56	Sagittarius
Apr 9	03:36	Capricorn

Apr 11	11:23	Aquarius
Apr 13	15:38	Pisces
Apr 15	16:46	Aries
Apr 17	16:11	Taurus
Apr 19	15:51	Gemini
Apr 21	17:50	Cancer
Apr 23	23:38	Leo
Apr 26	09:24	Virgo
Apr 28	21:44	Libra
May 1	10:41	Scorpio
May 3	22:47	Sagittarius
May 6	09:21	Capricorn
May 8	17:48	Aquarius
May 10	23:31	Pisces
May 13	02:19	Aries
May 15	02:48	Taurus
May 17	02:34	Gemini
May 19	03:38	Cancer
May 21	07:56	Leo
May 23	16:26	Virgo
May 26	04:16	Libra
May 28	17:11	Scorpio
May 31	05:07	Sagittarius
Jun 2	15:09	Capricorn
Jun 4	23:15	Aquarius
Jun 7	05:24	Pisces
Jun 9	09:26	Aries
Jun11	11:29	Taurus
Jun 13	12:24	Gemini
Jun 15	13:45	Cancer
Jun 17	17:25	Leo
Jun 20	00:45	Virgo

Jun 22	11:43	Libra
Jun 25	00:26	Scorpio
Jun 27	12:23	Sagittarius
Jun 29	22:05	Capricorn
Jul 2	05:24	Aquarius
Jul 4	10:52	Pisces
Jul 6	14:56	Aries
Jul 8	17:54	Taurus
Jul 10	20:10	Gemini
Jul 12	22:39	Cancer
Jul 15	02:43	Leo
Jul 17	09:39	Virgo
Jul 19	19:53	Libra
Jul 22	08:18	Scorpio
Jul 24	20:29	Sagittarius
Jul 27	06:21	Capricorn
Jul 29	13:13	Aquarius
Jul 31	17:40	Pisces
Aug 2	20:43	Aries
Aug 4	23:16	Taurus
Aug 7	02:01	Gemini
Aug 9	05:36	Cancer
Aug 11	10:42	Leo
Aug 13	18:03	Virgo
Aug 16	04:04	Libra
Aug 18	16:13	Scorpio
Aug 21	04:44	Sagittarius
Aug 23	15:20	Capricorn
Aug 25	22:35	Aquarius
Aug 28	02:34	Pisces
Aug 30	04:24	Aries

Sep 1	05:35	Taurus
Sep 3	07:30	Gemini
Sep 5	11:08	Cancer
Sep 7	16:59	Leo
Sep 10	01:10	Virgo
Sep 12	11:31	Libra
Sep 14	23:37	Scorpio
Sep 17	12:21	Sagittarius
Sep 19	23:51	Capricorn
Sep 22	08:18	Aquarius
Sep 24	12:55	Pisces
Sep 26	14:22	Aries
Sep 28	14:17	Taurus
Sep 30	14:34	Gemini
Oct 2	16:57	Cancer
Oct 4	22:27	Leo
Oct 7	07:03	Virgo
Oct 9	17:57	Libra
Oct 12	06:13	Scorpio
Oct 14	18:58	Sagittarius
Oct 17	07:03	Capricorn
Oct 19	16:52	Aquarius
Oct 21	23:02	Pisces
Oct 24	01:24	Aries
Oct 26	01:07	Taurus
Oct 28	00:11	Gemini
Oct 30	00:49	Cancer
Nov 1	04:48	Leo
Nov 3	12:44	Virgo
Nov 5	23:47	Libra
Nov 8	12:18	Scorpio
Nov 11	00:59	Sagittarius

Nov 13	13:00	Capricorn
Nov 15	23:30	Aquarius
Nov 18	07:14	Pisces
Nov 20	11:24	Aries
Nov 22	12:18	Taurus
Nov 26	11:07	Cancer
Nov 28	13:23	Leo
Nov 30	19:44	Virgo
Dec 3	06:01	Libra
Dec 5	18:31	Scorpio
Dec 8	07:11	Sagittarius
Dec 10	18:50	Capricorn
Dec 13	05:01	Aquarius
Dec 15	13:15	Pisces
Dec 17	18:52	Aries
Dec 19	21:38	Taurus
Dec 21	22:14	Gemini
Dec 23	22:18	Cancer
Dec 25	23:52	Leo
Dec 28	04:44	Virgo
Dec 30	13:37	Libra

Year 2008

DATE	TIME	SIGN OF ZODIAC
Jan 2	01:32	Scorpio
Jan 4	14:13	Sagittarius
Jan 7	01:43	Capricorn
Jan 9	11:13	Aquarius
Jan 11	18:44	Pisces
Jan 14	00:23	Aries
Jan 16	04:13	Taurus
Jan 18	06:30	Gemini

Jan 20	08:05	Cancer
Jan 22	10:20	Leo
Jan 24	14:48	Virgo
Jan 26	22:35	Libra
Jan 29	09:35	Scorpio
Jan 31	22:08	Sagittarius
Feb 3	09:52	Capricorn
Feb 5	19:10	Aquarius
Feb 8	01:46	Pisces
Feb 10	06:17	Aries
Feb 12	09:34	Taurus
Feb 14	12:19	Gemini
Feb 16	15:12	Cancer
Feb 18	18:51	Leo
Feb 21	00:06	Virgo
Feb 23	07:44	Libra
Feb 25	18:05	Scorpio
Feb 28	06:22	Sagittarius
Mar 1	18:33	Capricorn
Mar 4	04:24	Aquarius
Mar 6	10:53	Pisces
Mar 8	14:23	Aries
Mar 10	16:13	Taurus
Mar 12	17:54	Gemini
Mar 14	20:37	Cancer
Mar 17	01:04	Leo
Mar 19	07:25	Virgo
Mar 21	15:45	Libra
Mar 24	02:06	Scorpio
Mar 26	14:11	Sagittarius
Mar 29	02:43	Capricorn
Mar 31	13:34	Aquarius

Apr 2	20:55	Pisces
Apr 5	00:27	Aries
Apr 7	01:19	Taurus
Apr 9	01:27	Gemini
Apr 11	02:43	Cancer
Apr 13	06:29	Leo
Apr 15	13:06	Virgo
Apr 17	22:10	Libra
Apr 20	09:00	Scorpio
Apr 22	21:07	Sagittarius
Apr 25	09:47	Capricorn
Apr 27	21:27	Aquarius
Apr 30	06:11	Pisces
May 2	10:51	Aries
May 4	11:58	Taurus
May 6	11:17	Gemini
May 8	11:02	Cancer
May 10	13:10	Leo
May 12	18:48	Virgo
May 15	03:46	Libra
May 17	14:59	Scorpio
May 20	03:18	Sagittarius
May 22	15:55	Capricorn
May 25	03:51	Aquarius
May 27	13:38	Pisces
May 29	19:52	Aries
May 31	22:18	Taurus
Jun 2	22:06	Gemini
Jun 4	21:16	Cancer
Jun 6	22:00	Leo
Jun 9	02:01	Virgo
Jun 11	09:55	Libra

Jun 13	20:53	Scorpio
Jun 16	09:19	Sagittarius
Jun 18	21:51	Capricorn
Jun 21	09:33	Aquarius
Jun 23	19:32	Pisces
Jun 26	02:49	Aries
Jun 28	06:50	Taurus
Jun 30	08:03	Gemini
Jul 2	07:53	Cancer
Jul 4	08:15	Leo
Jul 6	11:04	Virgo
Jul 8	17:31	Libra
Jul 11	03:35	Scorpio
Jul 13	15:50	Sagittarius
Jul 16	04:20	Capricorn
Jul 18	15:40	Aquarius
Jul 21	01:07	Pisces
Jul 23	08:22	Aries
Jul 25	13:14	Taurus
Jul 27	15:55	Gemini
Jul 29	17:11	Cancer
Jul 31	18:21	Leo
Aug 2	20:59	Virgo
Aug 5	02:28	Libra
Aug 7	11:26	Scorpio
Aug 9	23:10	Sagittarius
Aug 12	11:42	Capricorn
Aug 14	22:56	Aquarius
Aug 17	07:46	Pisces
Aug 19	14:10	Aries
Aug 21	18:38	Taurus
Aug 23	21:48	Gemini

Aug 26	00:18	Cancer
Aug 28	02:51	Leo
Aug 30	06:18	Virgo
Sep 1	11:44	Libra
Sep 3	20:02	Scorpio
Sep 6	07:11	Sagittarius
Sep 8	19:45	Capricorn
Sep 11	07:19	Aquarius
Sep 13	16:04	Pisces
Sep 15	21:39	Aries
Sep 18	00:56	Taurus
Sep 20	03:17	Gemini
Sep 22	05:48	Cancer
Sep 24	09:13	Leo
Sep 25	13:52	Virgo
Sep 28	20:05	Libra
Oct 1	04:26	Scorpio
Oct 3	15:14	Sagittarius
Oct 6	03:48	Capricorn
Oct 8	16:03	Aquarius
Oct 11	01:31	Pisces
Oct 13	07:07	Aries
Oct 15	09:31	Taurus
Oct 17	10:25	Gemini
Oct 19	11:40	Cancer
Oct 21	14:35	Leo
Oct 23	19:40	Virgo
Oct 26	02:47	Libra
Oct 28	11:47	Scorpio
Oct 30	22:41	Sagittarius
Nov 2	11:13	Capricorn

Nov 5	00:01	Aquarius
Nov 7	10:43	Pisces
Nov 9	17:26	Aries
Nov 11	20:05	Taurus
Nov 13	20:11	Gemini
Nov 15	19:52	Cancer
Nov 17	21:07	Leo
Nov 20	01:12	Virgo
Nov 22	08:20	Libra
Nov 24	17:54	Scorpio
Nov 27	05:14	Sagittarius
Nov 29	17:48	Capricorn
Dec 2	06:44	Aquarius
Dec 4	18:23	Pisces
Dec 7	02:44	Aries
Dec 9	06:52	Taurus
Dec 11	07:33	Gemini
Dec 13	06:39	Cancer
Dec 15	06:22	Leo
Dec 17	08:35	Virgo
Dec 19	14:23	Libra
Dec 21	23:36	Scorpio
Dec 24	11:13	Sagittarius
Dec 26	23:56	Capricorn
Dec 29	12:42	Aquarius

Year 2009

DATE	TIME	SIGN OF ZODIAC
Jan 1	00:27	Pisces
Jan 3	09:50	Aries
Jan 5	15:46	Taurus
Jan 7	18:11	Gemini

Jan 9	18:14	Cancer
Jan 11	17:41	Leo
Jan 13	18:33	Virgo
Jan 15	22:30	Libra
Jan 18	06:20	Scorpio
Jan 20	17:30	Sagittarius
Jan 23	06:18	Capricorn
Jan 25	18:56	Aquarius
Jan 28	06:12	Pisces
Jan 30	15:25	Aries
Feb 1	22:08	Taurus
Feb 4	02:14	Gemini
Feb 6	04:05	Cancer
Feb 8	04:43	Leo
Feb 10	05:38	Virgo
Feb 12	08:33	Libra
Feb 14	14:50	Scorpio
Feb 17	00:53	Sagittarius
Feb 19	13:25	Capricorn
Feb 22	02:06	Aquarius
Feb 24	12:59	Pisces
Feb 26	21:24	Aries
Mar 1	03:33	Taurus
Mar 3	07:59	Gemini
Mar 5	11:07	Cancer
Mar 7	13:24	Leo
Mar 9	15:34	Virgo
Mar 11	18:46	Libra
Mar 14	00:22	Scorpio
Mar 16	09:21	Sagittarius
Mar 18	21:18	Capricorn
Mar 21	10:06	Aquarius

Mar 23	21:08	Pisces
Mar 26	05:03	Aries
Mar 28	10:09	Taurus
Mar 30	13:36	Gemini
Apr 1	16:30	Cancer
Apr 3	19:32	Leo
Apr 5	23:01	Virgo
Apr 8	03:22	Libra
Apr 10	09:23	Scorpio
Apr 12	18:00	Sagittarius
Apr 15	05:27	Capricorn
Apr 17	18:19	Aquarius
Apr 20	05:55	Pisces
Apr 22	14:09	Aries
Apr 24	18:46	Taurus
Apr 26	21:02	Gemini
Apr 28	22:38	Cancer
May 1	00:56	Leo
May 3	04:37	Virgo
May 5	09:51	Libra
May 7	16:48	Scorpio
May 10	01:49	Sagittarius
May 12	13:09	Capricorn
May 15	02:01	Aquarius
May 17	14:17	Pisces
May 19	23:30	Aries
May 22	04:40	Taurus
May 24	06:34	Gemini
May 26	06:58	Cancer
May 28	07:44	Leo
May 30	10:17	Virgo

Jun 1	15:17	Libra
Jun 3	22:43	Scorpio
Jun 6	08:23	Sagittarius
Jun 8	19:59	Capricorn
Jun 11	08:52	Aquarius
Jun 13	21:32	Pisces
Jun 16	07:51	Aries
Jun 18	14:20	Taurus
Jun 20	17:00	Gemini
Jun 22	17:12	Cancer
Jun 24	16:50	Leo
Jun 26	17:46	Virgo
Jun 28	21:24	Libra
Jul 1	04:18	Scorpio
Jul 3	14:10	Sagittarius
Jul 6	02:07	Capricorn
Jul 8	15:03	Aquarius
Jul 11	03:44	Pisces
Jul 13	14:40	Aries
Jul 15	22:30	Taurus
Jul 18	02:41	Gemini
Jul 20	03:51	Cancer
Jul 22	03:27	Leo
Jul 24	03:22	Virgo
Jul 26	05:25	Libra
Jul 28	10:56	Scorpio
Jul 30	20:10	Sagittarius
Aug 2	08:08	Capricorn
Aug 4	21:08	Aquarius
Aug 7	09:34	Pisces
Aug 9	20:23	Aries
Aug 12	04:49	Taurus

Aug 14	10:25	Gemini
Aug 16	13:13	Cancer
Aug 18	13:56	Leo
Aug 20	14:00	Virgo
Aug 22	15:12	Libra
Aug 24	19:16	Scorpio
Aug 27	03:16	Sagittarius
Aug 29	14:44	Capricorn
Sep 1	03:43	Aquarius
Sep 3	15:58	Pisces
Sep 6	02:14	Aries
Sep 8	10:17	Taurus
Sep 10	16:17	Gemini
Sep 12	20:19	Cancer
Sep 14	22:39	Leo
Sept 16	23:56	Virgo
Sep 19	01:26	Libra
Sep 21	04:52	Scorpio
Sep 23	11:43	Sagittarius
Sep 25	22:19	Capricorn
Sep 28	11:06	Aquarius
Sep 30	23:26	Pisces
Oct 3	09:20	Aries
Oct 5	16:33	Taurus
Oct 7	21:46	Gemini
Oct 10	01:48	Cancer
Oct 12	05:02	Leo
Oct 14	07:45	Virgo
Oct 16	10:29	Libra
Oct 18	14:22	Scorpio
Oct 20	20:49	Sagittarius
Oct 23	06:39	Capricorn

Oct 25	19:08	Aquarius
Oct 28	07:45	Pisces
Oct 30	17:56	Aries
Nov 2	00:44	Taurus
Nov 4	04:53	Gemini
Nov 6	07:42	Cancer
Nov 8	10:23	Leo
Nov 10	13:30	Virgo
Nov 12	17:22	Libra
Nov 14	22:24	Scorpio
Nov 17	05:22	Sagittarius
Nov 19	15:00	Capricorn
Nov 22	03:11	Aquarius
Nov 24	16:07	Pisces
Nov 27	03:10	Aries
Nov 29	10:34	Taurus
Dec 1	14:23	Gemini
Dec 3	16:00	Cancer
Dec 5	17:07	Leo
Dec 7	19:05	Virgo
Dec 9	22:47	Libra
Dec 12	04:31	Scorpio
Dec 14	12:25	Sagittarius
Dec 16	22:32	Capricorn
Dec 19	10:38	Aquarius
Dec 21	23:42	Pisces
Dec 24	11:39	Aries
Dec 26	20:26	Taurus
Dec 29	01:13	Gemini
Dec 31	02:45	Cancer

Year 2010

Date	Time	Sign of Zodiac
Jan 2	02:41	Leo
Jan 4	02:52	Virgo
Jan 6	04:58	Libra
Jan 8	10:00	Scorpio
Jan 10	18:10	Sagittarius
Jan 13	04:54	Capricorn
Jan 15	17:17	Aquarius
Jan 18	06:17	Pisces
Jan 20	18:36	Aries
Jan 23	04:39	Taurus
Jan 25	11:11	Gemini
Jan 27	14:01	Cancer
Jan 29	14:10	Leo
Jan 31	13:23	Virgo
Feb 2	13:42	Libra
Feb 4	16:55	Scorpio
Feb 7	00:03	Sagittarius
Feb 9	10:43	Capricorn
Feb 11	23:24	Aquarius
Feb 14	12:23	Pisces
Feb 17	00:30	Aries
Feb 19	10:55	Taurus
Feb 21	18:47	Gemini
Feb 23	23:28	Cancer
Feb 26	01:08	Leo
Feb 28	00:52	Virgo
Mar 2	00:31	Libra
Mar 4	02:11	Scorpio
Mar 6	07:36	Sagittarius

Mar 8	17:13	Capricorn
Mar 11	05:42	Aquarius
Mar 13	18:43	Pisces
Mar 16	06:32	Aries
Mar 18	16:29	Taurus
Mar 21	00:28	Gemini
Mar 23	06:16	Cancer
Mar 25	09:39	Leo
Mar 27	10:57	Virgo
Mar 29	11:21	Libra
Mar 31	12:41	Scorpio
Apr 2	16:52	Sagittarius
Apr 5	01:07	Capricorn
Apr 7	12:51	Aquarius
Apr 10	01:47	Pisces
Apr 12	13:31	Aries
Apr 14	22:55	Taurus
Apr 17	06:08	Gemini
Apr 19	11:39	Cancer
Apr 21	15:42	Leo
Apr 22	18:24	Virgo
Apr 23	20:16	Libra
Apr 27	22:28	Scorpio
Apr 30	02:36	Sagittarius
May 2	10:00	Capricorn
May 4	20:51	Aquarius
May 7	09:34	Pisces
May 9	21:29	Aries
May 12	06:48	Taurus
May 14	13:18	Gemini
May 16	17:45	Cancer
May 18	21:06	Leo

May 20	23:58	Virgo
May 23	02:49	Libra
May 25	06:17	Scorpio
May 27	11:15	Sagittarius
May 29	18:44	Capricorn
Jun 1	05:08	Aquarius
Jun 3	17:33	Pisces
Jun 6	05:49	Aries
Jun 8	15:41	Taurus
Jun 10	22:11	Gemini
Jun 13	01:50	Cancer
Jun 15	03:54	Leo
Jun 17	05:41	Virgo
Jun 19	08:13	Libra
Jun 21	12:13	Scorpio
Jun 23	18:10	Sagittarius
Jun 26	02:21	Capricorn
Jun 28	12:52	Aquarius
Jul 1	01:09	Pisces
Jul 3	13:44	Aries
Jul 6	00:29	Taurus
Jul 8	07:50	Gemini
Jul 10	11:38	Cancer
Jul 12	12:53	Leo
Jul 14	13:15	Virgo
Jul 16	14:24	Libra
Jul 18	17:42	Scorpio
Jul 20	23:48	Sagittarius
Jul 23	08:39	Capricorn
Jul 25	19:38	Aquarius
Jul 28	08:00	Pisces
Jul 30	20:41	Aries

Aug 2	08:13	Taurus
Aug 4	16:54	Gemini
Aug 6	21:50	Cancer
Aug 8	23:23	Leo
Aug 10	23:01	Virgo
Aug 12	22:42	Libra
Aug 15	00:26	Scorpio
Aug 17	05:34	Sagittarius
Aug 19	14:17	Capricorn
Aug 22	01:37	Aquarius
Aug 24	14:11	Pisces
Aug 27	02:49	Aries
Aug 29	14:35	Taurus
Sep 1	00:19	Gemini
Sep 3	06:50	Cancer
Sep 5	09:45	Leo
Sep 7	09:53	Virgo
Sep 9	09:01	Libra
Sep 11	09:21	Scorpio
Sep 13	12:52	Sagittarius
Sep 15	20:30	Capricorn
Sep 18	07:34	Aquarius
Sep 20	20:15	Pisces
Sep 23	08:47	Aries
Sep 25	20:16	Taurus
Sep 28	06:10	Gemini
Sep 30	13:45	Cancer
Oct 2	18:21	Leo
Oct 4	20:00	Virgo
Oct 6	19:51	Libra
Oct 8	19:52	Scorpio
Oct 10	22:09	Sagittarius

Oct 13	04:17	Capricorn
Oct 15	14:24	Aquarius
Oct 18	02:51	Pisces
Oct 20	15:23	Aries
Oct 23	02:29	Taurus
Oct 25	11:47	Gemini
Oct 27	19:14	Cancer
Oct 30	00:38	Leo
Nov 1	03:51	Virgo
Nov 3	05:19	Libra
Nov 5	06:15	Scorpio
Nov 7	08:27	Sagittarius
Nov 9	13:36	Capricorn
Nov 11	22:32	Aquarius
Nov 14	10:24	Pisces
Nov 16	22:58	Aries
Nov 19	10:04	Taurus
Nov 21	18:46	Gemini
Nov 24	01:14	Cancer
Nov 26	06:01	Leo
Nov 28	09:33	Virgo
Nov 30	12:15	Libra
Dec 2	14:43	Scorpio
Dec 4	17:59	Sagittarius
Dec 6	23:16	Capricorn
Dec 9	07:30	Aquarius
Dec 11	18:40	Pisces
Dec 14	07:14	Aries
Dec 16	18:49	Taurus
Dec 19	03:37	Gemini
Dec 21	09:22	Cancer
Dec 23	12:50	Leo

Dec 25	15:14	Virgo
Dec 27	17:38	Libra
Dec 29	20:49	Scorpio

Year 2011

DATE	TIME	SIGN OF ZODIAC
Jan 1	01:21	Sagittarius
Jan 3	07:39	Capricorn
Jan 5	16:08	Aquarius
Jan 8	01:57	Pisces
Jan 10	15:24	Aries
Jan 13	15:37	Taurus
Jan 15	13:23	Gemini
Jan 17	19:29	Cancer
Jan 19	22:16	Leo
Jan 21	23:10	Virgo
Jan 23	23:59	Libra
Jan 26	02:15	Scorpio
Jan 28	06:55	Sagittarius
Jan 30	14:04	Capricorn
Feb 1	23:21	Aquarius
Feb 4	10:24	Pisces
Feb 6	22:45	Aries
Feb 9	11:22	Taurus
Feb 11	22:20	Gemini
Feb 14	05:48	Cancer
Feb 16	09:14	Leo
Feb 18	09:39	Virgo
Feb 20	09:01	Libra
Feb 22	09:29	Scorpio
Feb 24	12:46	Sagittarius
Feb 26	18:32	Capricorn

Mar	1	05:14	Aquarius
Mar	3	16:47	Pisces
Mar	6	05:14	Aries
Mar	8	17:52	Taurus
Mar	11	05:31	Gemini
Mar	13	14:29	Cancer
Mar	15	19:33	Leo
Mar	17	20:53	Virgo
Mar	19	20:03	Libra
Mar	21	19:17	Scorpio
Mar	23	20:45	Sagittarius
Mar	26	01:57	Capricorn
Mar	28	11:00	Aquarius
Mar	30	22:38	Pisces
Apr	2	11:16	Aries
Apr	4	23:46	Taurus
Apr	7	11:21	Gemini
Apr	9	21:02	Cancer
Apr	12	03:37	Leo
Apr	14	06:40	Virgo
Apr	16	06:59	Libra
Apr	18	06:19	Scorpio
Apr	20	06:50	Sagittarius
Apr	22	10:24	Capricorn
Apr	24	17:59	Aquarius
Apr	27	04:57	Pisces
Apr	29	17:33	Aries
May	2	05:58	Taurus
May	4	17:09	Gemini
May	7	02:32	Cancer
May	9	09:35	Leo
May	11	13:59	Virgo

May 13	15:56	Libra
May 15	16:31	Scorpio
May 17	17:22	Sagittarius
May 19	20:16	Capricorn
May 22	02:32	Aquarius
May 24	12:24	Pisces
May 27	00:36	Aries
May 29	13:02	Taurus
May 31	23:56	Gemini
June 3	08:36	Cancer
June 5	15:03	Leo
June 7	19:33	Virgo
June 9	22:31	Libra
June 12	00:33	Scorpio
June 14	02:38	Sagittarius
June 16	05:59	Capricorn
June 18	11:47	Aquarius
June 20	20:45	Pisces
June 23	08:24	Aries
June 25	20:53	Taurus
June 28	07:56	Gemini
June 30	16:13	Cancer
July 2	21:43	Leo
July 5	01:15	Virgo
July 7	03:54	Libra
July 9	06:31	Scorpio
July 11	09:47	Sagittarius
July 13	14:14	Capricorn
July 15	20:30	Aquarius
July 18	05:13	Pisces
July 20	16:25	Aries
July 23	04:58	Taurus

July 25	16:34	Gemini
July 28	01:11	Cancer
July 30	06:16	Leo
Aug 1	08:41	Virgo
Aug 3	10:04	Libra
Aug 5	11:57	Scorpio
Aug 7	15:21	Sagittarius
Aug 9	20:38	Capricorn
Aug 12	03:47	Aquarius
Aug 14	12:54	Pisces
Aug 17	00:01	Aries
Aug 19	12:36	Taurus
Aug 22	00:53	Gemini
Aug 24	10:31	Cancer
Aug 26	16:09	Leo
Aug 28	18:13	Virgo
Aug 30	18:25	Libra
Sep 1	18:48	Scorpio
Sep 3	21:03	Sagittarius
Sep 6	02:03	Capricorn
Sep 8	09:42	Aquarius
Sep 10	19:26	Pisces
Sep 13	06:49	Aries
Sep 15	19:25	Taurus
Sep 18	08:06	Gemini
Sep 20	18:53	Cancer
Sep 23	01:55	Leo
Sep 25	04:49	Virgo
Sep 27	04:51	Libra
Sep 29	04:05	Scorpio
Oct 1	04:42	Sagittarius

Oct 3	08:16	Capricorn
Oct 5	15:18	Aquarius
Oct 8	01:13	Pisces
Oct 10	12:57	Aries
Oct 13	01:35	Taurus
Oct 15	14:15	Gemini
Oct 18	01:38	Cancer
Oct 20	10:06	Leo
Oct 22	14:41	Virgo
Oct 24	15:49	Libra
Oct 26	15:08	Scorpio
Oct 28	14:45	Sagittarius
Oct 30	16:39	Capricorn
Nov 1	22:08	Aquarius
Nov 4	07:18	Pisces
Nov 6	19:02	Aries
Nov 9	07:45	Taurus
Nov 11	20:10	Gemini
Nov 14	07:19	Cancer
Nov 16	16:17	Leo
Nov 18	22:19	Virgo
Nov 21	01:16	Libra
Nov 23	01:58	Scorpio
Nov 25	01:57	Sagittarius
Nov 27	03:04	Capricorn
Nov 29	07:02	Aquarius
Dec 1	14:45	Pisces
Dec 4	01:51	Aries
Dec 6	14:34	Taurus
Dec 9	02:52	Gemini
Dec 11	13:26	Cancer
Dec 13	21:48	Leo

Dec 16	03:58	Virgo
Dec 18	08:06	Libra
Dec 20	10:33	Scorpio
Dec 22	12:03	Sagittarius
Dec 24	13:47	Capricorn
Dec 26	17:14	Aquarius
Dec 28	23:45	Pisces
Dec 31	09:48	Aries

Year 2012

DATE	TIME	SIGN OF ZODIAC
Jan 2	22:16	Taurus
Jan 5	10:44	Gemini
Jan 7	21:05	Cancer
Jan 10	04:35	Leo
Jan 12	09:44	Virgo
Jan 14	13:28	Libra
Jan 16	16:33	Scorpio
Jan 18	19:29	Sagittarius
Jan 20	22:40	Capricorn
Jan 23	02:53	Aquarius
Jan 25	09:11	Pisces
Jan 27	18:28	Aries
Jan 30	06:28	Taurus
Feb 1	19:14	Gemini
Feb 4	06:04	Cancer
Feb 6	13:24	Leo
Feb 8	17:32	Virgo
Feb 10	19:54	Libra
Feb 12	22:01	Scorpio
Feb 15	12:56	Sagittarius
Feb 17	05:03	Capricorn

Feb 19	10:28	Aquarius
Feb 21	17:31	Pisces
Feb 24	02:48	Aries
Feb 26	14:29	Taurus
Feb 29	03:27	Gemini
Mar 2	03:08	Cancer
Mar 4	23:17	Leo
Mar 7	03:27	Virgo
Mar 9	04:50	Libra
Mar 11	05:24	Scorpio
Mar 13	06:53	Sagittarius
Mar 15	10:24	Capricorn
Mar 17	16:11	Aquarius
Mar 20	12:05	Pisces
Mar 22	09:57	Aries
Mar 24	17:43	Taurus
Mar 27	10:43	Gemini
Mar 29	23:07	Cancer
Apr 1	08:35	Leo
Apr 3	13:53	Virgo
Apr 5	15:32	Libra
Apr 7	15:17	Scorpio
Apr 9	15:12	Sagittarius
Apr 11	17:02	Capricorn
Apr 13	21:48	Aquarius
Apr 16	05:38	Pisces
Apr 18	15:59	Aries
Apr 21	04:05	Taurus
Apr 23	17:05	Gemini
Apr 26	05:42	Cancer
Apr 28	16:10	Leo
Apr 30	23:02	Virgo

May 3	02:04	Libra
May 5	02:20	Scorpio
May 7	01:39	Sagittarius
May 9	02:00	Capricorn
May 11	05:03	Aquarius
May 13	11:42	Pisces
May 15	21:45	Aries
May 18	10:03	Taurus
May 20	23:05	Gemini
May 23	11:31	Cancer
May 25	22:11	Leo
May 28	06:06	Virgo
May 30	10:46	Libra
June 1	12:31	Scorpio
June 3	12:32	Sagittarius
June 5	12:31	Capricorn
June 7	14:17	Aquarius
June 9	19:22	Pisces
June 12	04:21	Aries
June 14	16:22	Taurus
June 17	05:24	Gemini
June 19	17:34	Cancer
June 22	03:47	Leo
June 24	11:42	Virgo
June 26	17:15	Libra
June 28	20:32	Scorpio
June 30	22:04	Sagittarius
July 2	22:51	Capricorn
July 5	00:26	Aquarius
July 7	04:29	Pisces
July 9	12:14	Aries
July 11	23:30	Taurus

July 14	12:26	Gemini
July 17	00:31	Cancer
July 19	10:13	Leo
July 21	17:24	Virgo
July 23	22:38	Libra
July 26	02:29	Scorpio
July 28	05:18	Sagittarius
July 30	07:29	Capricorn
Aug 1	09:56	Aquarius
Aug 3	13:58	Pisces
Aug 5	20:58	Aries
Aug 8	07:28	Taurus
Aug 10	20:11	Gemini
Aug 13	08:27	Cancer
Aug 15	18:05	Leo
Aug 18	00:33	Virgo
Aug 20	04:45	Libra
Aug 22	07:54	Scorpio
Aug 24	10:50	Sagittarius
Aug 26	13:58	Capricorn
Aug 28	17:38	Aquarius
Aug 30	22:31	Pisces
Sep 2	05:37	Aries
Sep 4	15:41	Taurus
Sep 7	04:10	Gemini
Sep 9	16:49	Cancer
Sep 12	03:00	Leo
Sep 14	09:30	Virgo
Sep 16	12:55	Libra
Sep 18	14:46	Scorpio
Sep 20	16:34	Sagittarius
Sep 22	19:20	Capricorn

Sep 24	23:32	Aquarius
Sep 27	05:23	Pisces
Sep 29	13:14	Aries
Oct 1	23:26	Taurus
Oct 4	11:47	Gemini
Oct 7	00:45	Cancer
Oct 9	11:55	Leo
Oct 11	19:23	Virgo
Oct 13	23:02	Libra
Oct 16	12:06	Scorpio
Oct 18	12:26	Sagittarius
Oct 20	01:41	Capricorn
Oct 22	05:02	Aquarius
Oct 24	11:00	Pisces
Oct 26	19:31	Aries
Oct 29	06:15	Taurus
Oct 31	18:40	Gemini
Nov 3	07:43	Cancer
Nov 5	19:39	Leo
Nov 8	04:35	Virgo
Nov 10	09:35	Libra
Nov 12	11:10	Scorpio
Nov 14	10:52	Sagittarius
Nov 16	10:35	Capricorn
Nov 18	12:10	Aquarius
Nov 20	16:55	Pisces
Nov 23	13:12	Aries
Nov 25	12:18	Taurus
Nov 28	00:58	Gemini
Nov 30	13:55	Cancer
Dec 3	01:57	Leo

Dec 5	11:51	Virgo
Dec 7	18:35	Libra
Dec 9	17:51	Scorpio
Dec 11	22:22	Sagittarius
Dec 13	21:42	Capricorn
Dec 15	17:53	Aquarius
Dec 18	12:48	Pisces
Dec 20	07:43	Aries
Dec 22	18:25	Taurus
Dec 25	07:13	Gemini
Dec 27	20:06	Cancer
Dec 30	07:45	Leo

Year 2013

DATE	TIME	SIGN OF ZODIAC
Jan 1	17:35	Virgo
Jan 4	01:11	Libra
Jan 6	06:09	Scorpio
Jan 8	08:28	Sagittarius
Jan 10	08:54	Capricorn
Jan 12	09:01	Aquarius
Jan 14	10:49	Pisces
Jan 16	16:07	Aries
Jan 19	01:36	Taurus
Jan 21	14:04	Gemini
Jan 24	03:00	Cancer
Jan 26	14:20	Leo
Jan 28	23:27	Virgo
Jan 31	06:36	Libra
Feb 2	12:02	Scorpio
Feb 4	15:45	Sagittarius
Feb 6	17:55	Capricorn

Feb 8	19:16	Aquarius
Feb 10	21:19	Pisces
Feb 13	01:51	Aries
Feb 15	10:08	Taurus
Feb 17	21:50	Gemini
Feb 20	10:45	Cancer
Feb 22	22:12	Leo
Feb 25	06:52	Virgo
Feb 27	13:02	Libra
Mar 1	17:33	Scorpio
Mar 3	21:11	Sagittarius
Mar 6	00:14	Capricorn
Mar 8	03:01	Aquarius
Mar 10	06:19	Pisces
Mar 12	11:17	Aries
Mar 14	19:08	Taurus
Mar 17	18:09	Gemini
Mar 19	18:55	Cancer
Mar 22	06:50	Leo
Mar 24	15:49	Virgo
Mar 26	17:32	Libra
Mar 29	12:53	Scorpio
Mar 31	03:13	Sagittarius
Apr 2	05:35	Capricorn
Apr 4	08:41	Aquarius
Apr 6	13:00	Pisces
Apr 8	19:02	Aries
Apr 11	03:22	Taurus
Apr 13	14:13	Gemini
Apr 16	02:49	Cancer
Apr 18	15:13	Leo
Apr 21	01:08	Virgo

Apr 23	07:25	Libra
Apr 25	10:25	Scorpio
Apr 27	11:32	Sagittarius
Apr 29	12:21	Capricorn
May 1	14:19	Aquarius
May 3	18:25	Pisces
May 6	01:03	Aries
May 8	10:09	Taurus
May 10	21:21	Gemini
May 13	09:57	Cancer
May 15	22:38	Leo
May 18	09:33	Virgo
May 20	17:07	Libra
May 22	20:55	Scorpio
May 24	21:49	Sagittarius
May 26	21:28	Capricorn
May 28	12:48	Aquarius
May 31	00:30	Pisces
June 2	06:33	Aries
June 4	15:53	Taurus
June 7	03:32	Gemini
June 9	16:16	Cancer
June 12	04:58	Leo
June 14	16:26	Virgo
June 17	01:19	Libra
June 19	06:38	Scorpio
June 21	08:31	Sagittarius
June 23	08:08	Capricorn
June 25	07:26	Aquarius
June 27	08:32	Pisces
June 29	13:06	Aries

July 1	21:43	Taurus
July 4	09:22	Gemini
July 6	22:14	Cancer
July 9	10:48	Leo
July 11	22:12	Virgo
July 14	07:41	Libra
July 16	14:24	Scorpio
July 18	17:54	Sagittarius
July 20	18:39	Capricorn
July 22	18:07	Aquarius
July 24	18:22	Pisces
July 26	21:29	Aries
July 29	04:43	Taurus
July 31	15:42	Gemini
Aug 3	04:29	Cancer
Aug 5	16:58	Leo
Aug 8	03:57	Virgo
Aug 10	13:08	Libra
Aug 12	20:18	Scorpio
Aug 15	01:04	Sagittarius
Aug 17	03:25	Capricorn
Aug 19	04:07	Aquarius
Aug 21	04:43	Pisces
Aug 23	07:13	Aries
Aug 25	13:13	Taurus
Aug 27	23:08	Gemini
Aug 30	11:33	Cancer
Sep 2	00:01	Leo
Sep 4	10:43	Virgo
Sep 6	19:12	Libra
Sep 9	13:44	Scorpio
Sep 11	06:36	Sagittarius

Sep 13	09:56	Capricorn
Sep 15	12:05	Aquarius
Sep 17	13:58	Pisces
Sep 19	16:58	Aries
Sep 21	22:33	Taurus
Sep 24	07:34	Gemini
Sep 26	19:24	Cancer
Sep 29	07:57	Leo
Oct 1	18:52	Virgo
Oct 4	02:59	Libra
Oct 6	08:33	Scorpio
Oct 8	12:21	Sagittarius
Oct 10	15:17	Capricorn
Oct 12	18:00	Aquarius
Oct 14	21:06	Pisces
Oct 17	01:17	Aries
Oct 19	07:27	Taurus
Oct 21	16:14	Gemini
Oct 24	15:36	Cancer
Oct 26	16:12	Leo
Oct 29	03:45	Virgo
Oct 31	12:22	Libra
Nov 2	17:35	Scorpio
Nov 4	20:14	Sagittarius
Nov 6	21:44	Capricorn
Nov 8	23:30	Aquarius
Nov 11	02:36	Pisces
Nov 13	07:39	Aries
Nov 15	14:49	Taurus
Nov 18	12:07	Gemini
Nov 20	11:23	Cancer
Nov 22	23:56	Leo

Nov 25	12:11	Virgo
Nov 27	22:00	Libra
Nov 30	04:03	Scorpio

Dec 2	06:31	Sagittarius
Dec 4	06:49	Capricorn
Dec 6	06:53	Aquarius
Dec 8	08:34	Pisces
Dec 10	13:05	Aries
Dec 12	20:40	Taurus
Dec 15	06:41	Gemini
Dec 17	18:17	Cancer
Dec 20	06:48	Leo
Dec 22	19:19	Virgo
Dec 25	06:17	Libra
Dec 27	13:58	Scorpio
Dec 29	17:37	Sagittarius
Dec 31	18:01	Capricorn

Year 2014

DATE	TIME	SIGN OF ZODIAC
Jan 2	17:03	Aquarius
Jan 4	16:58	Pisces
Jan 6	19:45	Aries
Jan 9	02:24	Taurus
Jan 11	12:26	Gemini
Jan 14	00:25	Cancer
Jan 16	13:00	Leo
Jan 19	01:23	Virgo
Jan 21	12:43	Libra
Jan 23	17:43	Scorpio
Jan 26	03:13	Sagittarius
Jan 28	05:04	Capricorn

Jan 30	04:33	Aquarius
Feb 1	03:44	Pisces
Feb 3	04:55	Aries
Feb 5	09:46	Taurus
Feb 7	18:44	Gemini
Feb 10	06:33	Cancer
Feb 12	19:15	Leo
Feb 15	07:26	Virgo
Feb 17	18:22	Libra
Feb 20	03:33	Scorpio
Feb 22	10:12	Sagittarius
Feb 24	13:50	Capricorn
Feb 26	14:55	Aquarius
Feb 28	14:52	Pisces
Mar 2	15:40	Aries
Mar 4	19:12	Taurus
Mar 7	02:37	Gemini
Mar 9	13:33	Cancer
Mar 12	02:09	Leo
Mar 14	14:17	Virgo
Mar 17	00:46	Libra
Mar 19	09:13	Scorpio
Mar 21	15:39	Sagittarius
Mar 23	20:03	Capricorn
Mar 25	22:39	Aquarius
Mar 28	12:10	Pisces
Mar 30	01:54	Aries
Apr 1	05:20	Taurus
Apr 3	11:48	Gemini
Apr 5	21:40	Cancer
Apr 8	09:50	Leo

Apr 10	22:08	Virgo
Apr 13	08:33	Libra
Apr 15	16:20	Scorpio
Apr 17	21:44	Sagittarius
Apr 20	01:28	Capricorn
Apr 22	04:18	Aquarius
Apr 24	06:55	Pisces
Apr 26	10:01	Aries
Apr 28	14:23	Taurus
Apr 30	20:56	Gemini
May 3	06:13	Cancer
May 5	17:55	Leo
May 8	06:24	Virgo
May 10	17:19	Libra
May 13	01:07	Scorpio
May 15	05:44	Sagittarius
May 17	08:12	Capricorn
May 19	09:58	Aquarius
May 21	12:18	Pisces
May 23	16:01	Aries
May 25	09:28	Taurus
May 28	04:47	Gemini
May 30	14:13	Cancer
June 2	13:43	Leo
June 4	14:20	Virgo
June 7	02:01	Libra
June 9	10:38	Scorpio
June 11	15:23	Sagittarius
June 13	17:04	Capricorn
June 15	17:27	Aquarius
June 17	18:26	Pisces
June 19	21:26	Aries

June 22	03:03	Taurus
June 24	11:05	Gemini
June 26	17:05	Cancer
June 29	08:43	Leo
July 1	21:23	Virgo
July 4	09:43	Libra
July 6	19:33	Scorpio
July 9	01:24	Sagittarius
July 11	03:24	Capricorn
July 13	03:07	Aquarius
July 15	02:40	Pisces
July 17	04:07	Aries
July 19	08:42	Taurus
July 21	16:36	Gemini
July 24	02:59	Cancer
July 26	14:55	Leo
July 29	03:37	Virgo
July 31	16:09	Libra
Aug 3	02:57	Scorpio
Aug 5	10:19	Sagittarius
Aug 7	13:38	Capricorn
Aug 9	13:52	Aquarius
Aug 11	12:55	Pisces
Aug 13	13:00	Aries
Aug 15	15:58	Taurus
Aug 17	22:41	Gemini
Aug 20	08:45	Cancer
Aug 22	20:49	Leo
Aug 25	09:33	Virgo
Aug 27	21:54	Libra
Aug 30	08:53	Scorpio

Sep 1	17:17	Sagittarius
Sep 3	22:15	Capricorn
Sep 5	23:59	Aquarius
Sep 7	23:47	Pisces
Sep 9	23:33	Aries
Sep 12	01:17	Taurus
Sep 14	06:26	Gemini
Sep 16	15:24	Cancer
Sep 19	03:10	Leo
Sep 21	15:54	Virgo
Sep 24	03:59	Libra
Sep 26	14:29	Scorpio
Sep 28	22:50	Sagittarius
Oct 1	04:41	Capricorn
Oct 3	08:00	Aquarius
Oct 5	09:24	Pisces
Oct 7	10:07	Aries
Oct 9	11:44	Taurus
Oct 11	15:51	Gemini
Oct 13	23:30	Cancer
Oct 16	10:29	Leo
Oct 18	23:08	Virgo
Oct 21	11:12	Libra
Oct 23	21:10	Scorpio
Oct 26	04:40	Sagittarius
Oct 28	10:03	Capricorn
Oct 30	13:52	Aquarius
Nov 1	16:37	Pisces
Nov 3	18:53	Aries
Nov 5	21:33	Taurus
Nov 8	01:45	Gemini
Nov 10	08:38	Cancer

Nov 12	18:44	Leo
Nov 15	07:08	Virgo
Nov 17	19:30	Libra
Nov 20	05:31	Scorpio
Nov 22	12:19	Sagittarius
Nov 24	16:31	Capricorn
Nov 26	19:23	Aquarius
Nov 28	22:03	Pisces
Dec 1	01:14	Aries
Dec 3	05:15	Taurus
Dec 5	10:28	Gemini
Dec 7	17:34	Cancer
Dec 10	03:14	Leo
Dec 12	15:19	Virgo
Dec 15	04:05	Libra
Dec 17	14:52	Scorpio
Dec 19	21:55	Sagittarius
Dec 22	01:25	Capricorn
Dec 24	02:52	Aquarius
Dec 26	04:07	Pisces
Dec 28	06:35	Aries
Dec 30	10:56	Taurus

Year 2015

DATE	TIME	SIGN OF ZODIAC
Jan 1	17:09	Gemini
Jan 4	01:07	Cancer
Jan 6	11:03	Leo
Jan 8	22:58	Virgo
Jan 11	11:57	Libra
Jan 13	23:44	Scorpio
Jan 16	08:01	Sagittarius

Jan 18	12:04	Capricorn
Jan 20	12:59	Aquarius
Jan 22	12:48	Pisces
Jan 24	13:31	Aries
Jan 26	16:37	Taurus
Jan 28	22:36	Gemini
Jan 31	07:09	Cancer
Feb 2	17:41	Leo
Feb 5	05:46	Virgo
Feb 7	18:44	Libra
Feb 10	07:05	Scorpio
Feb 12	16:46	Sagittarius
Feb 14	22:24	Capricorn
Feb 17	12:13	Aquarius
Feb 18	23:47	Pisces
Feb 20	23:13	Aries
Feb 23	00:28	Taurus
Feb 25	04:54	Gemini
Feb 27	12:50	Cancer
Mar 1	23:34	Leo
Mar 4	11:58	Virgo
Mar 7	00:52	Libra
Mar 9	13:10	Scorpio
Mar 11	23:30	Sagittarius
Mar 14	06:40	Capricorn
Mar 16	10:14	Aquarius
Mar 18	10:58	Pisces
Mar 20	10:28	Aries
Mar 22	10:40	Taurus
Mar 24	13:22	Gemini
Mar 26	07:45	Cancer
Mar 29	05:48	Leo

Mar 31	18:12	Virgo
Apr 3	07:07	Libra
Apr 5	19:04	Scorpio
Apr 8	05:08	Sagittarius
Apr 10	12:47	Capricorn
Apr 12	17:44	Aquarius
Apr 14	20:12	Pisces
Apr 16	21:00	Aries
Apr 18	21:31	Taurus
Apr 20	23:28	Gemini
Apr 23	04:25	Cancer
Apr 25	13:13	Leo
Apr 28	01:07	Virgo
Apr 30	14:03	Libra
May 3	01:47	Scorpio
May 5	11:13	Sagittarius
May 7	18:16	Capricorn
May 9	23:22	Aquarius
May 12	02:53	Pisces
May 14	05:13	Aries
May 16	07:02	Taurus
May 18	09:27	Gemini
May 20	13:56	Cancer
May 22	21:42	Leo
May 25	08:52	Virgo
May 27	21:42	Libra
May 30	09:34	Scorpio
June 1	18:39	Sagittarius
June 4	12:50	Capricorn
June 6	05:02	Aquarius
June 8	08:16	Pisces

June 10	11:14	Aries
June 12	14:16	Taurus
June 14	17:51	Gemini
June 16	22:51	Cancer
June 19	06:22	Leo
June 21	16:59	Virgo
June 24	05:41	Libra
June 26	17:57	Scorpio
June 29	03:21	Sagittarius
July 1	09:11	Capricorn
July 3	12:21	Aquarius
July 5	14:23	Pisces
July 7	16:37	Aries
July 9	19:49	Taurus
July 12	12:16	Gemini
July 14	06:14	Cancer
July 16	14:15	Leo
July 19	12:47	Virgo
July 21	13:23	Libra
July 24	02:07	Scorpio
July 26	12:24	Sagittarius
July 28	18:47	Capricorn
July 30	21:40	Aquarius
Aug 1	22:36	Pisces
Aug 3	23:24	Aries
Aug 6	13:29	Taurus
Aug 8	05:40	Gemini
Aug 10	12:08	Cancer
Aug 12	20:52	Leo
Aug 15	07:45	Virgo
Aug 17	20:22	Libra
Aug 20	09:24	Scorpio

Aug 22	20:41	Sagittarius
Aug 25	04:22	Capricorn
Aug 27	08:03	Aquarius
Aug 29	08:51	Pisces
Aug 31	08:33	Aries
Sep 2	09:02	Taurus
Sep 4	11:48	Gemini
Sep 6	17:40	Cancer
Sep 9	02:36	Leo
Sep 11	13:55	Virgo
Sep 14	02:41	Libra
Sep 16	15:43	Scorpio
Sep 19	03:31	Sagittarius
Sep 21	12:33	Capricorn
Sep 23	17:51	Aquarius
Sep 25	19:43	Pisces
Sep 27	19:29	Aries
Sep 29	18:57	Taurus
Oct 1	20:03	Gemini
Oct 4	12:22	Cancer
Oct 6	08:31	Leo
Oct 8	19:50	Virgo
Oct 11	08:45	Libra
Oct 13	21:38	Scorpio
Oct 16	09:18	Sagittarius
Oct 18	18:52	Capricorn
Oct 21	01:38	Aquarius
Oct 23	05:18	Pisces
Oct 25	06:22	Aries
Oct 27	06:07	Taurus
Oct 29	06:24	Gemini
Oct 31	09:09	Cancer

Nov	2	15:48	Leo
Nov	5	02:22	Virgo
Nov	7	15:14	Libra
Nov	10	04:02	Scorpio
Nov	12	15:14	Sagittarius
Nov	15	00:21	Capricorn
Nov	17	07:24	Aquarius
Nov	19	12:21	Pisces
Nov	21	15:12	Aries
Nov	23	16:26	Taurus
Nov	25	17:15	Gemini
Nov	27	19:27	Cancer
Nov	30	12:47	Leo
Dec	2	10:09	Virgo
Dec	4	22:33	Libra
Dec	7	11:26	Scorpio
Dec	9	22:25	Sagittarius
Dec	12	06:46	Capricorn
Dec	14	12:59	Aquarius
Dec	16	17:45	Pisces
Dec	18	21:26	Aries
Dec	21	12:13	Taurus
Dec	23	02:31	Gemini
Dec	25	05:26	Cancer
Dec	27	10:31	Leo
Dec	29	18:58	Virgo

Year 2016

DATE		TIME	SIGN OF ZODIAC
Jan	1	06:41	Libra
Jan	3	19:36	Scorpio
Jan	6	06:56	Sagittarius

Jan 8	15:07	Capricorn
Jan 10	20:22	Aquarius
Jan 12	23:53	Pisces
Jan 15	02:48	Aries
Jan 17	05:48	Taurus
Jan 19	09:13	Gemini
Jan 21	13:28	Cancer
Jan 23	07:21	Leo
Jan 26	03:46	Virgo
Jan 28	14:59	Libra
Jan 31	03:50	Scorpio
Feb 2	15:50	Sagittarius
Feb 5	00:44	Capricorn
Feb 7	05:59	Aquarius
Feb 9	08:31	Pisces
Feb 11	09:55	Aries
Feb 13	11:35	Taurus
Feb 15	14:34	Gemini
Feb 17	19:24	Cancer
Feb 20	02:17	Leo
Feb 22	11:24	Virgo
Feb 24	22:41	Libra
Feb 27	11:26	Scorpio
Feb 29	23:56	Sagittarius
Mar 3	10:01	Capricorn
Mar 5	16:22	Aquarius
Mar 7	19:08	Pisces
Mar 9	19:40	Aries
Mar 11	19:44	Taurus
Mar 13	21:03	Gemini
Mar 16	00:56	Cancer
Mar 18	07:54	Leo

Mar 20	17:39	Virgo
Mar 23	05:23	Libra
Mar 25	18:09	Scorpio
Mar 28	06:46	Sagittarius
Mar 30	17:45	Capricorn
Apr 2	01:37	Aquarius
Apr 4	05:45	Pisces
Apr 6	06:46	Aries
Apr 8	06:10	Taurus
Apr 10	05:59	Gemini
Apr 12	08:06	Cancer
Apr 14	13:53	Leo
Apr 16	23:23	Virgo
Apr 19	11:24	Libra
Apr 22	00:17	Scorpio
Apr 24	12:46	Sagittarius
Apr 26	23:54	Capricorn
Apr 29	08:47	Aquarius
May 1	14:33	Pisces
May 3	17:04	Aries
May 5	17:10	Taurus
May 7	16:34	Gemini
May 9	17:24	Cancer
May 11	21:32	Leo
May 14	05:52	Virgo
May 16	17:33	Libra
May 19	06:29	Scorpio
May 21	18:48	Sagittarius
May 24	05:34	Capricorn
May 26	14:27	Aquarius
May 28	21:06	Pisces
May 31	01:09	Aries

June 2	02:46	Taurus
June 4	03:01	Gemini
June 6	03:41	Cancer
June 8	06:47	Leo
June 10	13:45	Virgo
June 13	00:33	Libra
June 15	13:18	Scorpio
June 18	01:34	Sagittarius
June 20	11:55	Capricorn
June 22	20:08	Aquarius
June 25	02:30	Pisces
June 27	07:08	Aries
June 29	10:03	Taurus
July 1	11:44	Gemini
July 3	13:20	Cancer
July 5	16:28	Leo
July 7	22:41	Virgo
July 10	08:32	Libra
July 12	20:52	Scorpio
July 15	09:14	Sagittarius
July 17	19:33	Capricorn
July 20	03:10	Aquarius
July 22	08:35	Pisces
July 24	12:33	Aries
July 26	15:37	Taurus
July 28	18:17	Gemini
July 30	21:09	Cancer
Aug 2	01:12	Leo
Aug 4	07:34	Virgo
Aug 6	16:56	Libra
Aug 9	04:51	Scorpio
Aug 11	17:24	Sagittarius

Aug 14	04:11	Capricorn
Aug 16	11:52	Aquarius
Aug 18	16:34	Pisces
Aug 20	19:18	Aries
Aug 22	21:19	Taurus
Aug 24	23:40	Gemini
Aug 27	03:06	Cancer
Aug 29	08:11	Leo
Aug 31	15:22	Virgo
Sep 3	00:55	Libra
Sep 5	23:38	Scorpio
Sep 8	01:20	Sagittarius
Sep 10	12:55	Capricorn
Sep 12	21:28	Aquarius
Sep 15	02:23	Pisces
Sep 17	04:22	Aries
Sep 19	04:58	Taurus
Sep 21	05:53	Gemini
Sep 23	08:33	Cancer
Sep 25	13:48	Leo
Sep 27	21:43	Virgo
Sep 30	07:52	Libra
Oct 2	19:43	Scorpio
Oct 5	08:26	Sagittarius
Oct 7	20:40	Capricorn
Oct 10	06:33	Aquarius
Oct 12	12:43	Pisces
Oct 14	15:08	Aries
Oct 16	15:04	Taurus
Oct 18	14:30	Gemini
Oct 20	15:28	Cancer
Oct 22	19:34	Leo

Oct 25	03:16	Virgo
Oct 27	13:51	Libra
Oct 30	02:01	Scorpio
Nov 1	14:43	Sagittarius
Nov 4	15:05	Capricorn
Nov 6	13:55	Aquarius
Nov 8	21:45	Pisces
Nov 11	13:45	Aries
Nov 13	02:24	Taurus
Nov 15	01:23	Gemini
Nov 17	00:57	Cancer
Nov 19	03:14	Leo
Nov 21	09:34	Virgo
Nov 23	19:42	Libra
Nov 26	08:01	Scorpio
Nov 28	20:46	Sagittarius
Dec 1	08:52	Capricorn
Dec 3	19:44	Aquarius
Dec 6	04:31	Pisces
Dec 8	10:15	Aries
Dec 10	12:41	Taurus
Dec 12	12:41	Gemini
Dec 14	12:08	Cancer
Dec 16	13:15	Leo
Dec 18	17:52	Virgo
Dec 21	02:39	Libra
Dec 23	14:32	Scorpio
Dec 26	03:19	Sagittarius
Dec 28	15:12	Capricorn
Dec 31	01:29	Aquarius

Year 2017

DATE	TIME	SIGN OF ZODIAC
Jan 2	09:57	Pisces
Jan 4	16:20	Aries
Jan 6	20:18	Taurus
Jan 8	22:06	Gemini
Jan 10	22:49	Cancer
Jan 13	00:08	Leo
Jan 15	03:52	Virgo
Jan 17	11:16	Libra
Jan 19	22:09	Scorpio
Jan 22	10:45	Sagittarius
Jan 24	22:43	Capricorn
Jan 27	08:36	Aquarius
Jan 29	16:10	Pisces
Jan 31	21:46	Aries
Feb 3	01:50	Taurus
Feb 5	04:44	Gemini
Feb 7	07:03	Cancer
Feb 9	09:41	Leo
Feb 11	13:52	Virgo
Feb 13	20:43	Libra
Feb 16	06:41	Scorpio
Feb 18	18:52	Sagittarius
Feb 21	07:08	Capricorn
Feb 23	17:17	Aquarius
Feb 26	00:24	Pisces
Feb 28	04:52	Aries
Mar 2	07:42	Taurus
Mar 4	10:05	Gemini
Mar 6	12:54	Cancer

Mar 8	16:45	Leo
Mar 10	22:07	Virgo
Mar 13	05:28	Libra
Mar 15	15:11	Scorpio
Mar 18	03:00	Sagittarius
Mar 20	15:31	Capricorn
Mar 23	02:28	Aquarius
Mar 25	10:06	Pisces
Mar 27	14:11	Aries
Mar 29	15:48	Taurus
Mar 31	16:40	Gemini
Apr 2	18:27	Cancer
Apr 4	22:13	Leo
Apr 7	04:20	Virgo
Apr 9	12:34	Libra
Apr 11	22:41	Scorpio
Apr 14	10:27	Sagittarius
Apr 16	23:04	Capricorn
Apr 19	10:52	Aquarius
Apr 21	19:43	Pisces
Apr 24	12:32	Aries
Apr 26	13:56	Taurus
Apr 28	13:39	Gemini
Apr 30	01:48	Cancer
May 2	04:12	Leo
May 4	09:46	Virgo
May 6	18:20	Libra
May 9	05:00	Scorpio
May 11	16:59	Sagittarius
May 14	05:37	Capricorn
May 16	17:50	Aquarius
May 19	03:52	Pisces

May 21	10:10	Aries
May 23	12:33	Taurus
May 25	12:15	Gemini
May 27	11:24	Cancer
May 29	12:12	Leo
May 31	16:16	Virgo
June 3	00:04	Libra
June 5	10:46	Scorpio
June 7	22:59	Sagittarius
June 10	11:36	Capricorn
June 12	23:45	Aquarius
June 15	10:17	Pisces
June 17	17:55	Aries
June 19	21:53	Taurus
June 21	22:44	Gemini
June 23	22:07	Cancer
June 25	22:06	Leo
June 28	12:41	Virgo
June 30	07:02	Libra
July 2	16:59	Scorpio
July 5	05:08	Sagittarius
July 7	17:44	Capricorn
July 10	05:35	Aquarius
July 12	15:51	Pisces
July 14	23:52	Aries
July 17	05:04	Taurus
July 19	07:31	Gemini
July 21	08:09	Cancer
July 23	08:33	Leo
July 25	10:32	Virgo
July 27	15:37	Libra
July 30	00:23	Scorpio

Aug 1	12:01	Sagittarius
Aug 4	00:36	Capricorn
Aug 6	12:15	Aquarius
Aug 8	21:56	Pisces
Aug 11	05:22	Aries
Aug 13	10:40	Taurus
Aug 15	14:06	Gemini
Aug 17	16:13	Cancer
Aug 19	17:55	Leo
Aug 21	20:25	Virgo
Aug 24	01:04	Libra
Aug 26	08:53	Scorpio
Aug 28	19:47	Sagittarius
Aug 31	08:18	Capricorn
Sep 2	20:06	Aquarius
Sep 5	05:28	Pisces
Sep 7	12:01	Aries
Sep 9	16:22	Taurus
Sep 11	19:29	Gemini
Sep 13	22:12	Cancer
Sep 16	01:09	Leo
Sep 18	04:52	Virgo
Sep 20	10:06	Libra
Sep 22	17:40	Scorpio
Sep 25	04:01	Sagittarius
Sep 27	16:24	Capricorn
Sep 30	04:40	Aquarius
Oct 2	14:26	Pisces
Oct 4	20:40	Aries
Oct 6	23:56	Taurus
Oct 9	01:44	Gemini
Oct 11	03:38	Cancer

Oct 13	06:41	Leo
Oct 15	11:19	Virgo
Oct 17	17:35	Libra
Oct 20	01:41	Scorpio
Oct 22	11:57	Sagittarius
Oct 25	00:12	Capricorn
Oct 27	12:59	Aquarius
Oct 29	23:46	Pisces
Nov 1	06:43	Aries
Nov 3	09:46	Taurus
Nov 5	10:26	Gemini
Nov 7	10:44	Cancer
Nov 9	12:29	Leo
Nov 11	16:41	Virgo
Nov 13	23:26	Libra
Nov 16	08:19	Scorpio
Nov 18	18:59	Sagittarius
Nov 21	07:14	Capricorn
Nov 23	20:14	Aquarius
Nov 26	08:04	Pisces
Nov 28	16:30	Aries
Nov 30	20:38	Taurus
Dec 2	21:21	Gemini
Dec 4	20:37	Cancer
Dec 6	20:37	Leo
Dec 8	23:08	Virgo
Dec 11	05:01	Libra
Dec 13	13:59	Scorpio
Dec 16	01:07	Sagittarius
Dec 18	13:33	Capricorn
Dec 21	02:29	Aquarius
Dec 23	14:42	Pisces

Dec 26	00:27	Aries
Dec 28	06:23	Taurus
Dec 30	08:31	Gemini

Year 2018

DATE	TIME	SIGN OF ZODIAC
Jan 1	08:10	Cancer
Jan 3	07:22	Leo
Jan 5	08:12	Virgo
Jan 7	12:14	Libra
Jan 9	20:05	Scorpio
Jan 12	07:04	Sagittarius
Jan 14	19:42	Capricorn
Jan 17	08:32	Aquarius
Jan 19	20:26	Pisces
Jan 22	06:27	Aries
Jan 24	13:39	Taurus
Jan 26	17:39	Gemini
Jan 28	18:57	Cancer
Jan 30	18:53	Leo
Feb 1	1913	Virgo
Feb 3	21:47	Libra
Feb 6	03:56	Scorpio
Feb 8	13:53	Sagittarius
Feb 11	02:21	Capricorn
Feb 13	15:11	Aquarius
Feb 16	02:41	Pisces
Feb 18	12:04	Aries
Feb 20	19:12	Taurus
Feb 23	00:07	Gemini
Feb 25	03:06	Cancer
Feb 27	04:42	Leo

Mar 1	05:57	Virgo
Mar 3	08:20	Libra
Mar 5	13:23	Scorpio
Mar 7	22:03	Sagittarius
Mar 10	09:52	Capricorn
Mar 12	22:44	Aquarius
Mar 15	10:12	Pisces
Mar 17	18:57	Aries
Mar 20	01:07	Taurus
Mar 22	05:30	Gemini
Mar 24	08:53	Cancer
Mar 26	11:45	Leo
Mar 28	14:30	Virgo
Mar 30	17:52	Libra
Apr 1	22:57	Scorpio
Apr 4	06:55	Sagittarius
Apr 6	18:01	Capricorn
Apr 9	06:50	Aquarius
Apr 11	18:40	Pisces
Apr 14	03:25	Aries
Apr 16	08:51	Taurus
Apr 18	12:02	Gemini
Apr 20	14:26	Cancer
Apr 22	17:09	Leo
Apr 24	20:40	Virgo
Apr 27	13:13	Libra
Apr 29	07:11	Scorpio
May 1	15:19	Sagittarius
May 4	02:06	Capricorn
May 6	14:48	Aquarius
May 9	03:11	Pisces
May 11	12:40	Aries

May 13	18:15	Taurus
May 15	20:43	Gemini
May 17	21:47	Cancer
May 19	22:10	Leo
May 22	02:03	Virgo
May 24	06:52	Libra
May 26	13:39	Scorpio
May 28	22:29	Sagittarius
May 31	09:26	Capricorn
June 2	22:06	Aquarius
June 5	10:53	Pisces
June 7	21:26	Aries
June 10	04:04	Taurus
June 12	06:53	Gemini
June 14	07:20	Cancer
June 16	07:20	Leo
June 18	08:40	Virgo
June 20	12:29	Libra
June 22	19:10	Scorpio
June 25	04:29	Sagittarius
June 27	15:52	Capricorn
June 30	04:37	Aquarius
July 2	17:31	Pisces
July 5	04:49	Aries
July 7	12:51	Taurus
July 9	16:58	Gemini
July 11	17:58	Cancer
July 13	17:31	Leo
July 15	17:31	Virgo
July 17	19:42	Libra
July 20	01:13	Scorpio
July 22	10:12	Sagittarius

July 24	21:48	Capricorn
July 27	10:41	Aquarius
July 29	23:28	Pisces
Aug 1	10:54	Aries
Aug 3	19:51	Taurus
Aug 6	01:32	Gemini
Aug 8	04:01	Cancer
Aug 10	04:17	Leo
Aug 12	03:59	Virgo
Aug 14	04:57	Libra
Aug 16	08:54	Scorpio
Aug 18	16:45	Sagittarius
Aug 21	04:00	Capricorn
Aug 23	16:55	Aquarius
Aug 26	05:32	Pisces
Aug 28	16:35	Aries
Aug 31	01:30	Taurus
Sep 2	8:01	Gemini
Sep 4	12:03	Cancer
Sep 6	13:54	Leo
Sep 8	14:29	Virgo
Sep 10	15:20	Libra
Sep 12	18:15	Scorpio
Sep 15	00:45	Sagittarius
Sep 17	11:07	Capricorn
Sep 19	23:51	Aquarius
Sep 22	12:27	Pisces
Sep 24	23:03	Aries
Sep 27	07:15	Taurus
Sep 29	13:26	Gemini
Oct 1	18:00	Cancer

Oct 3	21:12	Leo
Oct 5	23:19	Virgo
Oct 8	01:10	Libra
Oct 10	04:09	Scorpio
Oct 12	09:53	Sagittarius
Oct 14	19:17	Capricorn
Oct 17	07:36	Aquarius
Oct 19	20:20	Pisces
Oct 22	06:58	Aries
Oct 24	14:33	Taurus
Oct 26	19:41	Gemini
Oct 28	23:27	Cancer
Oct 31	02:42	Leo
Nov 2	05:47	Virgo
Nov 4	09:01	Libra
Nov 6	13:02	Scorpio
Nov 8	18:59	Sagittarius
Nov 11	03:54	Capricorn
Nov 13	15:45	Aquarius
Nov 16	04:41	Pisces
Nov 18	15:56	Aries
Nov 20	23:43	Taurus
Nov 23	04:10	Gemini
Nov 25	06:38	Cancer
Nov 27	08:35	Leo
Nov 29	11:08	Virgo
Dec 1	14:49	Libra
Dec 3	19:55	Scorpio
Dec 6	02:49	Sagittarius
Dec 8	12:01	Capricorn
Dec 10	23:39	Aquarius
Dec 13	12:40	Pisces

Dec 16	00:44	Aries
Dec 18	09:37	Taurus
Dec 20	14:34	Gemini
Dec 22	16:28	Cancer
Dec 24	16:58	Leo
Dec 26	17:50	Virgo
Dec 28	20:23	Libra
Dec 31	01:23	Scorpio

Year 2019

DATE	TIME	SIGN OF ZODIAC
Jan 2	08:58	Sagittarius
Jan 4	18:55	Capricorn
Jan 7	06:46	Aquarius
Jan 9	19:44	Pisces
Jan 12	08:18	Aries
Jan 14	18:31	Taurus
Jan 17	01:00	Gemini
Jan 19	03:44	Cancer
Jan 21	03:54	Leo
Jan 23	03:22	Virgo
Jan 25	04:02	Libra
Jan 27	07:31	Scorpio
Jan 29	14:33	Sagittarius
Feb 1	12:47	Capricorn
Feb 3	13:03	Aquarius
Feb 6	02:02	Pisces
Feb 8	14:34	Aries
Feb 11	01:28	Taurus
Feb 13	09:32	Gemini
Feb 15	14:03	Cancer
Feb 17	15:21	Leo

Feb 19	14:47	Virgo
Feb 21	14:17	Libra
Feb 23	15:56	Scorpio
Feb 25	21:19	Sagittarius
Feb 28	06:48	Capricorn
Mar 2	19:06	Aquarius
Mar 5	08:11	Pisces
Mar 7	20:27	Aries
Mar 10	07:10	Taurus
Mar 12	15:48	Gemini
Mar 14	21:49	Cancer
Mar 17	00:57	Leo
Mar 19	01:41	Virgo
Mar 21	01:28	Libra
Mar 23	02:16	Scorpio
Mar 25	06:06	Sagittarius
Mar 27	14:07	Capricorn
Mar 30	01:46	Aquarius
Apr 1	14:48	Pisces
Apr 4	02:56	Aries
Apr 6	13:06	Taurus
Apr 8	21:15	Gemini
Apr 11	03:31	Cancer
Apr 13	07:50	Leo
Apr 15	10:14	Virgo
Apr 17	11:22	Libra
Apr 19	12:40	Scorpio
Apr 21	15:59	Sagittarius
Apr 23	22:50	Capricorn
Apr 26	09:27	Aquarius
Apr 28	22:11	Pisces

May 1	10:24	Aries
May 3	20:18	Taurus
May 6	03:40	Gemini
May 8	09:06	Cancer
May 10	13:14	Leo
May 12	16:22	Virgo
May 14	18:51	Libra
May 16	21:26	Scorpio
May 19	01:21	Sagittarius
May 21	07:56	Capricorn
May 23	17:49	Aquarius
May 26	06:07	Pisces
May 28	18:32	Aries
May 31	04:43	Taurus

June 2	11:48	Gemini
June 4	16:17	Cancer
June 6	19:16	Leo
June 8	21:45	Virgo
June 11	00:29	Libra
June 13	04:02	Scorpio
June 15	09:03	Sagittarius
June 17	16:13	Capricorn
June 20	02:00	Aquarius
June 22	14:01	Pisces
June 25	02:38	Aries
June 27	13:32	Taurus
June 29	21:09	Gemini

July 2	01:24	Cancer
July 4	03:19	Leo
July 6	04:25	Virgo
July 8	06:07	Libra
July 10	09:28	Scorpio

July 12	15:05	Sagittarius
July 14	23:05	Capricorn
July 17	09:19	Aquarius
July 19	21:19	Pisces
July 22	10:02	Aries
July 24	21:42	Taurus
July 27	18:29	Gemini
July 29	11:31	Cancer
July 31	13:18	Leo
Aug 2	13:20	Virgo
Aug 4	13:30	Libra
Aug 6	15:31	Scorpio
Aug 8	20:35	Sagittarius
Aug 11	04:50	Capricorn
Aug 13	15:35	Aquarius
Aug 16	03:49	Pisces
Aug 18	16:33	Aries
Aug 21	04:37	Taurus
Aug 23	14:34	Gemini
Aug 25	21:05	Cancer
Aug 27	23:53	Leo
Aug 29	23:57	Virgo
Aug 31	23:08	Libra
Sep 2	23:35	Scorpio
Sep 5	03:08	Sagittarius
Sep 7	10:37	Capricorn
Sep 9	21:24	Aquarius
Sep 12	09:51	Pisces
Sep 14	22:32	Aries
Sep 17	10:31	Taurus
Sep 19	20:58	Gemini
Sep 22	04:50	Cancer

Sep 24	09:19	Leo
Sep 26	10:37	Virgo
Sep 28	10:03	Libra
Sep 30	09:42	Scorpio
Oct 2	11:44	Sagittarius
Oct 4	17:43	Capricorn
Oct 7	03:42	Aquarius
Oct 9	16:05	Pisces
Oct 12	04:46	Aries
Oct 14	16:24	Taurus
Oct 17	02:30	Gemini
Oct 19	10:43	Cancer
Oct 21	16:28	Leo
Oct 23	19:29	Virgo
Oct 25	20:20	Libra
Oct 27	20:29	Scorpio
Oct 29	21:58	Sagittarius
Nov 1	02:38	Capricorn
Nov 3	11:19	Aquarius
Nov 5	23:08	Pisces
Nov 8	11:49	Aries
Nov 10	23:18	Taurus
Nov 13	08:46	Gemini
Nov 15	16:15	Cancer
Nov 17	21:57	Leo
Nov 20	01:54	Virgo
Nov 22	04:19	Libra
Nov 24	05:58	Scorpio
Nov 26	08:11	Sagittarius
Nov 28	12:32	Capricorn
Nov 30	20:13	Aquarius

Dec 3	07:10	Pisces
Dec 5	19:44	Aries
Dec 8	07:29	Taurus
Dec 10	16:47	Gemini
Dec 12	23:23	Cancer
Dec 15	03:56	Leo
Dec 17	07:16	Virgo
Dec 19	10:04	Libra
Dec 21	12:57	Scorpio
Dec 23	16:34	Sagittarius
Dec 25	21:45	Capricorn
Dec 28	05:20	Aquarius
Dec 30	15:41	Pisces

Year 2020

DATE	TIME	SIGN OF ZODIAC
Jan 2	04:00	Aries
Jan 4	16:15	Taurus
Jan 7	02:11	Gemini
Jan 9	08:43	Cancer
Jan 11	12:16	Leo
Jan 13	14:06	Virgo
Jan 15	15:43	Libra
Jan 17	18:20	Scorpio
Jan 19	22:41	Sagittarius
Jan 22	05:00	Capricorn
Jan 24	13:20	Aquarius
Jan 26	23:44	Pisces
Jan 29	11:50	Aries
Feb 1	00:28	Taurus
Feb 3	11:29	Gemini
Feb 5	19:03	Cancer

Feb 7	22:45	Leo
Feb 9	23:39	Virgo
Feb 11	23:37	Libra
Feb 14	00:37	Scorpio
Feb 16	04:07	Sagittarius
Feb 18	10:37	Capricorn
Feb 20	19:42	Aquarius
Feb 23	06:37	Pisces
Feb 25	18:47	Aries
Feb 28	07:30	Taurus

Mar 1	19:21	Gemini
Mar 4	04:25	Cancer
Mar 6	09:27	Leo
Mar 8	00:47	Virgo
Mar 10	10:03	Libra
Mar 12	09:28	Scorpio
Mar 14	11:09	Sagittarius
Mar 16	16:25	Capricorn
Mar 19	01:16	Aquarius
Mar 21	12:33	Pisces
Mar 24	00:58	Aries
Mar 26	13:37	Taurus
Mar 29	01:38	Gemini
Mar 31	11:43	Cancer

Apr 2	18:26	Leo
Apr 4	21:18	Virgo
Apr 6	21:16	Libra
Apr 8	20:17	Scorpio
Apr 10	20:35	Sagittarius
Apr 13	00:05	Capricorn
Apr 15	07:37	Aquarius
Apr 17	18:29	Pisces

Apr 20	07:00	Aries
Apr 22	19:36	Taurus
Apr 25	07:20	Gemini
Apr 27	17:28	Cancer
Apr 30	01:06	Leo
May 2	05:35	Virgo
May 4	07:09	Libra
May 6	07:05	Scorpio
May 8	07:15	Sagittarius
May 10	09:38	Capricorn
May 12	15:38	Aquarius
May 15	01:24	Pisces
May 17	13:36	Aries
May 20	02:10	Taurus
May 22	13:36	Gemini
May 24	23:09	Cancer
May 27	06:33	Leo
May 29	11:40	Virgo
May 31	14:38	Libra
June 2	16:05	Scorpio
June 4	17:17	Sagittarius
June 6	19:44	Capricorn
June 9	00:54	Aquarius
June 11	09:31	Pisces
June 13	21:03	Aries
June 16	09:35	Taurus
June 18	21:00	Gemini
June 21	06:02	Cancer
June 23	12:33	Leo
June 25	17:05	Virgo
June 27	20:16	Libra
June 29	22:47	Scorpio

July 2	01:21	Sagittarius
July 4	04:48	Capricorn
July 6	10:08	Aquarius
July 8	18:12	Pisces
July 11	05:06	Aries
July 13	17:34	Taurus
July 16	05:19	Gemini
July 18	14:24	Cancer
July 20	20:16	Leo
July 22	23:40	Virgo
July 25	01:53	Libra
July 27	04:12	Scorpio
July 29	07:25	Sagittarius
July 31	11:58	Capricorn
Aug 2	18:11	Aquarius
Aug 5	02:27	Pisces
Aug 7	13:04	Aries
Aug 10	01:28	Taurus
Aug 12	13:46	Gemini
Aug 14	23:35	Cancer
Aug 17	05:38	Leo
Aug 19	08:20	Virgo
Aug 21	09:16	Libra
Aug 23	10:16	Scorpio
Aug 25	12:49	Sagittarius
Aug 27	17:37	Capricorn
Aug 30	00:37	Aquarius
Sep 1	09:34	Pisces
Sep 3	20:22	Aries
Sep 6	08:43	Taurus
Sep 8	21:27	Gemini
Sep 11	08:23	Cancer

Sep 13	15:32	Leo
Sep 15	18:37	Virgo
Sep 17	18:56	Libra
Sep 19	18:33	Scorpio
Sep 21	19:31	Sagittarius
Sep 23	23:16	Capricorn
Sep 26	06:08	Aquarius
Sep 28	15:34	Pisces
Oct 1	02:47	Aries
Oct 3	15:12	Taurus
Oct 6	04:02	Gemini
Oct 8	15:45	Cancer
Oct 11	12:24	Leo
Oct 13	04:56	Virgo
Oct 15	05:54	Libra
Oct 17	05:05	Scorpio
Oct 19	04:43	Sagittarius
Oct 21	06:43	Capricorn
Oct 23	12:17	Aquarius
Oct 25	21:18	Pisces
Oct 28	08:44	Aries
Oct 30	21:19	Taurus
Nov 2	09:59	Gemini
Nov 4	21:45	Cancer
Nov 7	07:18	Leo
Nov 9	13:30	Virgo
Nov 11	16:09	Libra
Nov 13	16:19	Scorpio
Nov 15	15:47	Sagittarius
Nov 17	16:34	Capricorn
Nov 19	20:25	Aquarius
Nov 22	04:06	Pisces

Nov 24	15:05	Aries
Nov 27	03:43	Taurus
Nov 29	16:16	Gemini
Dec 2	03:33	Cancer
Dec 4	12:53	Leo
Dec 6	19:46	Virgo
Dec 9	00:01	Libra
Dec 11	01:58	Scorpio
Dec 13	02:39	Sagittarius
Dec 15	03:35	Capricorn
Dec 17	06:27	Aquarius
Dec 19	12:39	Pisces
Dec 21	22:32	Aries
Dec 24	10:55	Taurus
Dec 26	23:32	Gemini
Dec 29	10:28	Cancer
Dec 31	18:58	Leo

APPENDIX II

YOUR BABY'S RISING SIGN

The following gives an approximation of your baby's Rising sign. This is normally a fairly complex calculation. Look up the month in which she was born, then find the time, and you will see the particular Rising sign. Note that if she is born toward the end of the month, the Rising sign may well have moved to the next sign. I must stress that this is only an approximate guide. For this reason, you should check out the Rising signs on either side and see which seems to best fit your child. Even better, you can obtain a free chart wheel for your baby on my web site www.chrissieblaze.com, in the Reports section to get the correct Rising sign. Alternatively, for an accurate birth chart, contact me or another professional astrologer.

JANUARY

12:25 a.m.	Libra
3:00 a.m.	Scorpio
5:30 a.m.	Sagittarius
7:40 a.m.	Capricorn
9:20 a.m.	Aquarius
10:40 a.m.	Pisces
11:50 a.m.	Aries
1:05 p.m.	Taurus
2:40 p.m.	Gemini
5:00 p.m.	Cancer
7:25 p.m.	Leo
10:00 p.m.	Virgo

FEBRUARY

1:00 a.m.	Scorpio
3:30 a.m.	Sagittarius
5:45 a.m.	Capricorn
7:15 a.m.	Aquarius
8:40 a.m.	Pisces
9:50 a.m.	Aries
11:05 a.m.	Taurus
12:45 p.m.	Gemini
3:00 p.m.	Cancer
5:20 p.m.	Leo
8:00 p.m.	Virgo
10:25 p.m.	Libra

MARCH

6:40 a.m.	Pisces
7:50 a.m.	Aries
9:25 a.m.	Taurus

10:45 a.m.	Gemini		7:05 p.m.	Scorpio
12:55 p.m.	Cancer		9:30 p.m.	Sagittarius
3:25 p.m.	Leo		11:45 p.m.	Capricorn
6:00 p.m.	Virgo			
8:25 p.m.	Libra		**JUNE**	
10:55 p.m.	Scorpio		12:40 a.m.	Pisces
1:25 a.m.	Sagittarius		1:50 a.m.	Aries
3:45 a.m.	Capricorn		3:05 a.m.	Taurus
5:20 a.m.	Aquarius		4:50 a.m.	Gemini
			7:00 a.m.	Cancer
APRIL			9:25 a.m.	Leo
1:45 a.m.	Capricorn		11:55 a.m.	Virgo
3:20 a.m.	Aquarius		2:25 p.m.	Libra
4:40 a.m.	Pisces		4:55 p.m.	Scorpio
5:55 a.m.	Aries		7:25 p.m.	Sagittarius
7:10 a.m.	Taurus		9:45 p.m.	Capricorn
8:50 a.m.	Gemini		11:20 p.m.	Aquarius
10:55 a.m.	Cancer			
1:20 p.m.	Leo		**JULY**	
4:05 p.m.	Virgo		1:05 a.m.	Taurus
6:20 p.m.	Libra		2:45 a.m.	Gemini
9:05 p.m.	Scorpio		5:10 a.m.	Cancer
11:30 p.m.	Sagittarius		7:25 a.m.	Leo
			10:00 a.m.	Virgo
MAY			12:25 p.m.	Libra
1:20 a.m.	Aquarius		3:05 p.m.	Scorpio
2:40 a.m.	Pisces		5:30 p.m.	Sagittarius
3:55 a.m.	Aries		7:45 p.m.	Capricorn
5:05 a.m.	Taurus		9:20 p.m.	Aquarius
6:45 a.m.	Gemini		10:40 p.m.	Pisces
9:00 a.m.	Cancer		11:50 p.m.	Aries
11:25 a.m.	Leo			
2:00 p.m.	Virgo		**AUGUST**	
4:25 p.m.	Libra		12:45 a.m.	Gemini

3:00 a.m.	Cancer		4:40 p.m.	Pisces
5:25 a.m.	Leo		5:50 p.m.	Aries
8:00 a.m.	Virgo		7:05 p.m.	Taurus
10:25 a.m.	Libra		8:55 p.m.	Gemini
12:55 p.m.	Scorpio		10:55 p.m.	Cancer
3:40 p.m.	Sagittarius			
5:45 p.m.	Capricorn		**NOVEMBER**	
7:20 p.m.	Aquarius		1:55 a.m.	Virgo
8:40 p.m.	Pisces		4:20 a.m.	Libra
9:55 p.m.	Aries		6:55 a.m.	Scorpio
11:05 p.m.	Taurus		9:35 a.m.	Sagittarius
			11:40 a.m.	Capricorn
SEPTEMBER			1:20 p.m.	Aquarius
1:10 a.m.	Cancer		2:35 p.m.	Pisces
3:25 a.m.	Leo		3:40 p.m.	Aries
5:55 a.m.	Virgo		5:15 p.m.	Taurus
8:25 a.m.	Libra		6:45 p.m.	Gemini
11:05 a.m.	Scorpio		9:10 p.m.	Cancer
1:30 p.m.	Sagittarius		11:25 p.m.	Leo
3:45 p.m.	Capricorn			
5:15 p.m.	Aquarius		**DECEMBER**	
6:40 p.m.	Pisces		12:00 a.m.	Virgo
7:50 p.m.	Aries		2:25 a.m.	Libra
9:00 p.m.	Taurus		4:55 a.m.	Scorpio
10:55 p.m.	Gemini		7:30 a.m.	Sagittarius
			9:45 a.m.	Capricorn
OCTOBER			11:20 a.m.	Aquarius
1:20 a.m.	Leo		12:35 p.m.	Pisces
4:10 a.m.	Virgo		1:45 p.m.	Aries
6:25 a.m.	Libra		3:00 p.m.	Taurus
8:55 a.m.	Scorpio		4:40 p.m.	Gemini
11:30 a.m.	Sagittarius		6:55 p.m.	Cancer
1:45 p.m.	Capricorn		9:35 p.m.	Leo
3:20 p.m.	Aquarius			

APPENDIX III

Your Baby's Nodes

2000 – 2020

DATE	NORTH NODE	SOUTH NODE
January 1, 2000 – April 5, 2000	Leo	Aquarius
April 6, 2000 – October 24, 2001	Cancer	Capricorn
October 25, 2001 – May 13, 2003	Gemini	Sagittarius
May 14, 2003 – December 26, 2004	Taurus	Scorpio
December 27, 2004 – June 22, 2006	Aries	Libra
June 23, 2006 – January 7, 2008	Pisces	Virgo
January 8, 2008 – July 27, 2009	Aquarius	Leo
July 28, 2009 – February 13, 2011	Capricorn	Cancer
February 14, 2011 – September 2, 2012	Sagittarius	Gemini
September 3, 2012 – March 22, 2014	Scorpio	Taurus
March 23, 2014 – October 10, 2015	Libra	Aries
October 11, 2015 – April 28, 2017	Virgo	Pisces
April 29, 2017 - November 16, 2018	Leo	Aquarius
November 17, 2018 - June 4, 2020	Cancer	Capricorn
June 5, 2020 – December 31, 2020	Gemini	Sagittarius

BIBLIOGRAPHY

Abadie, M.J. *Child Astrology: A Guide for Nurturing Your Child's Natural Abilities.* Destiny Books, Vermont, 1999.

Blaze, Chrissie. *Workout for the Soul: 8 Steps to Inner Fitness.* Aslan Publishing, CT, 2001.

Carroll, Lee and Jan Tober. *The Indigo Children.* Hay House, Carlsbad, California, 1999.

Choquette, Sonia, Ph.D. *The Wise Child.* Three Rivers Press, New York, 1999.

King, George and Richard Lawrence. *Realize Your Inner Potential.* The Aetherius Press, Los Angeles, 1996.

King, George. *Karma and Reincarnation.* The Aetherius Press, Los Angeles, 1985.

Lawrence, Richard. *The Little Book of Karma.* Thorsons Press, London, U.K., 2001.

Lawrence, Richard. *The Magic of Healing. How to Heal by Combining Yoga Practices with the Latest Spiritual Techniques.* Thorsons Press, London, U.K., 2002.

Lawrence, Richard. *Unlock Your Psychic Powers.* O Books,

Levine, Barbara Hoberman. *Your Body Believes Every Word You Say.* WordsWork Press, Fairfield, CT, 2000.

Salter, Joan. *The Incarnating Child.* Hawthorn Press, 1990.

Shroder, Tom. *Old Souls.* A Fireside Book, Simon & Schuster, Inc., New York, 1999.

Star, Gloria. *Optimum Child.* Llewellyn Publications, St. David's, MN, 1988.

Stern, Daniel N., M.D. *Diary of a Baby.* Basic Books, New York, 1990.

Weiss, Brian L., M.D. *Many Lives, Many Masters.* A Fireside Book, Simon & Schuster, Inc., New York, 1988.

RESOURCES

Visit www.chrissieblaze.com to obtain free in-depth monthly horoscopes, information about baby horoscope consultations with the author, and more.

NOTES

[1] In order to obtain an accurate birth chart, the exact time, date of birth, and location are required.

[2] *Embryology and World Evolution*, a series of lectures given by Dr. Karl Konig between October 15, 1965, and March 13, 1966.

[3] *Our Babies Ourselves: How Biology & Culture Shape the Way We Parent*, Meredith Small, Dell Publishing Company, 1999.

[4] To obtain a free astrological chartwheel giving the positions of all the planets, see the Resource Guide at the back of this book, or visit www.chrissieblaze.com.

[5] Although there will be similarities in temperament for two people born on the same day, the Rising sign is what we display to the world. Because the rising sign changes about every two hours, even a few hours' difference can make one person appear to be very different from another.

[6] Your child's Sun sign is a lot more than that, though it describes the way she expresses her inner self, the fundamental way she approaches life.

[7] Sixty to seventy percent of an adult's body weight is water.

[8] Bear in mind that this book can only offer a general guide to your baby's talents and potentials. Your evolving child is far more complex than you can ascertain from any book. I highly recommend that you have a full chart drawn up and interpreted for your baby by a professional astrologer.

[9] My own studies over eight years in the King's College, London, theological library led me to realize that reincarnation

was also originally a part of the teachings of the early Christian Fathers. In the fourth century A.D., much of the freedom of the Church was removed, along with this important doctrine, by the power-seeking Emperor Constantine and his wife.

[10] Dr. Stevenson is a medical doctor and had many scholarly papers to his credit before he began paranormal research. He is former head of the Department of Psychiatry at the University of Virginia and is director of the Division of Personality Studies at the University of Virginia.

[11] Dr. Brian L. Weiss, M.D., is a graduate of Columbia University and Yale Medical School. He is currently chairman of Psychiatry at the Mount Sinai Medical Center in Miami.

[12] *Many Lives, Many Masters.* Weiss, Brian L. A Fireside Book, Simon & Schuster, New York, 1988.

[13] The ancient study of the influence of numbers on human behavior.

[14] The Nodes of the Moon are not planets or physical bodies, but are mathematical points. They represent where the orbit of the Moon around the Earth crosses the Ecliptic (which is the apparent path of the Sun around the Earth). The North Node is the point where the Moon's orbit rises above the Elliptic, and the South Node is the point where the Moon's orbit falls below the Ecliptic. The North Node and the South Node are always exactly opposite each other in the chart.

[15] Our karmic pattern is the sum total of our thoughts and actions, and the state of our karmic pattern determines our future experiences. However, our karma is not inevitable; using awareness, intelligence, and spiritual knowledge, it can be changed or manipulated for the better. Refer to *Karma and Reincarnation* by Dr. George King, The Aetherius Society Press, Los Angeles.

[16] Joan Salter, *The Incarnating Child*, Hawthorn Press, 1990.

[17] Cleve Backster was founder of the CIA's polygraph, who helped develop interrogation techniques for the CIA.

[18] Metaphysicians believe that all life, from a rock to a sun, is living.

[19] IHM General Research Institute

[20] Most people do not use these three parts when they breathe but often only use just the upper part of their lungs.

[21] Dr. George King, Founder/President of The Aetherius Society. For more information, visit www.chrissieblaze.com or www.aetherius.org. All rights reserved. No reproduction in whole or part may be done without written permission from The Aetherius Society, 6202 Afton Place, Hollywood, CA 90028.

[22] Refer to *Workout for the Soul: 8 Steps to Inner Fitness*, by Chrissie Blaze. Aslan Publishing, 2001.

[23] *The Magic of Healing* by Richard Lawrence, Thorsons, March 2002.

[24] Prana, chi, or universal life forces are radiated constantly from the sun, and prana is the most important part of the air we breathe. Mystics say that prana is life.

[25] Lee Carroll and Jan Tober, *The Indigo Children: The New Kids Have Arrived*, Carlsbad, CA: Hay House, 1999.

[26] A nonprofit nonsectarian organization, whose main objective is to reach out and help these children. www.nfgcc.com.

[27] *The Indigo Children* by Lee Carroll and Jan Tober, Hay House, 2000.

[28] See www.indigodeath.com.

[29] *Workout for the Soul: 8 Steps to Inner Fitness* by Chrissie Blaze, Aslan Publishing, Inc., 2001.

BOOKS

O books
O is a symbol of the world, of oneness and unity. In
different cultures it also means the "eye", symbolizing
knowledge and insight, and in Old English it means "place
of love or home". O books explores the many paths of
understanding which different traditions have developed
down the ages, particularly those today that express
respect for the planet and all of life.

For more information on the full list of over 300 titles
please visit our website
www.O-books.net

SOME RECENT O BOOKS

How to Read Your Horoscope in 5 Easy Steps
Chrissie Blaze

Chrissie Blaze has written THE book for anyone interested in learning astrology, and she's done it in a lively and witty style. Reading this is like having your own personal astrology teacher close at hand. It's aimed at beginner astrologers but also offers insights and revelations for experienced astrologers. It's a must have in everyone's metaphysical library. **Dr. John Holder**, Chairman, Festivals for Mind-Body-Spirit, U.K.

9781846940729 160pp £9.99 $16.95

Mercury Retrograde
Your Survival Guide to Astrology's Most Precarious Time of Year
Chrissie Blaze

This exceptional treatment of how retrograde or stalled planets can stall your life offers yet more extraordinary proof that human beings are part of a giant energetic field of being. As one of astrology's brightest new stars Chrissie Blaze provides up much brilliant advice about how to navigate through life on hold. **Lynne McTaggart**, author of the bestselling *The Field*

9781846940736 240pp £9.99 $19.95

Superstar Signs
Sun Signs of Heroes, Celebrities and You
Chrissie Blaze

In our modern culture, everyone is fascinated by the lives of celebrities and they have become our modern day heroes. In this astrological guide to the Sun Signs, brief bios of these modern celebrities as well as heroes of the past, are used to illustrate the different qualities of the Sun Signs, Aries through Pisces. The aim of this book is as a fascinating guide to understanding more about the role of the Sun Signs.

9781846941252 400pp **£9.99 $19.95**

Saturn, Fatal Attraction
Adam Smith

This book is not just a brilliant book about astrology, it's also an incredible guide to life. It's spiritual, it's practical, it's spot on!
Jessica Adam, astrologer for *Vogue* and *Cosmopolitan*, author of *The New Astrology For Women*

190504786X 208pp £11.99 $24.95

The Last of the Shor Shamans
Alexander and Luba Arbachakov

The publication of Alexander and Luba Arbachakov's 2004 study of Shamanism in their own community in Siberia is an important addition to the study of the anthropology and sociology of the peoples of Russia. Joanna Dobson's excellent English translation of the Arbachakov's work brings to a wider international audience a fascinating glimpse into the

The Celtic Wheel of the Year
Celtic and Christian Seasonal Prayers
Tess Ward

This book is highly recommended. It will make a perfect gift at any time of the year. There is no better way to conclude than by quoting the cover endorsement by Diarmuid O'Murchu MSC, "Tess Ward writes like a mystic. A gem for all seasons!" It is a gem indeed. **Revd. John Churcher**, Progressive Christian Network

1905047959 304pp **£11.99 $21.95**

Tales of the Celtic Bards
Claire Hamilton

An original and compelling retelling of some wonderful stories by an accomplished mistress of the bardic art. Unusual and refreshing, the book provides within its covers the variety and colour of a complete bardic festival. **Ronald Hutton**, Professor of History, University of Bristol

9781846941016 320pp **£12.99 $24.95**

A Pagan Testament
The literary heritage of the world's oldest new religion
Brendan Myers

A remarkable resource for anyone following the Wicca/Pagan path. It gives an insight equally into wiccan philosophy, as well as history and practise. We highly recommend it. A useful book for the individual witch; but an essential book on any covens bookshelf. **Janet Farrar** and **Gavin Bone**, authors of *A Witches Bible, The Witches Goddess, Progressive Witchcraft*

9781846941290 384pp **£11.99 $24.95**

rapidly disappearing traditional world of the Shor Mountain people. That the few and very elderly Shortsi Shamans were willing to share their beliefs and experiences with the Arbachakov's has enabled us all to peer into this mysterious and mystic world. **Frederick Lundahl,** retired American Diplomat and specialist on Central Asia

9781846941276 96pp **£9.99 $19.95**

Shamanic Reiki
Expanded Ways of Workling with Universal Life Force Energy
Llyn Roberts and Robert Levy

The alchemy of shamanism and Reiki is nothing less than pure gold in the hands of Llyn Roberts and Robert Levy. Shamanic Reiki brings the concept of energy healing to a whole new level. More than a how-to-book, it speaks to the health of the human spirit, a journey we must all complete. **Brian Luke Seaward,** Ph.D., author of *Stand Like Mountain, Flow Like Water, Quiet Mind, Fearless Heart*

9781846940378 208pp **£9.99 $19.95**

The Way Beyond the Shaman
Birthing a New Earth Consciousness
Barry Cottrell

"The Way Beyond The Shaman" is a call for sanity in a world unhinged, and a template for regaining a sacred regard for our only home. This is a superb work, an inspired vision by a master artist and wordsmith. **Larry Dossey,** MD, author of *The Extraordinary Power Of Ordinary Things*

9781846941214 208pp **£11.99 $24.95**